Carnival
and Other Christian Festivals

Portions of this book have been abbreviated or otherwise adapted from previously published articles:
"Days of Saints and Virgins: The Hidden Theology of Patronal Saints Day Festivals," in *European Medieval Drama 1999*, ed. Sydney Higgins and Fiorella Paino (Camerino: Università degli Studi di Camerino, 2000)
"Masking the Site: The Fiestas de Santiago Apóstol in Loíza, Puerto Rico," *Journal of American Folklore* 114, no. 453 (2001)
"Corpus Christi in Cusco (Peru): Saint Sebastian and the Blue-Eyed Blacks," *The Drama Review* 47, no. 1 (2003)
"Carnival in Galicia: Scattered Ants, Whipped Backs, and Hammered Plowshares," *The Drama Review* 44, no. 3 (2000)
"The Impotence of Dragons: Playing Devil in the Trinidad Carnival," *The Drama Review* 42, no. 3 (1998)
"A Bolivian Morality Play: Saint Michael and the Sins of the Carnival Virgin," *European Medieval Drama* 5 (2001)

COPYRIGHT © 2003 BY THE UNIVERSITY OF TEXAS PRESS
Printed in the United States of America
First edition, 2003

Requests for permission to reproduce material from this work should be sent to Permissions, University of Texas Press, P.O. Box 7819, Austin, TX 78713-7819.

⊗ The paper used in this book meets the minimum requirements of ANSI/NISO Z39.48-1992 (R1997) (Permanence of Paper).

LIBRARY OF CONGRESS CATALOGING-IN-PUBLICATION DATA
Harris, Max, 1949–
   Carnival and other Christian festivals : folk theology and folk performance / by Max Harris.
        p.   cm. — (Joe R. and Teresa Lozano Long series in Latin American and Latino art and culture)
Includes bibliographical references and index.
   ISBN 0-292-70552-2 (alk paper) —
   ISBN 0-292-70191-8 (pbk. : alk. paper)
   1. Fasts and feasts.   2. Carnivals.   3. Festivals.   I. Title.
II. Series.
BV43 .H37   2003
263'.97—dc21   2003010315

To
Ann, Joel, and Matthew

Contents

Illustrations

PHOTOGRAPHS BY MAX HARRIS

Acknowledgments

My thanks are due, first, to the many thousands of folk artists who each year give so much to preserve, sustain, and develop the festive performances about which I write. Their work is far more important than mine.

Then, too, I owe my thanks to family members and friends who have traveled with me to fiestas. I have mentioned them only when the narrative required it, but they know that their presence added much joy to my research. This book is dedicated to my wife and sons.

Of the many other friends who deserve my thanks, I will mention just three who may not know how important a role they played in shaping this book. Milla Riggio invited me to go to Carnival in Trinidad. Stacy and Kevin Landon showed an early and encouraging interest in festive theology. Thank you all.

PART ONE

Days of Saints and Virgins

I.
Demons and Dragons
(CATALONIA)

FIERY DRAGONS and a clawed, bare-breasted serpent danced with devils, punctuating the night with fleeting visions of a world that we've been trained to think is hellish. Around the edges of the square, a crowd watched safely from behind a barrier of temporary metal railings. Where the circle of railings peeled back on itself, allowing devils guarded passage between an offstage alley and the square, I caught the eye of Marc Torras, the city's archivist and pyrotechnician. He invited me inside the barrier.

Squatting on the cobbled pavement, in the space of beasts and monsters, I could see more clearly: masked demons, dressed in fiery red and yellow suits, with fireworks in their hands and on their heads; winged, fire-breathing dragons, papier-mâché monsters each borne by a single man whose legs and feet alone were visible; the serpent, fanged and red-eyed, her flesh and breasts the pallid green of slime, likewise hefted by a single bearer. A long-necked giant mule, made of olive cloth stretched over a wooden frame, requiring several men to carry it, dropped its neck and, spinning, scattered a vicious circle of sparks. A bare-chested man in furred trousers and a bearded mask, topped with high, curving mountain goat's horns, briefly had the arena to himself. A flute played. Pan spoke to us, his voice amplified by loudspeakers. Most spectacular of all the monsters was the ox, a whirling, fire-spitting beast designed by Torras from two bulky pieces of an old ribbon-making loom, itself known as an "ox." The bearer's legs could just be seen amid the ambient flashes of light and thick clouds of smoke (Fig. 1.1).

Rockets shot into the air from the roof of the town hall. The smell of explosives was pervasive. When at last the show was over, the barriers were removed and the audience pressed into the heart of the square, now illuminated by streetlights. Devils, women, men, and children linked arms to dance in one big counterclockwise whirlpool to the joyous music of a band.

I was in Manresa, in the foothills of the Pyrenees above Barcelona, for the

1.1   Ox of fire. Manresa, 1995.

city's annual *festa major* (major feast day). What I had seen, that Saturday evening, was the *mostra del correfoc* (preview of the fire-running), a preliminary
display of the pyrotechnics that would be unleashed in full force on Monday night, when devils and monsters would run through the city streets, no
longer separated by barriers from onlookers but licensed to attack. Posted
notices warned citizens to board their windows and to remove their cars
from streets that lay along the route of the fire-running.[1]

Manresa's *festa major* is celebrated on the last weekend of August, within
a day or two of the city's patronal saints' day. Manresa has three patron
saints, Agnès, Fruitós, and Maurici, jointly known as els Cossos Sants (the
Holy Corpses). The relics of these Roman martyrs were transferred to the
city's new cathedral from the neighboring parish of Sant Fruitós de Bages,
where they had been languishing in relative neglect, on 30 August 1372.[2] In
1431 Manresa's guild of wool dressers, weavers, and tailors were given permission to celebrate the anniversary of that date with "dances, games [or
plays], illuminations and other things that may occur to them to solemnize
the festival."[3] Given the sponsoring guild, we can assume they wore elaborate costumes.

The "illuminations [*luminarias*]" may only have been decorative lights or
processional candles, but "a great snake [*culebra*] . . . blowing great flames

of fire from its mouth" had fought "many armed men" in royal festivities in Zaragoza as early as 1399. Pyrotechnics (to simulate artillery) and a fire-breathing griffin as large as a horse had appeared in the same venue in 1414. Demons and dragons were part of Barcelona's Corpus Christi procession by 1424, and during the same period, "little mortars and bombs" were being detonated for Corpus Christi in Manresa.[4] Given the conjunction of "illuminations" with "games" (jocs), it is tempting to think that light was partially provided, in this first of Manresa's festes majors, by fireworks and fiery monsters.

Until recently, the relics of the Cossos Sants were still borne through the city streets in an annual religious procession, preceded by the same spectacular figures that for years had led the consecrated host in the city's Corpus Christi procession. Among the traditional Catalan Corpus Christi and patronal saints' day figures recorded in Manresa are Saint Michael and a dozen adversarial devils; a winged, black, fire-breathing dragon; an "ox of fire" (bou de foc); and a giant mule (mulassa). All these, with the exception of Saint Michael, carried pyrotechnics. Additional fireworks were discharged along the route. Other traditional figures, of a less explosive nature, were a large, papier-mâché eagle, originally representing Saint John the Evangelist; giants, at first on stilts but later carried by an actor inside a huge wooden frame draped with oversized robes; dwarfs, with large papier-mâché heads; skirted hobbyhorses; and stick dancers.[5] No visibly female dragon or serpent (víbria) appears in the Manresa records, but she is well documented elsewhere in Catalonia.[6]

The last procession of the holy relics through Manresa was in 1966. The Corpus Christi procession, first held in 1322, ground to a similar halt in 1978. The correfoc was introduced in 1982.[7] I was there in 1995, when the only religious activity to commemorate the proximity of the patronal saints' day was a Sunday morning mass in the cathedral. Afterwards, the giants, dwarfs, and hobbyhorses joined the devils and the fiery monsters in a profane parade that led the worshipers away from the cathedral to the square, where castellers (human towers of acrobats) competed (Fig. 1.2). At night on Saturday and Monday, infernal pyrotechnics reigned unchallenged. The relics of the saints stayed safely in the crypt of the cathedral.[8]

Seated by the ox a few days earlier, its strings of fireworks still draped loosely on its back, Torras had explained to me the transformation of a procession of relics into an exaltation of demons and dragons. There had been, he said, "a change in the attitude of the people, a lessening of faith. People simply stopped coming out for the procession or they'd arrange to be away

1.2   *Castellers.* Manresa, 1995.

on vacation during the *festa major.*" Televisions and cars had compounded the problem. Before television, outdoor festivals had been the only entertainment. Now people had slick, fast-paced entertainment beamed into their homes. "And everybody has a car now. It's so much easier to leave town for the beach."

Secular modernization was not the only reason. Like most of Catalonia, in the political turmoil that preceded the Spanish Civil War, Manresa had been decidedly left-wing. After the municipal elections of April 1931, Manresa declared its allegiance to an independent Catalan Republic. In January 1932 miners and other workers briefly flew the black-and-red flag of the anarchist worker's party, the National Confederation of Labor (CNT), over the occupied town hall. Four years later, in February 1936, Manresa voted for the victorious left-wing Popular Front. When General Francisco Franco launched his military coup to save the conservative Catholic soul of Spain, anticlerical mobs in Manresa destroyed several churches and convents, barely sparing the cathedral.[9] Catalonia chafed bitterly under Franco's subsequent regime, which was characterized by a fervent Catholic triumphalism and a repressive opposition to regional autonomy. Franco's death in 1975 prompted a joyous resurgence of Catalan language and culture. I asked Torras whether the transformation of Manresa's *festa major* was a part of this reaction.

"Under Franco," he said, "attendance at Catholic holidays was obligatory and much Catalan folklore was banned. People avoided the religious processions if they could and, once they were no longer mandatory, ignored them. After the processions disappeared, we tried to revitalize the *festa* with profane elements that belong to Catalonia. Now, although some still go on vacation at the end of August, more are staying." Manresa's festive license of demons and dragons is no celebration of darkness. If Franco claimed the mantle of Catholic light, then to party as Catalan devils is a happy celebration of freedom.

Demons and dragons are a customary feature of saints' days and Corpus Christi festivals throughout Spain and its former empire. They are also common in Carnivals. Indeed, it is partly because of the presence of demons, dragons, and other masked transgressive figures that Carnival has been so often designated—by defenders and detractors alike—as a pagan or devilish season, a time of unrestrained indulgence before the ascetic penances of Lent.

Julio Caro Baroja, the father of Spanish Carnival studies, scorned the antiquarian notion that the masked figures and seasonal inversions of Carnival were "a mere survival" of ancient pagan rituals. Carnival, he argued, was first nurtured by the dualistic oppositions of Christianity. Where it survives—for when he wrote it had been banned in Spain by Franco—it still enacts those old antagonisms. "Carnival," he concluded, "is the representation of paganism itself face-to-face with Christianity."[10]

This view, often stated less sympathetically, is not exclusive to Roman Catholic countries, nor to those in which Carnival has faced recent governmental opposition. In Earl Lovelace's novel *Salt*, one of the characters claims to speak for Trinidad's fundamentalist Protestant community when, "fresh from an evangelical crusade across the island, [he] appeared on television condemning Carnival as devil worship and calling on all true Christians to keep their distance from it if they did not want to put their souls in peril."[11] Trinidad's Carnival receives lavish government funding and features costumed devils by the tens of thousands.

It is harder than it might seem, however, to draw a clear dividing line between such "Christian" festivals as Corpus Christi and patronal saints' days, on the one hand, and such "pagan" festivals as Carnival, on the other hand. A shared repertoire of masked characters and dramatic narratives and a common festive inclination to enact disorder makes for greater similarity than difference. Peter Burke, one of the more lucid historians of popular culture, has proposed that "there is a sense in which every festival [in early modern Europe] was a miniature Carnival because it was an excuse for disorder and because it drew from the same repertoire of traditional forms."[12]

Indeed, one of the ironies of festival studies is that a patronal saint's day whose official rhetoric is pious may in some respects be less constrained than a Carnival whose public rhetoric invokes the excesses of a pagan Bacchanal. Precisely because it claims to oppose civil and ecclesiastical authority, Carnival invites more determined diversion by those authorities (and their commercial backers) into nonthreatening channels than do patronal saints' days and such overtly religious and even triumphalist festivals as Corpus Christi. The latter, precisely because they claim to uphold official hierarchies, are sometimes freer to oppose them.

Sometimes, too, Carnivals and saints' days merge. In Oruro, Bolivia, devotion to the Virgen del Socavón (Virgin of the Mineshaft) migrated from the fixed festival of Candlemas (2 February) to the movable feast of Carnival. By delaying their public devotion to the Virgin until the four-day holiday before Ash Wednesday, Oruro's miners were able to enjoy a longer fiesta than if they had confined it to a single saint's day.[13] During Oruro's Carnival, thousands of devils dance through the streets before unmasking in the Sanctuary of the Mineshaft to express their devotion to the Virgin.

Evidently, the festive connotation of devils is not always demonic. In Manresa, the demons and dragons celebrate the restoration of liberty after a brutal civil war and subsequent dictatorship. In Oruro, as we shall see, the masked devils protest exploitation of indigenous miners by external forces and devote themselves to a Virgin who blesses the poor and marginalized. Festive disorder generally dreams not of anarchy but of a more egalitarian social order.

A further blurring of distinctions between "Christian" and "pagan" festivals arises if we grant the possibility, as Burke does, that Carnival may be better understood in relation to the Christmas season that begins it than to the Lenten season that displaces it. In many places the Carnival season still begins, as it has for centuries, in late December or early January. Tourists may not arrive until the last few days before Carnival Tuesday, but locals have been engaged in private preparations and escalating public merriment for several weeks by then.

Christmas itself was once marked by ceremonies of inversion. The Feast of Fools, widespread in medieval Europe, was traditionally associated with the Feast of the Holy Innocents on 28 December. Burke summarizes: "During the Feast of Fools a bishop or abbot of the fools would be elected, there would be dancing in the church and in the streets, the usual procession, and a mock mass in which the clergy wore masks or women's clothes or put their vestments on back to front, held the missal upside down, played cards, ate sausages, sang bawdy songs, and cursed the congregation instead of blessing them." (I am assured by friends in Catalonia that a boy bishop ceremony is still discreetly celebrated each year, on the feast day of Saint Nicholas on 6 December, some ten miles south of Manresa in the Monastery of Monsterrat. Marta Ibañez writes, "It is a remnant of the festivals of inversion, typical of the winter season, that culminate in Carnival.")[14] The reversal of hierarchies had an explicit theological justification. "Its legitimation," Burke explains, "was a line from the Magnificat, *Deposuit potentes de sedes et exaltavit humiles;* He hath put down the mighty from their seat and hath exalted the humble."[15]

The words, according to the Gospel of Luke, were first spoken by Mary in celebration of the coming birth of Christ (Luke 1:52). Burke points out that the whole Christmas season was once "treated as carnivalesque, appropriately enough from a Christian point of view, since the birth of the Son of God in a manger was a spectacular example of the world turned upside down."[16] The gradual dissociation of Carnival from Christmas, its confinement by the authorities—wherever possible—to the few days before Lent, and its demonization as a survival of pre-Christian pagan seasonal rites were the consequence of many forces, including the Renaissance penchant for imitating Roman festive practices, the sixteenth-century Reformation of the churches, the rise of a fastidious bourgeoisie, and the Romantic inclination to find pre-Christian seasonal rituals in peasant customs everywhere. It is a process that Burke calls "the triumph of Lent."[17]

We will return to the battle between the forces of Lent and those of Carnival later. For now, I simply want to observe that things are not always as they seem in festive celebrations. Carnival, condemned by the fundamentalist Caribbean preacher as "devil worship," may have its roots in the doctrine of the Incarnation. The festivities of Corpus Christi and patronal saints' days may, in some respects, be less restrained than Carnival. And all three provide a festive space for demons and dragons that may be symbols not of evil but of freedom.

The deliberate ambiguity of festive folk theater warrants careful attention. In an earlier book, I studied the widespread tradition of *moros y cristianos* ([mock battles of] Moors and Christians) in the light of James Scott's distinction between public and hidden transcripts. In the relationship between dominant and subordinate groups, the public transcript is what each may say and do in the presence of the other. The hidden transcripts of each side are what each may say and do in the absence of the other. Of particular interest to the student of folk theater are "the manifold strategies by which subordinate groups manage to insinuate their resistance, in disguised forms, into the public transcript."[18] The public transcript of Mexican mock battles between Moors and Christians is ordinarily the triumph of pale-skinned Catholics over dark-skinned heathens. This victory explains the early introduction of the theme to Mexico by the conquistadors. The hidden transcript is often that of reconquest: the expulsion of invading foreigners by the native owners of the land. This eviction explains the widespread adoption of the tradition by the indigenous peoples of Mexico: as Spanish Catholics drove out Moors, so might Mexican Indians drive out Spaniards.

The hidden transcript can be variously signaled. The dancers' masks may be reversed so that the Christian warriors have dark skin and the heathen villains have beards and rosy cheeks; the victorious Christian troops may be identified as Aztecs by decorative emblems sewn into their costumes; or the marginal actions of the "clowns" may undermine the scripted Spanish victory.[19] While the public transcript may be safely recorded in a prescribed text, the hidden transcript generally finds expression only in signs visible in performance.

Danzas (dances) and fiestas of Moors and Christians are not attached to any particular season of the year. I have seen them on patronal saints' days, at Corpus Christi, and during Carnival. One of my goals in this book is to apply the heuristic principle of public and hidden transcripts more broadly to the folk theater of these three festivals. It is not a matter of bringing prescriptive theory to the understanding of fiestas. The fiestas themselves take precedence over theory, but Scott's distinction helps me better explain what many years of participant observation of fiestas have taught me. In terms of methodology, for example, I have learned to pay more heed to the dramatic action of a fiesta and to the casual remarks of performers and audience than to the standard explanations offered to (and by) clergy, government agents, anthropologists, and other outsiders. I have learned to look for those details of performance that are quietly at odds with the public transcript, for it is amid these dissonances—just because they are apt to be regarded as innocuous, garbled, or irrelevant by scholars and others in authority—that folk performers are most likely to insinuate their hidden transcript into the public square.

But Scott's insight alone does not explain how—to use another phrase from my earlier book—I "read the mask" of a fiesta.[20] Several other insights have helped me place my observation of what lies hidden on the surface of fiestas in some kind of theoretical and methodological framework. In each of the first five chapters of this book, I offer an account of a particular patronal saints' day festival and use that account to introduce another principle that has helped me in their interpretation. My first concern is to understand the particular fiestas and, at the end of Part One, to come to some sort of general conclusion about such days of saints and virgins, but it seems kinder to the reader to scatter theory lightly through the opening chapters than to serve it in one dense initial lump. Having partied with saints and virgins in Part One, we turn our attention in Parts Two and Three to Corpus Christi and Carnival. In the process, we travel as far north as the lowlands of Belgium and as far south as the Bolivian Andes, passing along the way through various regions of Spain, the Caribbean, Mexico, and Peru.

Our first step, however, is a small one. On the Monday of Manresa's *festa major*, I drove the thirty miles downhill from Manresa to the Catalan wine-producing center of Vilafranca del Penedès. I missed Manresa's *correfoc*, arriving in Vilafranca in time for the last night of the novena, nine days of preparatory devotion before the opening of the town's *festa major* in honor of Saint Felix. After prayers, in the Basilica de Santa Maria, an orchestra of piano, cello, and eight violins struck up and a men's choir launched into the "Goigs a Sant Fèlix" (Joys to Saint Felix), a bright communal song of praise to the town's patron saint. The congregation, filling the building to capacity, loudly joined in the final chorus. Unlike Manresa, Vilafranca still celebrates its patron saint with gusto. But it does so without prejudice to demons and dragons. Afterwards, in the square outside, a suited dignitary told us that the *festa* promotes the unity of the sacred and the profane.

The next day, the profane *cercavila* (parade around the town) began at the north end of the Rambla Sant Francesc, a normally peaceful promenade lined with overhanging trees. By midday the *rambla* was canopied with a network of firecrackers, crisscrossing from tree to tree for more than a hundred yards. Spectators crowded both sides. When a policeman warned those of us at the south end to move, an old man protested vehemently. We stood firm. Someone at the north end ignited the web of firecrackers; billowing clouds of smoke and deafening explosions abruptly raced towards us. Instinctively, as if we were under sudden artillery attack, we all rushed backwards. After maybe five seconds—who was counting?—the terrifying noise and smoke stopped just a few feet short of our retreat. We looked at each other, relieved, a little embarrassed, and laughed.

Saint Michael, two dozen devils, and a fiery dragon emerged from the set-tling smoke, followed by bandits, an eagle, giants, dwarfs, numerous teams of folk dancers, human towers several stories high, and the town's brass band. The parade completed a circuit of the town, stopping often to dance before appreciative crowds. The mayor and his guests watched from the balcony of the town hall, which was draped with a prominent banner proclaiming the town's sympathies in the Balkan conflict: "Vilafranca per Bosnia" (Vilafranca for Bosnia) (Fig. 1.4). Spanish Christians rooted for the Muslims.

The profane figures of the *cercavila* were joined that evening by the sacred image of Saint Felix. Although the relics of the saint remain in the basilica, his sculpted image spends the year as a guest in the homes of his several stewards. The nighttime religious procession began at the house of his most recent host. Leading the procession, as it had for centuries, was the dragon. A single man, carrying the eight-foot-long body of a black winged dragon on his shoulders, spun on his feet while the dragon sprayed bright fire from its wing tips, back, mouth, and tail (Fig. 1.3). The dragon was accompanied by a large group of devils in horned and hooded costumes of brown sackcloth painted with flames, reptiles, and infernal monsters. The devils, too, scat-tered fire. In their midst walked a young girl in white, carrying a toy sword and shield. Like many a folk Saint Michael, she made no effort to restrict the progress of the devils.

In 1424 Barcelona's Corpus Christi procession began with the creation of the world, the fall of Lucifer, the dragon of Saint Michael, and a sword fight between twenty-three devils and an unspecified number of angels.[21] The first extant record of dragon, devils, and fireworks in the Vilafranca Cor-pus Christi procession dates from 1600.[22] After the relics of Saint Felix ar-rived in Vilafranca (1700) and he was named co-patron of the town (1776), festive emphasis shifted from Corpus Christi to the saint's annual feast day. The dragon first danced for Felix in 1779; the devils followed in 1816.[23] Saint Michael is little mentioned in the records. That the dragon and the devils were among the first traditional elements to accompany Saint Felix in pro-cession indicates their popular appeal. Saint Michael's subsidiary role was to recall—but rarely to enact—the necessary public transcript of archangelic victory. The popular appeal of demons does not lie in their official defeat.

There are, of course, practical reasons for beginning a procession with de-mons and a pyrotechnic monster: they clear the streets for the less threat-ening acts that follow, and they start the festivities with a spectacular bang rather than a pious whisper. But there are other reasons for the popularity of so many undefeated devils in Catalan festivals. Devils are thrice damned

1.3   Demons and dragon. Vilafranca del Penedès, 1995.

by those in power: they are the enemies of God; their very mode of representation in fiestas has long been condemned by church and state as a remnant of pagan ritual; and they embody human desires and behaviors that the
church represses. To dress as a devil and run unimpeded through the streets
is to step outside the authority of the church, to challenge its claims to absolute moral wisdom, and, in modern Spain, to distance oneself further from
Franco's Catholic triumphalism. It is not that Spaniards really want the devil
and his minions to win the cosmic battle (if they still believe in such a thing),
any more than they wish the Moors (whom they also love to act) had won
the territorial war. But to play the devil grants a certain festive freedom and
enacts a mild resistance to authoritative power. And so a pyrotechnic dragon
and undefeated devils led the procession in honor of Saint Felix.

    The procession stretched for a mile or more from the dragon to Saint Felix.
In between, in careful gradation from profane to sacred, defiant to compliant,
came the dances. Immediately following the devils was the *ball d'en Serralonga*, a traditional street play celebrating the escapades of the local bandit
hero Joan de Serralonga and his wife, Joana de Torrelles. Some thirty bandits
marched with Joan and Joana through the streets of Vilafranca, repeatedly
firing their arquebuses. The bandits also went undefeated. The earliest ex-

tant manuscript (1826) of the play is a copy of one written in 1820. Banned at least once in the late nineteenth century, the *ball d'en Serralonga* had died out by the 1920s. It was revived in 1980, five years after the death of Franco sparked a broad recuperation of Catalan folk performances.[24]

Traditional masked Corpus Christi figures came next. The eagle, like the dragon, was fashioned out of painted papier-mâché. Larger, less active, and less exciting than its infernal counterpart, it rested on the shoulders of a single man but required additional manual support. Once the symbol of Saint John the Evangelist, the eagle is now more likely to denote local autonomy. Two regal giants followed, made of wooden frames clothed with oversized robes and topped with papier-mâché heads, each borne by a single dancer who peered out through a thigh-high grille. Then came eight dwarfs (*nans*) and four big heads (*caps grossos*), each dancer creating the impression of diminutive size by wearing a disproportionately large papier-mâché head.

Skirted hobbyhorses formed a bridge to the unmasked (and therefore less threatening) dances that followed. All the horses were ridden by young women. Each rider was concealed from the waist down by an oval, hooped cotton skirt. In front of her upper body, a papier-mâché equine neck and head protruded. Like their fifteenth-century Barcelona predecessors, sponsored by the confraternity of cotton weavers, the Vilafranca hobbyhorses are known as *cotonines* (little cotton-[skirted horses]).

Many of the unmasked dancers carried modified weapons or instruments (shepherd's crooks, short sticks, flowered hoops, or tambourines) in what may once have been pyrrhic dances. The *bastoners* (stick dancers) performed a carefully choreographed dance of rapidly clashing sticks. One of the dancers told me afterwards that their distant predecessors had replaced traditional swords with more readily available cart wheel spokes.[25] The *pastorets* (little shepherds) struck the ground and one another's wooden crooks in rapid-fire movements that threatened, if they missed, to fracture wrists and ankles. Then they formed an unbroken circle of interweaving shepherds, linked by crooks, who wove a wooden knot on which one of their number was raised shoulder high. The *figuetaires* (makers of faces),[26] lacking weapons, pulled noses and slapped hands and faces with their bare hands before delivering a final phallic fist gesture. Another unarmed troupe wove ribbons round a portable maypole in the *ball de les gitanes* (dance of the gypsies). Yet another divided into several circles of two men and two women apiece to perform an elegant *ball pla* (plain dance, i.e., without leaps).[27]

Then came three teams of *castellers*. Vilafranca is justly proud of its *castellers*, according them an almost religious status as markers of commu-

1.4 Processional *castellers* in front of the town hall. Vilafranca del Penedès, 1995.

nal identity. Hence their place in the procession close to the image of Saint Felix. Each team consisted of a hundred or more men, women, and children who built human towers several stories high. The heavyweights among them formed a base of concentric human circles that supported a narrowing tower of younger and more lightweight members. The last to climb the wavering tower was a young child, often no more than five or six years old, who clambered up the backs of the other *castellers* to stand at the top. In procession (Fig. 1.4), the human tower moved forward several yards or even rotated on its axis before dismantling (or collapsing). The towers form a striking image of communal interdependence, involving male and female, young and old, in a complex series of movements in which there is no room for individual flamboyance and each part must depend on all the others. To be a *casteller* is to submit to the good order of the whole. And yet the goal of all this order is a striking image of the reversal of conventional social hierarchy: the tower is supported on the backs of adult males hidden in the base and at its visible pinnacle is a small child, often female.

Even closer to Saint Felix was an explicitly religious variation on the *castellers:* the misleadingly named *ball de la moixiganga* (mummers' dance). Some twenty-five men and boys formed acrobatic towers representing scenes from the Passion of Christ: Jesus in prayer, the scourging, the mock coronation with thorns, two versions of the crucifixion, the deposition, and the burial. When not in formation, the men and boys processed in sober double file, bearing candles. The first record of such a display in Vilafranca dates from 1713. The dance lapsed between 1905 and its revival in 1985.[28]

Finally came the image of Saint Felix, surrounded by candles, on a litter quietly borne by four men in suits. This Felix, the best known of the sixty-six who share that happy name in the pages of the *Roman Martyrology*, was a Roman priest martyred under Diocletian, ca. 304. On his way to execution, the priest was joined by an unidentified stranger who volunteered to join him in death. The pair are known in the literature of sanctity as Felix and Adauctus (the added one).[29]

The procession thus stretched from the demonic to the sainted, from the lawless to the orderly, from loud and scattered fire to silent and contained candles. Just as the *castellers* represented the mutual interdependence of different parts in the formation and sustenance of a complex whole, so did the entire procession, with its mixture of saints and demons, dwarfs and giants, fiery dragons and civic dignitaries in somber suits. Even the ostensibly pyrrhic dances represented mutual cooperation rather than conflict. In an intricate series of dance steps and clashing sticks, each performer had to depend for his or her safety on the skill and care of the others. So it was with the procession as a whole: were the demons or the bandits to be excluded, the processional balance would be as surely lost as would the balance of the *castellers* if any member of the tower stepped out of place.

Lest the extended procession be mistaken for a visual argument that the coexistence of demons and saints depends on keeping them as far apart as possible, the climactic entry of Saint Felix to the basilica brought all the parts together in a single spectacle. Arriving at the basilica, the dragon, devils, and bandits waited to the north of the stone steps leading to the church's west door. The dancers and *castellers* gradually filled the open square behind them. By the time the *moixiganga* and the saint reached the foot of the steps, there was barely room for performers or spectators, packed shoulder to shoulder, to move anywhere in the square. The saint stood to the south of the steps, the *moixiganga* in the middle.

Suddenly, the dragon and the demons exploded into action, hurling fire in all directions, Joan de Serralonga and his gang shot arquebuses in the air, giants whirled, drums beat, dancers jumped, a cascade of white fire poured down from the roof of the church over its facade, the *moixiganga* formed a mimetic tower, and Felix was carried up the steps into the basilica. The *moixiganga* followed in sacred formation. The procession thus turned itself inside out, with the sacred rear passing through the profane front in a moment of shared celebration. The crowd rushed into the basilica behind the *moixiganga*. A few minutes later, there was not even standing room inside. At the front, a choir several hundred strong led the congregation in singing the "Goigs a Sant Fèlix." Many of those in the choir were still in costume, including Joan de Serralonga himself.

The following night, a second, virtually identical procession began and finished at the basilica. After wending its way through Vilafranca's streets, it once more concluded with a spectacular entry to the church. I missed the third procession, leaving Vilafranca on the last day of August for my next patronal saint's day festival. I gather from Vilafranca's program that the procession took Felix from the basilica, through the streets, to the house of his first steward for the following year. A grand show of fireworks welcomed him.

Felix had thus spent just two nights in the basilica before resuming his role as a perpetual house guest in the community. Like many patron saints, Felix identifies more readily with the people, with whom he spends his time, than with the institution of the church. Twice, as he does each year, he had sanctioned a festive invasion of the church in proclamation of a vision of human community more tolerant than official theological dogma and more inclusive than antagonistic political ideologies. Whereas traditional Christian theology tends to see both corporate history and individual psychology as a dualistic struggle between good and evil, the folk theology of Vilafranca's *festa major* offers an alternative vision in which differences, rather than being set at odds with one another, are encompassed in a single mutually interdependent whole. Whereas political ideologies tend to see human society as a bloody battleground between good and evil, the political vision of Vilafranca's *festa major* pleads instead for tolerance. Sympathy for the embattled Muslims of Bosnia, heirs to the Turks so long feared and fought by Spain, was a specific application of this vision.

At least, this is how I saw it. But a cautious reader may ask whether I am not simply imposing my own meaning on another's fiesta. In the absence of any explicit interpretation (written or oral) by local informants, how do I know what the fiesta signifies? In Manresa—thanks to the good offices of María-Angels Clotet, a friend in the town hall—I was able to speak with Marc Torras and several others intimately involved with the festivities. In Vilafranca, I had no such contact. I read the definitive work on the town's dances and processional figures by a local scholar, Francesc Bové, and I spoke with several performers, most of whom told me what Bové had already published in 1926. Only the official who opened the *festa* by declaring that it celebrated the unity of the sacred and the profane offered any explanation of the fiesta as a whole.

But I don't believe that lack of insider information renders a fiesta unintelligible to an observant outsider. Before stating my case positively, it is worth pointing out that the traditional anthropological reliance on local informants can be misleading. The information gleaned may now be nothing more than the recycled speculation of a previous scholar. Such is the case, for example, with English morris dancers who almost uniformly embrace the discredited theory of Cecil Sharp that the morris has its origins in pre-Christian seasonal ritual.[30] To be informed by a rural morris dancer that he is engaged in an ancient fertility rite does not make it so.

Even more important, perhaps, is the reluctance of a subordinate people to reveal the hidden transcript of a performance to an outsider, let alone to one whose skin color identifies him as one of the dominant caste. While this is less of a problem for a European scholar in England or Spain than it is for the same person in Bolivia or Puerto Rico, it is always a danger. Insiders tend to offer outsiders the public transcript. Even in Vilafranca, I was more likely to be offered the conventional platitude that the *festa* was in honor of Saint Felix than I was to be told that it entailed a complex negotiation with orthodox theology and the aftermath of a military dictatorship. In Manresa, Torras only spoke of Franco when I pressed him.

Finally, what is articulated in performance may never be rendered explicitly in words even by the performer himself. This is not just a matter of allowing the hidden transcript to remain implicit. It is also a question of media. Just as a painter may speak more clearly in paint than in theory, so a group of folk performers may express themselves more skillfully in performance than when one of their number explains the performance to an outside investigator. When the folklorist Dorothy Noyes arrived in Berga, thirty miles uphill from Manresa, full of a scholar's questions about the town's Corpus Christi festival—known as the Patum—she was told repeatedly, "La Patum s'ha de viure. T'hi ficaràs o no?" (One has to live the Patum. Are you going in there or not?)[31] To insist on the primacy of words is to insist on translation into the medium of the scholar. Much may be lost in the translation.

Conversation with performers can be invaluable, but it is no guarantee of understanding and it is no substitute for reading the mask of the performance itself. By definition, there is no textual documentation of a hidden transcript, and spoken clues to its identity are not there simply for the asking. It is my experience that windows onto the hidden transcript are more likely to swing open unexpectedly in response to a naive question in a casual conversation than they are in the context of a formal interview. But if I really want to fathom a fiesta's hidden transcript, I must watch for its display, not in text or speech, but in performance.

This, then, is my second heuristic principle: the hidden transcript—and hence the full complexity of meaning—of a fiesta is accessible in performance even if it is not confirmed by explicit textual or verbal statement. Or, to put it another way, folk performances bear sufficient signification in themselves if outsiders will but take the time to learn to understand them. Careful scholarship about the history of a fiesta and its constituent parts— and not just local legends endorsed by poor scholarship—certainly help the investigator, although there is no guarantee that meaning is constant from one generation to the next. Annual folk performances are fluid, responsive to their changing social, political, economic, and religious contexts, but a knowledge of their history at least guards against misleading public transcripts grounded in a fabricated history. Knowledge of the present social context helps, too, but this is a two-way street. In several cases, a fiesta has provided me with insight into current social tensions not otherwise articulated in public. In sum, conversations with performers and other local residents add to my understanding, as do careful historical research and a knowledge of current social dynamics, but in the end it is the performance itself that must be allowed to speak, even in the absence of any verbal confirmation of its meaning.

Support for my conviction that words are not the final interpretive authority can be drawn from the field of art history. In a brilliant essay, first published in 1983, Leo Steinberg drew attention to the previously unremarked fact that in Renaissance art Christ's penis was not only portrayed— as had rarely been the case in medieval art—but that attention was drawn to it and, most astonishing of all, that it was frequently erect. He argued that this was not just a matter of increased naturalism but that it advanced a theological argument for the full humanity and sinlessness of Christ. Chastity without ability would have been impotence, not commendable restraint.

In defending his argument against the generally skeptical and the specifically prudish, Steinberg had to wrestle with the fact that there was little contemporary textual support for his position. He did so by pointing out that, in the nature of the case, writers and preachers could discreetly avoid the issue of Christ's genitalia but painters, when representing him as a human baby or a naked victim of crucifixion, could not. Either they implicitly feminized him, or they rendered him fully male and fully human. Renaissance painters took the latter course, he suggested, for good theological reasons. The absence of textual support had more to with the relative media than with the novelty of Steinberg's position.

He went further, acknowledging that one of the secondary motives of his study was "to remind the literate among us that there are moments, even in a wordy culture like ours, when images start from no preformed program to become primary texts. Treated as illustrations of what is already scripted, they withhold their secrets."[32] An auxiliary purpose of my own book is to make the same case for fiestas. Fiestas are primary texts that withhold their secrets from those who insist on what Steinberg calls "verbal corroboration." "Our material," he writes, in language that applies almost as well to the field of festival studies, "are images that speak not in tongues but in shapes and gestures, images that transmit conscious decisions, solutions invented by artists, approved by peers and patrons and enforced by habit and acquiescence."[33] Folk performers may not always be quite so self-conscious about their decisions as Renaissance painters, but they are artists nonetheless, and their works are primary texts that will always be in danger of misunderstanding when scholarly interpreters privilege verbal commentary over the performances themselves.

Given the nature of public and hidden transcripts, folk performers may prefer it this way. It means that scholars are more likely to accept and perpetuate the public transcript. But there is always a hunger to be understood, especially when political danger has subsided. After all, in the absence of textual corroboration, the performers can always retreat, if necessary, to a public denial of the supposed hidden transcript. But I have found they are just as likely to be delighted when I hazard a guess as to their intent. They may only grin, but they let me know when I'm right.

None of this guarantees that my uncorroborated—or loosely corroborated —readings of fiestas are correct. It only argues that my attempt should not be deemed misguided from the outset. I cannot, as Steinberg could, reproduce complete paintings by way of supporting evidence, but I will do my best to describe each fiesta in as much detail as space allows, thereby giving readers the opportunity to assess my reading of the data for themselves. I will also draw attention to what corroboration is available. But, in the end, my readings will have to be judged not on the weight of verbal corroboration but on the evidence of the primary texts themselves: the fiestas.

2.

Flowers for Saint Tony
(ARAGON)

WHILE WORKING on the music for his ballet suite *The Three-Cornered Hat*, the Spanish composer Manuel de Falla visited the small Aragonese town of Fuendetodos (Zaragoza), where he was treated to a midday banquet in the town hall. Intending to honor both Falla and the musical traditions of the region, a diva in his party stepped outside onto the balcony and sang, with a skill honed on the concert stage, the Aragonese *jota* from Falla's *Seven Spanish Songs*. The members of the packed crowd in the square below greeted her highbrow rendition of their popular music with puzzled silence. They didn't recognize it as a *jota*. That night, in the narrow streets of Fuendetodos, Falla heard the young men of the town sing traditional *jotas* with a passion that evoked fervent applause. He understood the earlier silence of the crowd and was deeply moved. The final dance of *The Three-Cornered Hat*, which Diaghilev's Ballets Russes opened in London in July 1919, is set to a sparkling *jota* that owes much to Falla's time in Fuendetodos.[1]

Many years later, not far from Fuendetodos, I had a similar awakening. I knew that folk theater was as capable as any professional theater of embodying profound human emotions and addressing complex social issues, but I was not yet fully aware of folk theater's rich theological dimension. My appreciation of folk theology, like Falla's admiration of his country's folk music, first took conscious form in Aragon. It happened in September 1995, during a fiesta mass in honor of San Antolín in Sariñena (Huesca), some eighty-five miles by road from Fuendetodos and about twice as many from Vilafranca del Penedès. I had left Vilafranca before the third procession of Saint Felix to be in Sariñena for the start of its own more tranquil saint's day festival.

The first night of the fiesta was full of romance. Six musicians playing guitars, mandolins, and a ukelele joined two master singers of the traditional *jota* in a tour of the narrow, cobbled streets of the old town.[2] Under sparkling stars, they serenaded old women in doorways and young girls on balconies, weaving personal names into traditional love lyrics and singing to all—of whatever age or beauty—with splendid passion. Some responded in kind. A wrinkled widow, her eyes shining, sang an ardent love song. A younger woman stepped into the street and sang a powerful *jota*. Householders provided food and drink for the performers and the crowd. We ate bread, ham, and cheese and drank wine from a common skin, throwing our heads back, raising the wineskin high, and pouring a thin stream of airborne liquid into our mouths. Once, turning a corner, we were met by a group of boys who blocked the street and hefted one of their number, no more than twelve years old, onto their shoulders. Solo, he sang a *jota* that impressed even the masters. Long after midnight, while the *joteros* were still making their romantic rounds, I wandered back to my hotel and fell happily asleep.

The next morning, I followed the fiesta parade from the eastern edge of town to the central Plaza de España. The baton-twirling majorettes, the town's marching band, and the six young queens of the fiesta (*mairalesas*), waving at the crowd from their tractor-drawn float, were recent innovations.[3] An older tradition was represented by the sixteen men and eight boys who performed an intricate stick dance (Fig. 2.1). The men wore checked bandannas, red and green sashes crossed over white shirts, black knickers, white lace stockings, bells strapped onto their right calves, and lightweight dancing sandals.[4] The boys substituted blue sashes and white cotton skirts trimmed with lace. To an outsider, the skirts appear to feminize the boys, but Jaime Martín Coto, the *maestro* of the dance team, assured me that the boys were initiates into a religious rite and were dressed in the manner of candidates for the priesthood. Similar white dresses, with "liturgical antecedents," were the common costume of sixteenth-century ritual dancers.[5] They are still worn by adult male dancers in both Graus (Huesca) and Peñíscola (Castellón). Music for the dance was supplied by a single bagpiper.[6]

The dancers were followed by a comic devil and his seven-year-old apprentice *diablito* (little devil). In the past, the devil used to lift young women's skirts with his pitchfork, but "the presence of the majorettes . . . has rendered this redundant."[7] Instead, the devil tried to sweep up watching children with his fork. Unlike his Catalan kin, Sariñena's devil sows discord rather than freedom; he therefore bears no fireworks and inspires no fear. Social order may be threatened, but evil doesn't win in folk fiestas.

When we reached the Plaza de España, the devil delivered a speech. My neighbor in the audience explained, "He's telling the people to do bad things." The town historian countered with the story of Sariñena's patron

2.1 Stick dancers. Sariñena, 1995.

saint, Antolín. Townspeople wore sprigs of basil in their lapels, guarding themselves against the powers of evil with its sweet perfume.[8] Then the mayor fired a rocket from the balcony of the town hall. Like Falla, I ate lunch with the mayor and his guests. No one sang me a song, but I was invited to deliver a ceremonial kiss on both cheeks to each of the *mairalesas.*

That night, the *joteros,* joined by the twelve-year old soloist of the night before, took to the stage beneath the town hall balcony. There were folk dancers, too, including some whose dance told the story of the siege of Zaragoza by the forces of Napoleon. The guitars imitated the rapid fire of artillery. Shortly before midnight, a small crowd gathered outside the parish church in the nearby Plaza del Salvador to sing the ballad of San Antolín. A statue of the saint, dressed for the occasion in the same red and green sashes and checked bandanna as the town's stick dancers, smiled on us from the doorway of the church. We sang of a pilgrim who had brought the severed finger of the saint to Sariñena from Pamiers, on the French side of the Pyrenees, where Antolín had been born and martyred. After begging alms, the pilgrim had tried to leave Sariñena, but all the town's bells began miraculously to ring. The pilgrim was unable to move and the finger of San Antolín has remained in Sariñena ever since.[9]

2.2   Processional statue of San Antolín. Sariñena, 1995.

The next day (September 2) was Antolín's feast day. A second statue of the saint, easier to carry because much lighter and less valuable should it fall, was borne in short procession from the Plaza de España to the church. Antolín stood in aromatic basil and, once again, wore a bandanna round his neck (Fig. 2.2). He was accompanied by suited dignitaries from the mayor's office and the twenty-four dancers, who now clashed swords rather than sticks. Outside the church, the *mairalesas* waited, along with other women in traditional Aragonese festive dress. When Antolín arrived, they followed him into the church for the fiesta mass. A throng of worshipers carried offerings of flowers and fruit up the nave, through an honor guard of dancers, to the altar.[10] A priest and his assistant received the gifts and offered worshipers a reliquary, containing Antolín's finger, to kiss. As they turned to leave, the worshipers faced the original statue of San Antolín. Many, as they passed, patted his feet affectionately.

As the stream of townspeople greeted Antolín, I noticed a statue of Christ the King high in the ornate *retablo* behind the altar. Enthroned in dominant majesty, a ruler's scepter in one hand and a diminutive orb in the other, he stared out over our heads. Not only could we not bring him flowers or pat his feet, we couldn't even make eye contact with him.

Was the pictured distance of Christ, I wondered, a cause of the proximity of Antolín? The central Christian story that God in Christ became a human being is radically at odds with the organizational assumptions of a hierarchical church. For the Son of God to divest himself of power and become the squalling human child of poor parents is a move that challenges mortal presumptions of rank. It promises, if the generalization of the Magnificat is to be believed, a toppling of the mighty and a tumultuous exaltation of the humble. Embarrassed by this divine challenge to good order, Christian art commissioned by the powerful all too often sanitizes the nativity, removing the dirt of poverty and portraying the baby as a king to whom homage is already due. The infant Christ of icons challenges no social order; he has shrunk but not lost rank.

Church art largely disregards the daily life of Jesus. Neither Vermeer's domestic *Christ in the House of Martha and Mary* nor Steen's boisterous *Wedding Feast at Cana*, to cite just two examples of paintings that portray Jesus in a common social setting, were created to be hung in church. Art commissioned by the powerful to be displayed in consecrated space prefers to pass directly from a sanitized nativity to a bloody crucifixion. The adult Christ restores good order only when he models to the powerless from the cross the virtues of patient suffering. Art that decorates the walls of churches teaches us that Jesus is Immanuel (God with us) in our suffering but not in our resistance. Where are the great church paintings of Jesus driving moneychangers from the temple? There may be good theological reasons why paintings of the cross outnumber paintings of the cleansing of the temple, but they are reinforced by other, more suspect political and economic motives.

Nor do paintings of a bloody Christ encourage us to take much pleasure in created things. They might, if the surrounding action showed forgiven human beings rejoicing in their freedom, but they tend instead to tell us life is full of violence, a vale of tears to be endured in expectation of the disembodied joys of heaven. The theme is reinforced by pictures of the fall. Masaccio's fresco of the *Expulsion* (ca. 1425–1428), in the Brancacci Chapel of the Carmelite Church in Florence, is perhaps the best of many mournful paintings on the topic. But where are the great Christian testimonies in paint to the sensual pleasures of Adam and Eve before the fall? Hieronymus Bosch's *Tryptich of the Garden of Delights* (ca. 1510) hardly counts, for there the creation of Eve in the first panel leads directly—without pleasure—through the dark and stagnant monster-spawning pond beneath her feet to the riot of bizarre sexuality in the central panel. The dire apocalypse depicted in the final panel passes judgment.[11]

Church art tends to power and judgment. Sponsored artists raise the resurrected Christ to his eternal throne, where he rules over all things, endorsing the privileges of human rulers to whom he delegates a measure of his own authority. Further justifying the fear of the ruled towards the men who rule them, the reigning Christ is often shown in final judgment. In the French cathedral of Albi (Tarn), a vast mural—possibly painted by anonymous Flemish contemporaries of Bosch—portrays such a scene in agonizing detail. Over fifty feet wide and forty-five feet high, Albi's *Last Judgment* (1474–1500) was one of the largest single paintings produced in the late Middle Ages. Although the mural has now lost its central section, in which a gigantic Christ loomed over doomsday, most of the demonic inquisition remains, a veritable nightmare of torments spread across the full width of the cathedral's western wall.[12]

Less than a hundred yards away, in the former bishop's palace, the visitor can see a very different kind of painting. Henri de Toulouse-Lautrec was born in Albi in 1864. The Palais de La Berbie contains room after glorious room of his works. Like Jesus, Toulouse-Lautrec did not scorn the company of prostitutes and sinners but gave them dignity in his art. It would not be hard to make the case that Toulouse-Lautrec's painterly love of fallen human beings is more consistent with the doctrine of the Word made flesh than is the monstrous vision on the walls of the cathedral.

When Christian art and rhetoric recruited the Son of God as a terrifying ally of hierarchical power, the folk turned to Jesus's mother. It is no accident that popular devotion to Mary grew dramatically during the late Middle Ages, when the dominant image of Christ was that of supreme ruler and universal judge. As Christ receded to an awe-inspiring throne, the Virgin Mary comforted his subjects. Her prayers and pleas, they hoped, would temper his stern justice.

But popular devotion to Mary is not a simple matter, for Mary, too, has been exalted high above her earthly station to the rank of heavenly queen and co-mediatrix. One can argue that this ascension fulfills the pregnant Mary's prophecy of social reversal, for now an unwed teenaged mother rules. If, as Henry Adams wrote, the medieval bishop of Chartres "was much more afraid of Mary than he was of any Church Council ever held,"[13] then the topsy-turvy justice of the Magnificat had gained a foothold in a patriarchal world. But one can also claim that in her exaltation Mary ceases to be one of us. Immaculately conceived, perpetually virgin, wholly sinless, she becomes a patroness, if not of male power, then of unattainable female purity. The Mary being lifted up to heaven by a choir of angels in Rubens's *The Assumption of the Holy Virgin*—the altarpiece in Antwerp Cathedral—is not one who has displaced the mighty from their seat. She is one who is joining their ranks.

If church art and its sponsors have suppressed the subversive implications of the Incarnation, appropriating Christ and his mother for their own more conservative ends, then perhaps patronal festivals of saints and virgins are a move in the opposite direction, a defiant effort by the folk to reclaim the liberating implications of the Incarnation, to bring divine humanity back down to earth. Local festive Virgins are not the universal Virgin of church dogma or of Counter-Reformation art. Each has a local name. She may be Our Lady of the Virtues or the Virgin of the Snows, but she is never the Virgin unspecified. When her skin is darkened, lowering her social rank, she is known affectionately as *la morenica* (the little dark one). She rarely lives in the parish church but has a chapel of her own, where she is cared for by a local confraternity. She is, in short, not *the* Virgin but *our* Virgin. The archbishop of Valladolid once remarked of anticlerical iconoclasts, "These people would be ready to die for their local Virgin, but would burn that of their neighbors at the slightest provocation."[14]

Or, if the exalted Virgin Mary still seems somewhat out of reach, the folk turn to a saint. According to Peter Brown, the cult of the saints began "when Mediterranean men and women, from the late fourth century onwards, turned with increasing explicitness for friendship, inspiration and protection in this life and beyond the grave, to invisible beings who were fellow human beings and whom they could invest with the precise and palpable features of beloved and powerful figures in their own society."[15] The saints are local, and they are, like the Jesus of the gospels if not of church art, one of us. They are good friends who lived godly lives among us and have gone ahead to speak on our behalf. Their relics and their images bespeak their continued presence with us. Just as they do with a named Virgin, so Spanish towns and villages claim their patron saints as their own, often dressing them in local costume or according them local nicknames.

So it was in Sariñena. Antoine de Pamiers had become Antolín, or Tony, of Sariñena. Tony was no distant ruler or fastidious ascetic. He liked flowers, fruit, sweet-smelling herbs, and colorful costumes. If he didn't go out with the *joteros,* it wasn't because he disapproved. He came to his own church door when we called and enjoyed the ballad that we sang him on his steps. He dressed like "our" dancers and went around the town with us. Antolín approved of simple human pleasures. I have seen many Spanish patron saints endorse such entertainment. In Trevélez, high in Andalusia's Sierra Nevada, San Antonio de Padua stops and turns to watch the fireworks that repeat-

edly greet his nighttime procession through the village. And in Llanes, on
the Asturian coast, San Roque and his dog are carried to the main square to
see costumed children perform an intricate pilgrim dance that ends with five
children, each exalted on a knot of sticks, leading the town in a joyous cry of
"¡Viva Llanes!" and "¡Viva San Roque y su perro!" (Long live San Roque and
his dog!).

Some would call all this idolatry, but the biblical prohibition against the
worship of idols arguably forbids false images, not images as such. It is an
article of Christian faith that Jesus, as the Son of God, is "the image of the invisible God" (Colossians 1:15). Whether the distant king high in the *retablo* or
the friendly saint in dancer's dress better represents this image in the parish
church of Sariñena is open for discussion. That one is named Christ and the
other Antolín does not decide the issue.

It may be that the transformation of Christ by church artists and their
sponsors into an advocate for hierarchies of power is the worst kind of fab-
rication of false images. And it may be that Tony's affable endorsement of
the town's festivities aligns him well with a God who chose to become, of
all things, "flesh" (John 1:14) and, thus embodied, to save a wedding party by
turning six huge jars of water into first-class wine (John 2:1-11). The early
church too soon forgot the view of the Hebrew scriptures that romance is
to be enjoyed (Song of Songs), that happiness is an extended family around
a table (Psalm 127), and that the promised consummation may be compared
to "a feast of rich food for all peoples, a banquet of aged wine—the best of
meats and the finest of wines" (Isaiah 25:6). Sariñena's patron saint licenses
a folk theology that might have seemed strange to the historical Antoine de
Pamiers but not to a Jew raised, like Jesus, in a culture where sacrificial offerings made possible communal feasts. To sing romantic *jotas*, to drink wine,
to eat well, and to dance freely may be a profoundly religious act of gratitude
to God.

The popular elements in patronal saints' day festivals, like Carnival, have
often been demonized as pagan or heretical. Sariñena's feast of San Antolín
suggests an alternative hypothesis. Could it be that popular religious festivals offer a source of theological wisdom, otherwise unarticulated and therefore unnoticed by formal theology, that is worthy of a place alongside sacred
text, reason, and ecclesiastical tradition? Such a perspective would partly
balance the standard sources of theology, which privilege clerical exegesis,
educated reason, and authoritative legitimation of tradition.

Historically, even the clergy have at times resisted the construction of
theology from the top down. One could argue that the better impulses of

both the Protestant Reformation and the Second Vatican Council consti-
tuted such a challenge. But the most notable recent challenge has been in
those Latin American base communities where liberation theologians have
encouraged uneducated lay Catholics to interpret the Bible freely in the light
of their own immediate social experience.[16] Taking my hypothesis seriously
would extend the commitment of liberation theology to give voice to the
marginalized by attending carefully to a medium in which folk communities
have always spoken, albeit in ways that have made their intentions appear
innocuous or garbled to clergy, anthropologists, and other outsiders. I make
no claims for the authority or constancy of folk theology, only for the balance
it provides. Like other theological endeavors, it is shaped by flawed human
beings and washed by cultural currents.

This, then, is my third heuristic principle: fiestas afford a fertile opportunity for the insinuation of a hidden transcript of folk theology into the public
transcript of formal Catholic devotion. Such hidden theological transcripts,
visible in performance rather than in text, offer a corrective to the public
theology of church ritual, preaching, and art, especially where the latter have
been largely shaped by those in power. To ignore this hidden theological transcript is to ignore a vital clue to the multifaceted meaning of the festival.

Neither the folk performance nor the folk theology of Sariñena's festival
ended with its mass. Afterwards, the lightweight image of San Antolín was
taken to the Plaza de España and placed on a pedestal at one end of a temporary stage beneath the town hall's balcony. There he joined us in enjoyment of a *coloquio* (play) of Moors and Christians. Unlike many Spanish folk
performances since the death of Franco, Sariñena's *coloquio* is not a revival but has been performed continuously since the sixteenth or seventeenth
century. Only during the four years of the Civil War (1936–1939) was it sus-
pended.[17] As a "religious act," it used to be performed in the square in front
of the church but was moved to a stage in front of the town hall in 1976, so
that more people could see it well. The date suggests an attempt to divest
the play of any taint of religious triumphalism it may have acquired under
Franco.

The play is part of a longer performance that includes *mudanzas* (dance
movements), *dichos* (satirical verses), and the *coloquio* itself. Confusingly for
English speakers, the performance as a whole is known as the *dance*, which
in Aragon designates not a dance (*danza*) but a particular complex of traditional performance activities. The *dance* began with sixteen adult dancers
and four skirted boys, known as *volantes* (initiates or flyers),[18] forming two
facing lines along the length of the stage. In front of the dancers, the May-

2.3   The Turkish and Christian generals lead their troops in a brief sword fight.
Sariñena, 1995.

oral and Rabadán (First and Second Shepherds) engaged in a brief comic dialogue. The former represented the wisdom of age, the latter the impetuosity
of youth.[19] The young Rabadán prejudicially reported the imminent arrival
of an army of Turks so ugly that he thought at first they were the furies of hell
and, as he ran away, his socks fell down in fear. (In Spanish folk performance,
Turks and Moors are interchangeable.) Afterwards, the troupe danced, wielding first sticks and then swords.

The Christian General arrived to reassure the shepherds that the Turks
were not "infernal furies" but "men like us." The Turkish General followed
and, after bantering with the shepherds, demanded tribute of his Christian
adversary, whom he repeatedly identified as Charlemagne.[20] Each general
told the other that he really didn't want to fight. The Christian promised the
Turk that if only he'd be baptized, the Christian would gladly serve him "as
a brother and a friend." Nevertheless, the two generals engaged in a series of
vaunting speeches that erupted periodically into brief sword fights between
the two lines of adult dancers (Fig. 2.3). The *volantes* had left the stage and
one line of dancers had added Moorish hats and tunics to their dress.

The battles were brief. Given the skill with swords displayed earlier, we
might have expected longer pyrrhic dances. But each clash was quickly interrupted by one or the other general shouting, "¡Quietos turcos y cristianos!"
(Be quiet, Turks and Christians!), or some such admonition to truce. It was

clear they'd rather talk than fight. Finally, an angel, played by a small boy in white satin and wings, stopped the fighting altogether. He called on the Christians to show compassion and the "noble" Turks to put their faith in Christ and his mother, Mary. The Turks agreed and the angel called on all his "sons" to "embrace like brothers," a command happily obeyed by both teams of dancers.[21] The devil, furious at this outbreak of peace, was told to "go to hell" by the young angel, who threatened him with a toy sword. Then, a fire-cracker stunned the devil into terrified submission. A few moments later, he died. The Christian General joyfully embraced his Turkish counterpart as a "new Christian."

The *coloquio* was followed by further danced *mudanzas* and a set of *dichos* or comic stories in verse, delivered by the Mayoral, about the year gone by in Sariñena. One old man told me that the *dichos* were especially good this year, because the first shepherd threw in "some real Aragonese words and the mayor couldn't do anything about it because it's fiesta." Castilian, as it's spoken in Madrid, is the official but not the traditional language of Aragon. In using Aragonese words, the Mayoral was implicitly positioning Sariñena (like the Moors) on the margins of centralized Spain. The performance closed with two final *mudanzas.* One ended with four boys standing on a knot of swords, formed by the other dancers around the first shepherd's neck, and a fifth standing even higher on the other boys' clasped hands. In the other, four *volantes* turned somersaults over the swords held low between the two rows of adult dancers.[22]

Sariñena was repeatedly invaded by Moors and Christians between the first Moorish conquest of the town in 714 and its final Christian reconquest in 1228.[23] The river that runs through the town still bears the Arabic name Alcanadre. Although the scars of these battles have long since healed, the trauma of a more recent Moroccan invasion lingers. The local historian Arturo Morera tells the story of the town in a novel whose imagined hero lives for many centuries, converting from one faith to another as the opposing armies sweep through. Changing to Christianity for the last time, he refuses to malign his Muslim neighbors: "I'm a friend of the Muslims not *because* of their faith but because I'm a friend of all good people of whatever religion or no religion at all who want to live in peace and brotherly love."[24]

Many centuries later, in March 1938, Franco's planes subjected Sariñena to a fierce aerial bombardment that drove out the Republican army and cleared the way for Nationalist ground troops, including many Moroccan volunteers, to seize the town. Morera's hero remembers the earlier Moorish invasions: "[Back then] the Muslims were my friends. I could not have imagined that, eight centuries later, new Mohammedan mercenaries would have made me so recoil."[25] Born in 1921, Morera was in "bitter exile" at the time of the attack.[26]

After the war Franco actively encouraged festivals of Moors and Christians, seeing in them a popular expression of his own Spanish Catholic triumphalism. Such a public transcript allowed the *moros y cristianos* to survive when Carnival was banned, but it is not the reason they are staged by folk performers. My own study suggests that the Spanish tradition embodies a popular longing for *convivencia*, the capacity of people to live together in difference. The battles end not with slaughter but with Moors and Christians living at peace with those who are enemies no longer.[27] This is certainly the case in Sariñena, where the fights are short-lived; the Turks, even before conversion, are not only "men like us" but "noble"; and "old" and "new" Christians finally embrace as "brothers." The official referent may be twelfth-century religious warfare, but I suspect the unspoken referent is the more recent conflict fueled by Catholic and anti-Catholic ideology. Folk theater cannot yet refer directly to the Civil War.

The street party in honor of San Antolín lasted until the early hours of the following morning. Some time after midnight, a small crowd watched a display of fireworks in a modern square to the east of town. Afterwards, to the exuberant music of an impromptu brass band, the audience marched back through town to the oval Plaza del Salvador outside the parish church. More people thronged the plaza than I'd seen at any one time during the entire fiesta. Many more hung from balconies and windows. The official program had nothing scheduled. Someone mentioned donkey races.

A small trailer backed into the square, dropped its ramp, and unloaded six frightened donkeys. The already dense crowd pushed back towards the outer buildings and the central promenade to clear a cobbled course around the oval. Six riders mounted the donkeys and urged them round in either direction. After a chaotic lap or two, others took the first jockeys' places. Donkeys changed direction, collided, slipped, skidded, and tried to flee into the crowd. Onlookers cheered, laughed, and slapped rumps to drive the reluctant animals faster. I stayed an hour or so, during which time I saw no organized competition and was offered no explanation but hilarity. The patronal saint's day festival, it seemed—assured of the benevolence of God in Antolín and of the possibility of peace between contemporary "Moors" and "Christians"—had slipped into a Carnival. The townspeople loved it.[28] A little after 2:30 A.M., I was one of the first to leave. I don't think Antolín came out to watch, but he can't have slept much while we partied outside in his honor.

3.
El Mas Chiquito de To' Los Santos
(PUERTO RICO)

THANKS TO THE pioneering work of the Puerto Rican scholar Ricardo Alegría and to the scale and exuberance of their processions, the Fiestas de Santiago Apóstol en Loíza (Festivals of Saint James the Apostle in Loíza) are among the best known patronal saints' day celebrations in the Spanish-speaking Caribbean. Little devils with translucent colored bat wings, wielding sticks with paper bags that once were bladders, march in front of smaller saints whose size belies their status. Spanish knights in pale-faced masks wear paper flowers in their hats. Ancestral spirits harness skirted mules, while cross-dressed crazy women sweep the streets and offer their outrageous, padded bums for sodomy. Although the fiestas are named after both a saint (Santiago) and a town (Loíza), only one of the designations is fully warranted. The other masks a hidden transcript, legible in performance, of folk theology. I saw the fiestas in July 1997.

Alegría's brief but invaluable documentary film (1949), his substantial book on the fiestas (1954), and his summary article in the *Journal of American Folklore* (1956) have long been the unchallenged source of interpretation of Loíza's festivities. Neither the work of subsequent scholars and filmmakers nor the elaborate programs published annually by the mayor's office in Loíza offer any evidence of disagreement with Alegría's reading.[1] Although Alegría carefully qualified his speculative account of the fiestas with such phrases as "it would be natural to suppose that" and "it is possible to believe that,"[2] his provisional conclusions have been accepted without question by subsequent scholars, filmmakers, and local officials. Alegría (and all who rely on him) claim that the fiestas draw their strength from a syncretic mixture of Spanish mock battles between Moors and Christians, on the one hand, and imported Yorùbá deities and masks, on the other.

My fourth heuristic principle comes into play here. Official explanations, especially when backed by uncontested scholarship, should be regarded with considerable suspicion. Such explanations often turn out to be dignifying histories, simultaneously giving a patina of age to the festivities and masking the hidden transcript that drives their repeated popular staging. By Alegría's own admission, the European and African traditions whose traces he claims to have uncovered now have no meaning for those who take part in the fiestas. Not only do I believe that he is wrong about the historical roots of the fiestas, but I believe that his account obscures the much more vibrant social and theological commentary to which the fiestas do in fact give lively dramatic form.

The starting point for my own understanding of the fiestas lies in a deceptively simple observation. The festivities are uniformly ascribed to Loíza despite the fact that they happen in Medianía, some three miles away. Or, to be more precise, they take place on the road from Loíza to Medianía, gathering strength in both numbers and vitality as they travel eastward from one to the other. The true location of the fiestas is thus masked by their public designation. I believe that the fiestas are rooted, at least in part, in long-standing and continuing tensions between the comparative social prestige of Loíza and Medianía.

Loíza was one of the first colonial settlements on the island. Black slaves were brought to Loíza as early as 1519 to work in gold mining and, when the gold deposits ran out, in the cultivation of sugarcane. By the middle of the eighteenth century, Loíza and its surroundings had the highest concentration of blacks on the island. The pueblo itself was small, boasting only two stone buildings (the church and the government office) and a population of a few white officials and their mulatto and free black neighbors. White owners lived, with their black slaves, on the adjoining sugarcane plantations. A growing population of free blacks spread eastward along the coast in the area now known as Medianía.[3] With the demise of the sugar industry in the middle of the nineteenth century and the abolition of slavery in 1873, the economy of the region changed, but the demographics remained much the same. Although for administrative purposes Medianía is now considered a barrio of Loíza, it is the old pueblo of Loíza that remains the seat of official power. "Loíza," I was told, "is where the bureaucrats are: the mayor, the teacher, the priest, and so on. Medianía is where the poorer people live."

The region as a whole is still one of the deepest pockets of Afro-Caribbean culture on the island,[4] more isolated than its location fifteen miles east of the capital of San Juan would suggest. A minor road leaves the main highway five miles inland, joins the coast at Loíza, turns eastward to Medianía, and then loops back to rejoin the main highway. Until recently only a ferry crossed the river that separates Loíza from the rutted coastal road that leads more directly, if no more quickly, to San Juan.

The origins of the festival are uncertain. The official patron saint of Loíza since 1645 has been Saint Patrick. The church in Loíza, the oldest parish church on the island, is still devoted to San Patricio. It is the much newer parish church in Medianía that is named after Santiago Apóstol. Despite the efforts of nineteenth-century immigrant Irish plantation owners to popularize Patrick's feast day (17 March), the black population has always preferred Santiago. There are several possible reasons for this. First, a feast day that falls in the middle of Lent has limited potential for exuberant popular celebration. Second, so the story goes, a miraculous image of Santiago was found in the trunk of a cork tree in Medianía sometime around 1832. And third, if we are to believe Alegría, the traditional representation of Santiago as a warrior on horseback reminded the black community of similar images of the Yorùbá god Shangó.[5]

But there is no evidence for Alegría's claim. Even Alegría admits that "no visible traces of the worship of African gods survive in Loíza today: the names of Shangó and Ogún have no meaning for its current inhabitants."[6] In the absence of present evidence, he concocts a mythical history. "It would be natural to suppose," he writes, that the early black population of Loíza, when required to fight with the Spaniards against invading Carib Indians and European pirates, "identified the warrior Saint [of Spain] . . . with the African war gods." A similarity of attributes "could well have led to a fusion of the two conceptions." "But," he concedes, in a final twist of circular reasoning, "if such a process of syncretism took place in Loíza . . . , the only affirmative evidence that remains is the devotion of the present population to the Saint."[7]

Alegría's speculative reconstruction unravels over the simple fact that the early black population of Loíza was not Yorùbá. While establishing the ethnic origins of a slave population is uncertain at best, documentary evidence suggests—as one might expect from the history of the transatlantic slave trade in general—that the majority of sixteenth-century Puerto Rican slaves came from the West African coast between modern Senegal and Liberia and that a broadening stream of slaves from Congo and Angola began to arrive in Puerto Rico as the sixteenth century drew to a close.[8] Most of those from Congo and Angola were Bantu. Traffic in Yorùbá slaves, shipped for the most part from the Bight of Benin in southwestern Nigeria, was virtually unknown at this period. A few may have arrived by the second half of the seventeenth century, but substantial numbers of Yorùbá only began to arrive in the Americas in the late eighteenth and early nineteenth century. Of these, most went to Brazil and Cuba.[9]

Manuel Álvarez Nazario, in his exhaustive study of African vocabulary in Puerto Rican Spanish, finds little evidence of Yorùbá influence. "It is possible," he writes, "that an appreciable number of Yorùbá arrived in Puerto Rico in the last third of the eighteenth and the beginning of the nineteenth centuries, just as in Cuba. Nevertheless, during this period, and indeed for as long as the slave trade endured into the nineteenth century, the bulk of the slaves imported into [Puerto Rico] . . . seem to have been of Bantu origin, . . . as can be seen from the etymologies of the great majority of African words that have survived in popular Puerto Rican Spanish."[10] Ironically, the only evidence that Álvarez Nazario offers of a Yorùbá presence in Puerto Rico is Alegría's claim that the Fiestas de Santiago Apóstol in Loíza bear traces of the Yorùbá god Shangó.[11]

But Alegría's claim owes more to the scholarly influences under which he was writing than to any actual evidence in Puerto Rico.[12] As a graduate student at the University of Chicago, Alegría worked closely with the Yorùbá specialists Melville Herskovits and William Bascom at nearby Northwestern University. From them he acquired not only a regional interest but also a political agenda, for Herskovits consciously directed his research against the widespread conviction that slavery had stripped Africans in the New World of all vestiges of their original culture.[13] Like many worthy "demythologizers," Herskovits has been accused of "erring on the side of overstatement."[14] The same charge may be leveled against Alegría, who completed his studies in Chicago in 1947, two years before he filmed the Loíza fiestas.

Even the details of his mentors' work do not advance Alegría's cause. Herskovits, in an article cited by Alegría, makes the general point that African Catholics in the New World syncretize Catholic saints and African gods but finds Shangó identified with Santa Barbara rather than Santiago. Bascom, in his study of Shangó in the New World, finds links between Shangó and Saints Jerome, John, Michael, Barbara, Peter, and George but not James (Santiago).[15] Alegría is therefore reduced to comparing the images of Santiago in Loíza with a Nigerian wood sculpture of Shangó on horseback, but even this is challenged by recent experts on the art of the African diaspora. Judith Bettelheim writes, "There is no tradition of wood sculpture resembling this manner of depicting Shangó in either Cuba or Puerto Rico." Henry Drewal adds, "There are representations [in Cuba] of Shangó on horseback, but these are linked to images of Santa Barbara on horseback, in armor, in front of a castle."[16]

The devotion to Santiago in Loíza, in short, has nothing to do with Shangó. It more likely derives from the saint's ambiguous role in the mythology of Spanish colonialism. On the one hand, Santiago is the patron saint of Spain, supernatural leader of Christian troops against dark-skinned heathen, and archetypal hero of white Spanish Catholic triumphalism: in each of the three processional images of Santiago in Loíza, a diminutive, pale-faced Santiago sits astride a rearing white horse, beneath whose forefeet lie one or two severed black Moorish heads. On the other hand, Santiago is a native warrior who opposes external rule, for he gained his earliest and most famous victories not in wars of conquest but of reconquest, displaying his military prowess during Spain's long campaign to expel the Moors. Official approval of Santiago's role as defender of the faith is thus matched by subordinate appropriation of his role as liberator. It is not, I suspect, the old public transcript of the differing skin colors of Santiago and his victims that appeals to those in Medianía but the almost equally venerable hidden transcript of his defeat of oppressive outside forces.

A similar ambiguity governs relationships among the three processional images of Santiago, whose status depends on the social location of the viewer. Seen from Loíza, the official hierarchy ranks them according to size and in the order in which they first appear: Santiago de los Hombres (Saint James of the Men), Santiago de las Mujeres (Saint James of the Women), and Santiago de los Niños (Saint James of the Children). Men thus rank above women, women above children, larger above smaller, and first above last. Santiago de los Hombres is honored on the first day of the processions (Fig. 3.1). Although only eighteen inches tall, he is the largest of the three images, the only one that begins its journey by processing westward—led by priests—into Loíza, and the only image now allowed inside the parish church of Saint Patrick.[17] Seen from Medianía, where each image spends the year in the house of its respective *mantenedora* (guardian), the popular hierarchy privileges Santiago de los Niños (Fig. 3.2). Nine inches tall, he is the image that miraculously appeared in the cork tree and is believed to be a potent worker of miracles on behalf of the powerless (all of whom, regardless of age, are treated as children by the powerful). Because each of the other images drops out after sharing its day of honor with those officially ranked beneath it, Santiago de los Niños reigns alone on the last day of the fiestas, when the greatest number of people take part.

On the morning of 24 July, I visited the home of Santiago de los Hombres. Despite the official designation of the fiestas, he lives not in Loíza but in Medianía Baja, the closest of the two Medianías to Loíza. The daughter

3.1 Santiago de los Hombres. Medianía, 1996.

of his *mantenedora* was putting the final touches to his costume. She told me that her mother had inherited the role of guardian from her own mother thirty-seven years ago.

In the late afternoon, while the sun was still oven-hot even in the shade of the flame red poinciana trees, a small procession formed up and headed west from the *mantenedora*'s house. A jeep with a huge papier-mâché mask mounted on its hood led the way, followed by a small group of pilgrims. A woman carried a scarlet and gold banner that proclaimed, "Viva Santiago Apóstol." Two others carried the image of Santiago de los Hombres. A brass band on a flatbed truck brought up the rear. Halfway to Loíza, two priests in white cassocks and red stoles joined the procession.[18] Thereafter, devotional songs alternated with the band's *pasodobles*. The number of participants grew along the way but never reached much more than a hundred. A scattering of onlookers watched us pass.

Reaching Loíza, the procession traveled counterclockwise around the main square before entering the church. After a brief priestly exhortation and a congregational song, the worshipers dispersed. The saint was left alone indoors. In Loíza's nearby sports stadium, the mayor pronounced the fiestas open, reminding the people of Loíza that theirs is a festival in honor of Santiago and not a Carnival. The first procession had conformed to official expectations.

The next morning challenged them. A company of some one hundred fifty *vejigantes* assembled in the streets west of the town center. The *vejigantes* are the most colorful of the festival's processional characters. Describing themselves as *diablitos* (little devils), they wear loose-fitting, multicolored body suits that reveal, when the wearer raises his arms, an arc of translucent material that connects sleeve to side like bat wings. Their faces are hidden behind elaborate masks, most of which are carved from coconut shells and given exaggeratedly African features such as flattened noses and thick lips (Fig. 3.3). Others, borrowed from the *vejigantes* of the island's largest Carnival at Ponce, are shaped from papier-mâché and give form to fantastic monsters. All are brightly painted and have multiple horns longer than the mask itself. The name of the characters derives from the *vejiga* (bladder) on a stick that they used to carry. Some still carry inflated paper bags or balloons.

Although Alegría admits that "it is no longer possible in Loíza to prove the existence of an artistic tradition that derives its elements from the vigor of African art," he proposes that the style of the *vejigante* masks was influenced by traditional Yorùbá masks. Once again he argues from an assumed resemblance to a mythical history: "Like the Yorùbá masks, those from Loíza represent grotesque faces showing extreme expressions, are polychrome, and the details are painted with great elaboration. The facial traits are exagger-

3.2   Santiago de los Niños. Medianía, 1996.

3.3 *Vejigantes*. Loíza, 1996.

ated, especially the mouths and eyes, which are generally ovoid in shape."[19] Making a characteristic leap of the imagination, he concludes, "It is possible to believe that in Loíza . . . the influence of the African sculpture was maintained in the slave descendants and manifested itself in the artistic opportunities which the fiesta offered."[20]

Given the ethnicity of early slaves in Puerto Rico, this is improbable. It also misrepresents Yorùbá style. Bascom writes, "Compared to many African cultures, Yorùbá carving is relatively naturalistic and restrained, and for this reason, has not been appreciated by those who prefer the abstract or grotesque."[21] Yorùbá Egúngún masks, which incorporate the grotesque to satirize such antisocial figures as drunkards, prostitutes, or enemies, are an exception to this general rule, but even they do not provide a model for the masks in Loíza. After a visit to Loíza, Drewal wrote, "Yorùbá do not use coconuts for carving, and there is no widespread tradition of [placing] horns on Yorùbá masks. . . . [I saw] no clear or explicit links to Yorùbá masking [in Loíza]."[22] A more plausible explanation is that the coconut masks, like the fantastic papier-mâché masks, have their roots in the island's Carnival tradition. The coconut masks suggest a kind of carnivalesque ethnic caricature, exaggerating and thereby mocking the traditional white colonist's association of dark skin and the demonic.

Alegría is also persuaded that the *vejigantes* once fought another of the festival's masked characters, the pale-faced *caballeros* (gentlemen) (Fig. 3.4).

"It would appear," he writes, without offering any evidence for his suggestion, "that formerly the *caballeros* were the Saint's escort and performed certain pantomimes representing battles between themselves and Santiago Apóstol on the one hand and the Moors on the other." These may, he adds, have resembled the *fiestas de moros y cristianos* "still celebrated in Mexico."[23] Although such mock battles between Moors and Christians were staged in colonial Puerto Rico, neither they nor the elaborate ritual dances and large-scale battles of the Mexican tradition bear more than a superficial resemblance to Loíza's festivities.[24]

I know, for instance, of no example of the tradition anywhere in which the Moors have carried bladders. These were instead the common property of the medieval fool and are still carried by Carnival maskers in parts of Europe.[25] Moreover, while there is no historical evidence of Puerto Rican *vejigantes* taking part in mock battles, there is ample testimony to their participation in civic spectacles, masquerades, and Carnivals. A *vejigante* in a "ridiculous costume" took part in San Juan's festivities of May 1747 belatedly celebrating the coronation of Ferdinand VI of Spain. The account notes, "Those who in Europe are called *diablitos* go by the name of *begigantes* [sic] in this island."[26] One nineteenth-century observer in San Juan remembered, among the maskers who filled the streets of the city every Sunday in June, "an infinite number of blacks dressed as demons to whom they give the name of *vejigante*." Their role then included the exchange of sung pleasantries with small boys who followed them.[27] And Louis Bonafoux, in 1879, reported seeing in Puerto Rican Carnivals "companies of *vejigantes*, whose humor consists of lashing with large bladders the first biped they meet."[28] *Nenen de la ruta*, a film made in 1956, shows the Loiceño *vejigantes* flourishing inflated bladders and accompanied by a chorus of small boys,[29] but neither this nor the earlier film made by Alegría shows any sign of a mock battle.

When I asked a group of *vejigantes* if they represented Moors, they regarded my suggestion as very strange.

"No," they said. "We're *diablitos*. We're opposed to Santiago. The *caballeros* defend Santiago."

"Do you fight?" I asked.

"Yes, with swords," they replied.

"But I've not seen you fight."

"No," they told me. "That's just the story. We don't actually fight. Really, we get on fine with the *caballeros* and Santiago. We're friends."

The story may be Alegría's, repeated now for fifty years. Although, on the existing evidence, I can no more prove my hypothesis than Alegría can his, my best guess is that the *vejigantes* and *caballeros* are carnivalesque figures of independent, although complementary, origins, both representing ethnic caricatures, whose coincidental juxtaposition in Loíza invited the later rationalization of a shared origin in the tradition of Moors and Christians. The *locas* (madwomen), *viejos* (ancestors), and other carnivalesque characters who join the parades strengthen my hypothesis but expose a weakness in Alegría's, for not even he supposes that they originated in mock battles between Moors and Christians.

The *vejigantes'* parade through Loíza on 25 July was led by youngsters clad as Taino Indians and by girls dressed as nineteenth-century African slave women. The *vejigantes* followed, hooting and spreading their wings. A small truck brought up the rear, its voluminous loudspeakers blaring Caribbean dance music, including one song that I recognized as the winning Road March of the 1996 Trinidad Carnival.[30] The joyous parade of Indians, Africans, and demons passed counterclockwise around the town hall, main square, and parish church, encircling the "trapped" Santiago de los Hombres and reclaiming the streets for those whose costumes declared their festive opposition to traditional colonial and ecclesiastical measures of value.

The next day was the day of Santiago de los Hombres. In the heat of the early afternoon, the officially privileged image of Santiago was taken from the Church of Saint Patrick and set out, with a few devotees and the brass band on a truck, for Medianía. There were no priests. A group of *vejigantes* started from the edge of town, far ahead of the image. After a while, the first *caballeros* joined the procession, walking between Santiago and the *vejigantes*.[31]

The *caballeros* wore wire-mesh masks, each painted with pale skin, blue eyes, and a thin mustache to caricature aristocratic Spanish features. Their hats were decorated with large plumes or paper flowers and mirrors; long, multicolored ribbons flowed down before and behind (Fig. 3.4). Their uniforms of cape, jacket, and trousers, all in flowered or checked material, "conjure[d] up the image of a harlequin" rather than a warrior.[32] They carried no weapons. According to Alegría, the *caballero*'s costume is more expensive than the *vejigante*'s, restricting the former role to "those who can count on greater economic resources,"[33] but the reverse was true of the masks and costumes that I priced in the Ayala family store in Medianía.[34] Although the tourist trade may have affected the relative prices of masks over the last fifty years—with the more spectacular *vejigante* masks fetching higher prices—I suspect that the costumes mock rather than reflect hierarchies of class and ethnicity.

3.4 *Caballeros.* Loíza, 1996.

As the religious procession made its way towards Medianía, more and more revelers, in and out of costume, joined the parade that preceded it. *Vejigantes* and *caballeros* proliferated. *Viejos* and *locas* came out in fewer numbers. The former traditionally wore ragged clothes and masks made of paper or cardboard shoe boxes. Now they are just as likely to wear store-bought plastic werewolf or ghoul masks. Denoting ancestral spirits rather than old men, their plastic Halloween masks are neither concessions to modernity nor generic Carnival disguises but specific updates of an old tra-dition.[35] Homage is traditionally paid to ancestors as the procession passes the cemetery on the outskirts of Loíza. The *locas* used to be cross-dressed men, with exaggerated padding before and behind, who alternately flirted with men in the crowd and swept the streets with short brooms, pretending to gather dust in biscuit tins. They were thus a parody of both the domes-ticated woman and the woman of the street.[36] Nowadays, they tend more simply to be camp drag queens.

By the time we reached Medianía, several hundred jovial pilgrims were walking ahead of the image in a kind of mobile street party. Hundreds more lined the streets to watch. As the religious tail of the procession neared the house where Santiago de los Niños lodged, four bearers carried him into the

street to face Santiago de los Hombres. The two images approached one another, each preceded by a flag bearer. Three times the ensigns genuflected,
swirling their flags in a figure eight design, while behind them the bearers
of the images also genuflected, making each Santiago dip in greeting to the
other. The crowd applauded. As Santiago de los Niños fell in behind his
senior namesake, the procession continued eastward. At the house of the
mantenedora of Santiago de las Mujeres, a similar salutation took place before the women's Santiago joined the procession between Santiago de los
Hombres and Santiago de los Niños.[37]

In the center of Mediania Alta, where the crush of marchers and onlookers was most dense, the procession turned left into the neighborhood of
Las Carreras. When the images reached the site of the sacred cork tree (now,
sadly, dead), they turned to face back down the street that runs a few hundred
yards from the main road to the beach. Fireworks shot high in the sky. Three
men on horseback trotted the full length of the street from the main road
bearing the images' gold and scarlet standards. Then the procession retraced
its route, leaving each of the images with its respective *mantenedora* and
shrinking in numbers until it reached the house of Santiago de los Hombres.
There the procession dissolved, leaving in its wake a series of street parties
that drank and danced to loud music outside the bars and the houses of the
saints.

In the dusty front courtyard of the Ayala store, I watched a group of four
drummers call solo dancers into the open space in front of the drums for
bailes de bomba (drum dances). In a joyous musical contest, each dancer
improvised an intricate routine, challenging the lead drummer to reproduce its complex rhythm.[38] Mistaken as he may be about the source both of
Loiceño devotion to Santiago and of the design of *vejigante* masks, Alegría
is right about the *bailes de bomba* being "of African origin."[39] But they are
not Yorùbá. When Charles Walker saw the dance performed by African-born
slaves in Ponce in 1836, he observed, "It is the dance of their native land and
they accompany the music with songs in the Congo language."[40] Many of the
names still in use for the *bailes de bomba* are "of probable Bantu origin."[41]

Before I left the courtyard, I bought one of Raul Ayala's *vejigante* masks.
Then, slowly, I walked the three miles back to Loíza, where I ate in a fast-
food restaurant whose walls were decorated with ornate *vejigante* masks and
splendid paintings of the fiestas by the Mediania artist Samuel Lind. I had
earlier visited Lind's studio in Mediania, where we had spoken at length
about the fiestas, his paintings, and his designs for the annual festival poster
and program cover. But it was not so much his paintings or our conversa-

tion that helped me better understand the fiestas. It was his more modest preparation of a church bulletin.

The next morning, I attended Sunday mass in Medianía. It was a friendly, informal service, at the end of which birthdays were celebrated and visitors, including myself, introduced. Lind's festive calligraphy on the front of the bulletin praised Santiago, in the local dialect,[42] as "protector of the poor, kind to women, and affectionate to children," who had come to Loíza "pa' gozá y sufri' con nojotro" (to rejoice and suffer with us). Santiaguito de los Niños, it added, is "el mas gracioso y chiquito de to' los Santos" (the most gracious and the smallest of all the saints). Brief expositions of the scripture readings for the day proposed that acceptance of God as sole Father and Lord is "the best guarantee that there may be brotherhood among men and that no one may claim to be lord over another" and called us to "reject, like Jesus, all temptation to triumphalism, above all in the political and social order." In Medianía, the church has embraced the God of the Magnificat who unseats the mighty and exalts the meek. It is no wonder that the parades and processions of the fiestas repeatedly enact a joyous exodus from Loíza, where the plantation owners worshiped and the "bureaucrats" still hold sway, to Medianía, where God sends the smallest and most gracious of the saints to dwell with the poor.

After church, Santiago de las Mujeres was bundled into a car and driven to Loíza to lead the second exodus. That afternoon, instead of walking all the way from Loíza, I waited at the house of Santiago de los Niños for the procession to arrive. Numbers were up slightly from the previous day. *Locas* in particular were more plentiful, pairs of cross-dressed, lipsticked young men walking arm in arm, their biological gender sometimes betrayed by thin mustaches. When Santiago de las Mujeres arrived, he was greeted with flag-swirling and genuflection by his smaller namesake, who then fell in behind him. There was no sign of Santiago de los Hombres. "He's finished," I was told. In Las Carreras, two riders delivered the scarlet and gold banners to their respective bearers. Then the parade again returned the images to their *mantenedoras* and dissolved into serial street parties. At the house of Santiago de las Mujeres, crowds milled in the street, some dancing to recorded music, others drinking and talking. Santiago and his white horse stood beribboned and ignored on the front porch.

On the third and final day of the processions, I walked from the house of Santiaguito's *mantenedora* to meet the oncoming parade. For a mile or more, the road was packed with *caballeros, vejigantes, viejos, locas,* and a wide range of generic Carnival characters, all outnumbered by the multitude of festive marchers in everyday clothes. I joined the parade with one of the livelier groups, clustered around a kind of bicycle rickshaw pulling a sound system rather than a passenger seat. The group danced eastward, whistling, jumping, and shouting to the rhythm of the loudspeakers. The star of the show was an athletic *loca*, well over six feet tall, with blackened face, exaggerated pink lipstick, pink head scarf, and long, brown cotton dress, who swept the road with the traditional broom and biscuit tin. At one point, he stopped the bicycle and danced on a small platform over the front wheel, facing backwards and salaciously waving his outrageously padded behind at the crowd in front. When someone jumped onto the platform to attempt mock sodomy, the *loca* mimed both shock and pleasure. He was a fine actor who played his part with obscene energy and imagination.

In the heart of Medianía Alta, I waited for Santiago de los Niños. No flag-waving and saintly curtsy had interrupted his progress today. As the sole surviving Santiago, he was obligated to recognize no parental, larger, or more authorized image. Instead, he had shepherded the final exodus from Loíza alone, picking up more and more exuberant revelers en route, until he now arrived, tiny protector of the poor, the women, the children, the dead, the little devils, the crazy, and the cross-dressed, in the midst of a jubilant party of the marginalized, held in his honor. Even the *caballeros* had abandoned their claims to higher rank, leaving the privileged confines of Loíza to join their brothers and sisters in Medianía. As a sop to the bureaucrats and clergy left behind, if it helped to win their own freedom, the revelers were happy to pay lip service to the pretense that the festival was taking place in Loíza.

Santiago de los Niños wound through the back lanes of Las Carreras, the gardens lining his route ablaze with flowers, to the site of the cork tree where he had once been found. After his standard had been ridden, unchallenged, up the long street from the main road, he returned slowly to his *mantenedora*'s. The band played *pasodobles*. I rode with friends in the back of the masked jeep that led the procession. *Locas* waved to us from the street. A skirted hobbyhorse, ridden by a *viejo* in traditional paper mask, danced alongside.[43] The parish priest of Medianía, in street clothes, walked happily with the people.

Outside the *mantenedora*'s house, a packed crowd watched the star *loca* put on a display of exuberant sexual mimicry. A sixty-year-old *vejigante* told me that each year, for the fiestas, he returns to Medianía from New York. He had learned his role from his father and his grandfather (who came from Africa) and was now passing it on to his son. Later, as I watched the *bailes de bomba* in the Ayala courtyard, the members of the family served us drinks and *bacalaitos* (thin cod fritters). When I finally left, the street party in honor of Santiago de los Niños, from which none are excluded but those who think themselves too good, was still in full swing in Medianía.

I had found no evidence that, for those in the streets in Medianía, the Fiestas de Santiago Apóstol signify an appropriation of ancestral Yorùbá art or of Spanish mock battles between Moors and Christians. The Fiestas de Santiago Apóstol are instead rooted in the mixed soil of local tensions, Carnival, and Christianity. There is the long-standing and continuing tension between the comparative social prestige of Loíza and Medianía. There is a Carnival tradition that challenges conventional hierarchies of power. And there is a reading of the Christian narrative that insists that none, however marginalized by those who dominate human society, be excluded from God's festivities.

Jesus told the parable of a rich man who served a banquet. He told his servants, "Go out quickly into the streets and alleys of the town and bring in the poor, the crippled, the blind, and the lame. . . . Go out to the roads and country lanes and make them come in, so that my house will be full" (Luke 14:21–23). In Medianía, during the Festival of Santiaguito de los Niños, the folk theologians of the streets add the crazy women, the dead, the devils, and the cross-dressed.

4.
The Cross-Dressed Virgin on a Tightrope
(MEXICO)

IN DECEMBER 1998, I was one of a reported six million pilgrims who visited the basilica of Guadalupe in Mexico City to celebrate the annual feast day of the Virgin of Guadalupe (12 December).[1] That's more people than live in the entire country of Denmark, greater than the combined populations of Puerto Rico and Trinidad and Tobago, and about equal to the population of Israel. Arguably, this densely packed fiesta exalts not one sacred woman but three.

The basilica sits at the point where the northern causeway that once crossed Lake Texcoco from the Mexica (Aztec) island capital of Tenochtitlan abutted the mainland hill of Tepeyac.[2] According to the sixteenth-century Franciscan ethnographer Bernardino de Sahagún, Tepeyac was the site of a preconquest temple where the Mexica worshiped Tonantzin, whom he called "the mother of the gods." Recent scholars have questioned the existence both of the temple and of Tonantzin, but Sahagún's assertion has been so often quoted that it is widely believed.[3]

The association of Christianity's own "mother of God" with Tepeyac began—so the story goes—in 1531, when the Virgin Mary was seen four times on the hillside by a poor, baptized Indian by the name of Juan Diego. Mary asked that a temple be built for her at Tepeyac and invited Juan Diego to relay her request to the bishop of Mexico. To impress the skeptical bishop, the Virgin conjured roses out of season: when Juan Diego opened his cloak in the episcopal palace, a profusion of fresh flowers scattered over the floor. The cloak, made of maguey fiber, was miraculously imprinted with the Virgin's image.

A chapel dedicated to the Virgin of Guadalupe was built at Tepeyac sometime in the sixteenth century.[4] After the lake was drained in the early seventeenth century, a grand highway was constructed linking the center of Mexico City to the shrine of Guadalupe. A colonial basilica was completed in 1709. In the 1950s the surrounding buildings were razed and the space paved to form an atrium the size of several football fields. Listing and unsafe, the old golden-domed basilica remains but has been functionally replaced by a larger, modern basilica, consecrated in 1976, its concrete roof swept back like hair pinned tight and crowned with an inverted shuttlecock.[5] The site is one of the most venerated in the Catholic world.

Juan Diego's cloak, bearing Mary's image, hangs in state, framed in glass, high on the modern basilica's western wall. The Virgin's head is bowed, her hands clasped in prayer. Dressed in a blue robe adorned with stars and surrounded by rays of sunlight, she stands on a crescent moon. She is immediately visible to anyone entering by one of the eastern doorways. At the foot of the wall beneath her image, a moving walkway slowly transports devotees, necks craned, past the object of their gaze. The hands and face of the image are brown-skinned. Known as *la morena* (the dark one), the Mexican Virgin of Guadalupe is "a dark Virgin on a poor Indian's cloak."[6] By papal decree, she is also queen of Mexico and empress of the Americas. Popularly, she is every Mexican's mother. On the outside of the basilica and on thousands of T-shirts is emblazoned "¿No estoy yo aquí que soy tu madre?" (Am I, your mother, not here?).

Mary is supposed to have asked the question of Juan Diego in Nahuatl: "cuix àmo nican nicà nimoNantzin?"[7] Her use of the indigenous language is significant. The first Nahuatl account of the appearances, Luis Laso de la Vega's *Nican mopohua* (1649), repeatedly stresses that Juan Diego was "a humble commoner, a poor ordinary person [*maçehualtzintli*]," that is, a poor Indian.[8] The story presents a marked difference between the attitude to the Indian of the bishop and his court, on the one hand, and that of the Virgin, on the other. Whereas the Virgin initiates contact with Juan Diego, appearing alongside his habitual paths and "waiting for him" when he returns,[9] Juan Diego has to go out of his way to see the bishop, who lives in a palace and always keeps his Indian supplicant waiting. The bishop gives orders to all and sundry, but the Virgin makes requests. The bishop employs servants who block access to him, spy on Juan Diego, and deliver false reports. The Virgin's visits with Juan Diego are unmediated.

The Virgin tells Juan Diego, "I am the compassionate mother of you and of all you people here in this land, and of the other various peoples who love me, who cry out to me, who seek me, who trust me. There [in the temple to be built at Tepeyac] I will listen to their weeping and their sorrows in order to remedy and heal all their various afflictions, miseries, and torments."[10] When Juan Diego apologetically tells Mary, on her fourth appearance, that he has no time to stop since he's rushing to summon priestly help for his sick uncle, she replies, "Do not be concerned, do not fear the illness, or any other illness or calamity. Am I, your mother, not here?" At that very moment, the text assures us, the uncle recovered.[11] Unlike the Spanish bishop, the dark-skinned "mother of the very true deity [*in ninantzin in huel nelli Teotl*]"[12] extends motherly compassion to all the peoples of Mexico.

On the face of it, the *Nican mopohua* would seem to speak of the mother of God's sympathy for Indians in an ecclesiastical context dominated by Spanish-born clergy. The account, however, was written not by a native Nahuatl speaker but by a Creole priest, born in Mexico of Spanish descent. This fact, as we shall see, complicates its interpretation. The identity of Mary as "compassionate mother," however, appeals across racial, ethnic, and class boundaries.

Popular Catholic devotion to Mary expresses the human need to experience God as sympathetic and close at hand rather than as distant, impassive, and judgmental. Some Christians would rather imagine God as a nurturing mother than as a male potentate. The biblical narrative does not preclude this impulse. On one occasion, God compares himself to a mother comforting her child (Isaiah 66:13). On another, Jesus glosses the Psalmist's longing to "take refuge in the shelter of [God's] wings" (Psalms 57:1, 61:4) by telling Jerusalem, "How often have I longed to gather your children together, as a hen gathers her chicks under her wings" (Matthew 23:37). The wisdom of God is personified at length in feminine terms (Proverbs 8), a gendered identity Jesus does not hesitate to own when he says of himself, "Wisdom is proved right by her actions" (Matthew 11:19). While maternal and other feminine images of God are unquestionably outweighed in the biblical narrative by paternal and masculine images—the story was, after all, mostly written by men—the feminine side of God is not entirely suppressed. The folk theology of popular religious festivals affirms it.

This longing to experience God as mother was amply borne out by the crowds at the basilica on the morning of 11 December. Lines of pilgrims who had arrived on buses, trucks, bicycles, and foot formed on the steps of the basilica. As space cleared, those at the front of the queue were ushered inside to shuffle slowly forward and to lay their offerings at the altar. Celibate priests on a balcony, dipping brushes, sprinkled holy water on inferior devotees. The cloaked Virgin never left her wall. Framed, exalted, she was out of reach. The people came to gaze on her, their passage through her sanctuary directed by officials of the church. Her guarded immobility distinguished this fiesta from every other saint's day festival I'd seen.

Given the likely authorship of her founding narrative and the subsequent history of her manipulation by Creole clergy, this should not surprise us. For all the rhetoric of a dark-skinned Virgin extending compassion to a poor Indian, Guadalupe's image was from the beginning the property of Creole clergy, a source of Creole satisfaction that the Virgin had appeared in Mexico and not in Spain. The story of Juan Diego and the apparitions in Tepeyac was first published by two Creole priests, Miguel Sánchez and Luis Laso de la Vega, in 1648 and 1649. Before that, "there is no clear evidence for the story" or for any "strong Indian devotion" to the image.[13]

For well over a century, "the providential story of Guadalupe's apparition" remained "more popular among Creole clergymen . . . than among Indian villagers."[14] Despite frequent Indian resistance, the priests used the story and the image of Guadalupe as a pious sign to try to draw the Indians into a centralized church in which the Indians held little or no power. In 1760, for example, the Indians in Tejupilco (Estado de México) "lodged a complaint against their *cura* [parish priest] for forcing them to hold an annual celebration commemorating the apparition." Their counterparts in Zacualpan (Estado de México) "suspected in 1757 that their priests were introducing feast days in honor of Guadalupe as a way to increase their incomes."[15] It was only after another Creole priest, Miguel Hidalgo, adopted her image as the symbol of his incipient rebellion against Spanish rule in 1810 that the Virgin of Guadalupe began to win acceptance, even among the Indians, as the mother of all Mexico. The clergy have still not relinquished control of her original image.

Outside the basilica, the hierarchy of dancers reflected a similar tendency among today's urban Mexicans to value constructed images of Indians more highly than they do the Indians themselves. Several indigenous groups were dancing. Totonac *quetzales* from the state of Veracruz, accompanied by a single musician with a pipe and tabor, wore huge circular headdresses whose colors recalled the rainbow of colors flashing from the play of sunlight on the plumage of the sacred quetzal bird. Nahua *inditos* (little Indians) from the state of Puebla, accompanied by a fiddle and a guitar, wore fringed, broad-brimmed hats, festooned with flowers and dangling ribbons. In their midst, a cross-dressed boy sucking a lollipop danced the part of Maringuilla. Maringuilla or Malinche, the name given to female dance characters throughout Mexico, represents a mother goddess and the female companion of a messianic Moctezuma.[16] She is the third sacred woman who, along with the Virgin Mary and Tonantzin, plays an important role in the annual celebrations at the basilica.

Nearby, thirty *santiaguitos* (little Santiagos) posed for a group photograph

4.1   Santiago (Armando Espinosa). Basílica de Guadalupe, 1998.

with their own framed reproduction of the Virgin. Many of the dancers carried swords. Santiago himself wore a pale-faced, bearded mask, crowned with golden sun rays and a small cross (Fig. 4.1). A small girl in white satin, the *angelito* (little angel), or "guardian," of Santiago, slowly flapped her feathered wings. Their presence at the basilica once documented, the *santiaguitos* performed an elaborate narrative dance, one of many Mexican variants of choreographed battles between Moors and Christians. The *maestro* of the troupe, Armando Espinosa, told me that the group had come from San Luis Huexotla (Estado de México), where they'd dance again a few days later in their own more intimate fiesta. He invited me to join them. I said I'd try.

Like so many dances performed by Christian Indians in Mexico, these dances are syncretic, blending elements of European and autochthonous traditions into forms that do not permit the easy separation of imported Catholic and precontact indigenous elements. References to native quetzals, on the one hand, or the use of European fiddle and guitar, on the other, are no definitive guide to a dance's pedigree. The sainted knight of Spain wears both cross and sun rays. Whatever their origins may be, they are now indigenous Christian dances performed by Catholic Indians.

The same is not true of the more ostentatiously but less genuinely Indian

4.2 A *danza azteca* in honor of the Virgin. Basilica de Guadalupe, 1998.

dances that were also beginning to fill the atrium. Known generically as *danzas aztecas* (Aztec dances), they were being performed by urban, middle-class mestizos and mestizas in costumes loosely based on pictures of Aztec warriors and dancers from the old codices (Fig. 4.2). The dancers wore cloaks, tunics, and chasubles sewn with Aztec designs. Many carried wooden *macanas* (obsidian-edged Aztec swords) and shields covered in gaudy brocade. Their expensive feather headdresses included plumes plucked overseas from ostriches and other exotic birds. Young drummers beat out a loud and insistent rhythm on reproduction Aztec *huehetl* and *teponaztli* drums. The drums looked authentic, but their sound had nothing of the subtlety of genuine Native American drumming. The choreography of the dances was a rhythmic shuffle, allowing the participation of young and old, trim and overweight. Although a few individuals performed fast and fancy leaps, the dances as a whole lacked the sophisticated footwork and skilled coordination of the *quetzales* or the *santiaguitos*.

The *danzas aztecas* are self-conscious attempts, as many participants told me, to revive "the dances of our [Aztec] ancestors." They are far from authentic. "As well developed as we know it was both before and after the conquest," James Lockhart has concluded, Aztec dance has left too little "tangible evidence" to yield any certain reconstruction.[17] The urban mestizo's ideas about his Aztec ancestors are culled as much from popular films, posters, newspapers, and magazines—and from Hollywood representations of Native Americans—as they are from the ancient codices and subsequent scholarship. To put it unkindly, the *danzas aztecas* resemble a cross between a Plains Indians powwow and the gaudy fantasies of a Las Vegas costume designer. The performers are not living tradition bearers but escapees from the alienation of daily routine to a world of "invented ethnicity."[18] The pursuit of urban middle-class success can make us hanker sometimes after noble savagery.

More numerous and more flamboyant than the Catholic Indian dances, the *danzas aztecas* demanded greater space and drew larger crowds. The drumming of the former drowned out the quiet music of the latter. Urban Mexican contempt for the cultural products of unsophisticated rural Indians marginalized real Indians in the name of a romantic, middle-class vision of Mexico's indigenous past. Once again, for all the rhetoric of a dark Virgin appearing to a poor Indian, the dynamics of the basilica and its image favored those Mexicans whose ethnicity is less rather than more indigenous. In the *danzas aztecas*, urban mestizos defiantly assert the value of a native heritage they despise in the flesh of their Indian neighbors.

As night fell, scattered floodlights came on. Seething with people, the atrium was growing hard to navigate. Aztec dances proliferated. Sharing a blanket with an Indian family, I watched instead a Nahua *danza de moros y cristianos* from Santiago de Tiopantlan (Puebla). Flawless footwork and rapid hand movements produced some of the best sword dancing I've seen. Clashing swords sparked. The Moors wore tunics in the Spanish national colors of red and yellow, the Christians in the Mexican colors of red, white, and green. The dancers grinned when I remarked on their surreptitious national identities. "Of course," they said. A small boy in white—another Maringuilla—represented "the angel of the Christians," one of the dancers told me. "She stops the war. The war can't pass her." So, with the help of Malinche, Christian Mexico resisted pagan Spain.

By midnight so many pilgrim travelers had bedded down in the churchyard, squeezing dancers into shrinking circles and pedestrians into compressed alleyways, that it was barely possible to move. I watched a group of *concheros* begin their long preparatory rites. The dance, named after the *concha* (a stringed instrument made from an armadillo shell) carried by the dancers (Fig. 4.3), is an older, generally lower-class antecedent of the *danzas aztecas*. Less aggressive in its claims to be reviving the dances of the ancestors, the *danza de los concheros* nevertheless preserves, if Martha Stone's account of her induction into the dance cult in the 1940s is to be believed, pre-

4.5 *Gracejos* (*danza de los negritos*). Basílica de Guadalupe, 1998.

thick, animal-skin chaps, and masks made of animal skin (Fig. 4.5) or molded
rubber. Over their shoulders hung coiled thirty-foot rope whips. The "monsters" were called *gracejos* (witty speakers), an ironic designation since they
"spoke" only in high-pitched whistles and hoots. After each round of the
dance, a pair of *gracejos* uncoiled their whips and fought one another. Taking
turns, one unleashed a cracking shot while the other leaped to avoid the
stinging blow. The trick was to wrap the tip of the whip around the unguarded back of an opponent's lower legs. Whipping battles are popular in
the Andes, but these were the first I had seen in Mexico. After a couple of
hours, all the dancers approached the door of the basilica on their knees. The
fiddler removed his baseball cap and, so great was his devotion to the Virgin,
openly wept.

Even more intriguing was the *danza de los maromeros* (dance of the tightrope walkers) from Acatlan (Guerrero). Two dozen men, wearing bright red
breeches, white shirts, and red peaked hats fringed in yellow, erected a tightrope between two sets of crossed poles thirty feet apart. The structure col-
lapsed at least once while the rope was being tested. Satisfied at last that the
contraption was safe, one of the *maromeros* climbed the crossed poles. Sit-
ting in the joint, twelve feet above the ground, he was handed a thick wooden
balance bar almost as long as the rope. Standing slowly, he stepped onto the

rope. The balance bar dipped to one side. He adjusted his grip. Gaining in confidence, he walked to the middle of the rope and stood for a while, gently bobbing up and down. A brass band began to play. Beneath the rope, the other *maromeros* commenced a merry, bouncing dance. The man on the tightrope also started to dance, leaping a couple of feet in the air, crossing and uncrossing his feet as he did so.

Several dancers took turns on the rope. At one point, two *maromeros* stepped onto the rope together, facing one another, sharing the same balance bar, and carefully synchronizing their jumps. Then, slowly and simultaneously, they lay on their backs on the rope, raised themselves on their shoulders, and waved their feet in the air. The star dancer of the troupe was the Malinche, a cross-dressed man in sneakers, long pink skirt, and dark glasses (Fig. 4.6). A second troupe of *maromeros* danced a hundred yards away. Their Malinche, resting, seated, on the gently bouncing cord, flung hard candy to the crowd. Pretty girls asked for more and, grinning, he obliged.[22]

In the late afternoon, two teenaged girls in sequins and dyed ostrich

4.6 Malinche prepares to dance the tightrope (*danza de los maromeros*). Basilica de Guadalupe, 1998.

feathers approached me and asked for money. They said they had no bus fare home. I told them I'd pay their bus fare if they'd talk to me about their *danza.* They alluded to Tonantzin.

"She's the reason why we dance."

I feigned surprise. "I thought you were dancing for the Virgin."

"But Tonantzin and the Virgin are the same," the younger girl replied.

"And does your priest agree with this?"

"He'd say the same or else our parents wouldn't let us dance to her."

The older girl joined in. "We dance the steps our forebears offered to the sun."

"The sun?" I asked.

"Sí. Claro."

I pressed on. "But now you're dancing for the Virgin?"

"Yes. The Virgin is the partner of the sun."

"Who told you this?"

"Our *capitán.* He studies books about the gods. He reads about our ancestors and teaches us these things."

I gave them each a bunch of coins. They ran off giggling. I think they'd won a bet.

The younger girl's equation of Tonantzin and the Virgin of Guadalupe struck me at first as a conventional observation that Guadalupe had replaced the Aztec "mother of the gods" once worshiped on the same site. Perhaps this was all the girl meant. But her priest's endorsement of the shared identity of Christian Virgin and Nahuatl Tonantzin suggests another possibility. Louise Burkhart has recently proposed that Tonantzin ("our honored mother") was nothing more than a postconquest Nahuatl name for the Virgin Mary: "The Indians were not perpetuating memories of pre-Columbian goddesses but were projecting elements of their Christian worship into their pre-Christian past, conceptualizing their ancient worship in terms of Mary."[23] The girl's captain, immersed in "books about the gods," may claim retrospectively that the "Virgin is the partner of the sun," but her Catholic priest counters with the more orthodox assertion that Tonantzin and the Virgin "are the same." The former is only the Virgin's name in Nahuatl. "Tonantzin is Mary," Burkhart writes, "Mary is Tonantzin."[24]

From anything but a devoutly Mexican Catholic point of view, both Tonantzin and the quasi-divine Virgin of Guadalupe are mythical figures. So is Malinche. All three testify to the human need to experience God as mother. And all three are linked, in varying degree, with the sacred space at Tepeyac. Tepeyac is the home of Tonantzin and of the Mexican Virgin of Guadalupe.

The day of Guadalupe attracts a disproportionate number of dances in which Malinche plays a part.

The sacred identity of Malinche in ritual Mexican dances has been woefully misread by scholars, who have too readily identified her with the Indian woman of the same name who served as Cortés's mistress and translator. The Malinche of the European conquest narratives is a figure of considerable ambivalence in the Mexican psyche: a traitor to her people, the victim of European male rape, and the tainted mother of the first mestizo.[25] The Malinche of the dances is a much more powerful, positive figure. In conquest dances, she is the partner not of Cortés but of a messianic Moctezuma. Together, they embody the divine rulers of the spirit realm. When Malinche appears without Moctezuma, she is a goddess of fertility, the partner of the rain god Tlaloc.[26]

The dance character's name may derive, like the mountain in the state of Tlaxcala now known as La Malinche, from the Aztec goddess Matlalcueye. But it may just as well derive from the name of the dominant female figure in Spanish Catholicism, María. Nahuatl lacks the r sound, converting it to l, and tends to replace the glottal stop between two vowels with an n. The suffix -tzin connotes honor or reverence. "Blessed María" thus becomes in Nahuatl "Malintzin," or, in Hispanicized Nahuatl, "Malinche."[27] The fact that in the dances the female character may equally be called Maringuilla (little Mary) seems to confirm the link between Malinche and the Virgin Mary. Just as there is easy slippage in the popular mind between the Virgin of Guadalupe and a real or imagined Aztec goddess named Tonantzin, so the Malinche of the dances may represent at different times—or even simultaneously—a figure from indigenous mythology and the Catholic Mother of God.

There are, then, three overlapping identities for the single complex female figure who draws so many pilgrims to the basilica on the Day of Guadalupe. There is, first, the Virgin of Guadalupe. Although her original image hangs high and unmoving on the west wall of the basilica, many dance troupes have their own portable banner or framed image of the Virgin (see Fig. 4.2 above). In this more personal form, she travels with the dancers to and from their homes and, like Antolín of Sariñena, happily watches them dance. Virtually omnipresent, the Virgin of Guadalupe adorns dancers' costumes and spectators' T-shirts, poses on posters and calendars, and dwells in homes, offices, garages, and bus stations throughout Mexico and the Mexican diaspora. The clergy may retain the original image, but they cannot keep the Virgin from living with her people.

Second, there is Tonantzin. Once, perhaps, nothing more than a Nahuatl name for Mary, Tonantzin is now widely believed to be the name of a goddess worshiped by the Aztecs on the hill of Tepeyac. This, therefore, is the identity adopted for the mother goddess by those middle-class mestizos who want to put down fictitious roots in the religion of their indigenous ancestors. Tonantzin does not go inside the basilica but remains outside. She is "the partner of the sun" and patron of the *danzas aztecas*.

Finally, there is Malinche or Maringuilla. She enjoys a deeper intimacy with the dancers than even Tonantzin or the multiplied images of the Virgin. Malinche doesn't stand by, watching the dances. She joins in. She is the companion of every soldier in the *danza de los concheros*. She is the little angel who "stops the war" from harming indigenous Christian Mexico in the dance of Moors and Christians. In the *danza de la conquista*, she is the partner of the Moctezuma who goes undefeated by the Spaniards. And, in the *danza de los maromeros*, she is the cross-dressed Virgin on a tightrope, inciting the merriment of brass bands and dancers and happily throwing candy to the crowd.

Why is she cross-dressed? Perhaps for no other reason than the traditional reluctance of male folk performers to expose their women to the immodesty of public performance. Or is it possible that the folk theologians of indigenous Mexico have, unconsciously perhaps, found a playful way to enact the idea that a traditionally masculine God has a distinctly feminine side? In any case, it is this multifaceted Virgin of Guadalupe, slipping surreptitiously across racial, class, and gender barriers, who is the "mother of all Mexico." It is she, rather than the solitary image that hangs in the basilica, who is the object of worship in this constructed, crowded, and contested sacred space.

The annual festivities at the basilica of Guadalupe illustrate my fifth heuristic principle: large-scale urban fiestas tend to be the most contested. This is especially so when the public transcript of the festival claims to privilege indigenous, "primitive," ancient, exotic, or other peoples generally excluded, impoverished, or otherwise marginalized by modern urban life. Such public transcripts of authentic otherness tend to conceal a hidden transcript of more ordinary aspirations.

At the basilica of Guadalupe, this hidden transcript has belonged neither to the most dominant social group (colonial peninsular clergy and, more recently, a prosperous urban upper class) nor to the most subordinate group (rural Indians) but to those in between (colonial Creole clergy and a struggling mestizo middle class). This middle class has sought validation within the sacred time and space of the basilica and its fiesta just because, at all other times and places, it has been excluded from the ranks of the dominant. The middle class, moreover, is itself divided. Urban mestizos, dressed as honored "Aztec ancestors," now compete for fleeting local status with clerical guardians of maternal deity. The latter control the basilica, the former dominate the atrium.

Although the resentment of the middle class has been directed at those above, its small gains have come at the expense of those below. Indians drawn, at first with reluctance but finally with devotion, into the orbit of the basilica have been restricted by those who claim to represent them as priests or as Aztec dancers. Despite the rhetoric of its public transcript, the festival at the basilica has never been the property of the heirs of Juan Diego. Even the founding narrative rewarded Juan Diego only with the lifetime privilege of serving as a sweeper in the Virgin's temple.[28] Since then, Indians have remained at the center of the basilica's official rhetoric and on the margins of its official power.

But "poor ordinary people" are rarely passive in such festive struggles. Persuaded of the power of Guadalupe, the Indians of central Mexico have assured themselves of access to that power by contesting the centralization of her image. They have done so, first, by multiplying her names. They gave her both a Nahuatl name (Tonantzin) and a Hispanicized Nahuatl name (Malinche). The former has gradually been appropriated by indigenist mestizos. The latter, because it carries too many negative connotations for mestizos, has largely remained the property of Catholic Indians. At the basilica of Guadalupe, the mother of God has become three persons: Mary, Malinche, and Tonantzin.

Rendered fertile by the contest for her power, each has given birth to multiple and varied images. Mary appears on group banners and individual "tattoos, . . . medicine bottles, liquor bottles, key chains, paper weights, magnets, bottle openers, lamps, posters," and T-shirts.[29] Tonantzin disguises herself as Mary, concealing within the form of the Christian Virgin an autochthonous deity and even (according to some feminists) a "sex goddess."[30] Malinche is a little angel, a tightrope dancer, the companion of soldiers, and the consort of Moctezuma, appearing in many dances at once. The three women are all over the place at the basilica, and they go home with the pilgrims. Power thus spreads from the single sacred image, controlled by clergy, to the many images that live daily with the folk. Power is refracted and diffused; sacred space is decentralized. If the more powerful control the sacred image at the center of the sacred space, the less powerful multiply the images, extending power to the margins.

This tactic should not surprise us, for we have already seen the multiplication of images, albeit on a smaller scale, in Medianía. There, the popular Santiago de los Niños contests the power of the clerically favored Santiago de los Hombres, while Santiago de los Mujeres provides a kind of intermediary distraction. Even more significant, it may have been a similar impulse that gave rise to folk celebrations of days of saints and virgins in the first place. I suggested earlier that the gradual multiplication and domestication of images of saints and virgins was a form of resistance to the manipulation of standardized images of Christ and the Virgin by those in power. Taking issue with images of distant rule, patient suffering, and impossible purity, the folk multiplied saints and virgins, enabling each community to have its own more benevolent image of divine proximity and human joy. Sacred time and space became local and human, complicating clerical control. The multiplication of images at the basilica of Guadalupe reproduces and extends this pattern, imagining God as a compassionate mother who condescends to have her picture hung in an official gallery but much prefers to travel everywhere to console, defend, and party with her children.

5.
A Polka for the Sun and Santiago
(MEXICO)

TWO DAYS LATER, my wife and I drove from Mexico City to San Luis Huexotla. Finding at first no sign of the *santiaguitos* whom we had seen at the basilica of Guadalupe, we parked our car in a quiet square beside the village's colonial church, built in the mid-sixteenth century on the ruins of an old pyramidal temple. The church adjoins the small Franciscan convent to which Gerónimo de Mendieta retired in 1595 to write his *Historia eclesiástica indiana.* The convent was built over the old Aztec ceremonial plaza, erasing the sacred space of one religion with that of another. Other Aztec ruins, including a fortified wall twenty feet high and eight feet thick, reportedly built in 1409, lay nearby.[1]

Huexotla has been continually inhabited for eight hundred fifty years. According to Sahagún's informants, the first nomadic Chichimeca to arrive in the region of Lake Texcoco "settled in the place that is now called Huexotla," a claim supported by a published list of Huexotla's rulers that extends for more than five hundred years before the Spanish conquest.[2] Archaeological evidence suggests, a little more conservatively, that permanent occupation of the site began around 1150. Even so, Huexotla is nearly two hundred years older than Tenochtitlan/Mexico City and was once a city of considerable stature. Estimates of its population in the fourteenth and fifteenth centuries range from 11,750 to 23,500. Although the center of local political power later shifted to Texcoco, Huexotla was still an important ceremonial center at the time of the Spanish conquest.[3]

Hernan Cortés visited Huexotla in January 1521. In those days, it was possible to travel all the way from Huexotla to Tenochtitlan by water. Huexotla lay a mile or two upstream from the eastern shore of Lake Texcoco; Tenochtitlan was twenty miles away across the lake.[4] Huexotla has shrunk in size and importance since then. Its population, which had dwindled to 660 in 1698, was still only 2,786 in 1977.[5] Visiting in 1834, the English traveler Charles

Latrobe called Huexotla an "ancient but decayed town . . . , now reduced to a mere Indian hamlet."[6] Nevertheless, its residents are conscious of its mixed Aztec and colonial heritage, characteristically adding the name of San Luis, its European patron saint,[7] to its older Nahuatl name. Thus they identify the village as both Indian and Catholic. Unlike Tepeyac, San Luis Huexotla has a proven early history of both indigenous and Catholic devotion. Its *danza de los santiaguitos* reflects that dual heritage.

Walking downhill beside the churchyard, we rounded a corner into the Calzada de los Aztecas, passed a stilled carousel, and found the festival: two brass bands, two troupes of dancers, and a chapel, its whitewashed facade ablaze with flowers. Armando Espinosa, the *maestro* of the *santiaguitos,* grinned hugely when he saw us. To our right, as we looked down from the chapel steps, Armando's troupe danced on an elongated, covered, makeshift stage across the street. Directly to our left, against the stone wall that extended from the chapel, a second troupe was dancing on an open stage. Each group had its own musicians. Brass, woodwind, and percussion had replaced the older violin, guitar, and drum around 1928.[8] The second troupe had split off from the first some twenty years earlier, "in a kind of envy," according to Armando, "wanting their own *cuadrilla* [group]."

The two groups danced to the same music and wore almost identical costumes. The Christians wore black *charro* trousers, straw hats or broadbrimmed sombreros, and short capes decorated with Christian symbols: the face of Jesus, the Virgin of Guadalupe, Santiago on his white horse, the cross, the eucharistic bread and wine. Each carried a sword in his right hand and a small cross in his left. The Moors wore plumed fezzes and long capes decorated with contrary symbols: the sun, moon, and stars, the signs of the Zodiac, a dragon. Some added the national symbol: an eagle, a snake in its beak and its wings spread, perched on a cactus. Each Moor carried a scimitar, sword, or machete.

Casting was flexible. At the basilica, Armando had played the double role of Santiago and the Christian King (see Fig. 4.1 above). Here, he played the Moorish General Sabario (see Fig. 5.4 below). There, Armando's brother had played Sabario, but here he was in charge of fireworks. The girl who had played the *angelito* at the basilica had been replaced by a boy, whose white robe grew progressively more grubby as the day wore on. The masks, too, were interchangeable. The Santiago of the newer group was now wearing the mask that the older Santiago had worn at the basilica.

When we arrived, shortly after midday, the *santiaguitos* had been dancing for four hours. The morning *danza* was performed without words. Armando told us that the dance represented a "true history" of the clash between the Moors of Granada and the Christians of Toledo, a claim that the scripted dialogue of the evening performance would support. But, as Jesús Jáuregui observed after watching a similar *danza de los santiaguitos* in nearby San Pablo Ixáyotl, the text of the dance has become "something extraneous, rigid, and lifeless."[9] It is in the more flexible signs of gesture, dance, and costume that the hidden transcript is displayed. In Huexotla, the costumes declared the "Moors" to be devoted to the sustenance of the heavenly bodies. The eagle on the cactus derived from Aztec legend. The dragon may have recalled the fire serpent wielded, according to some readings of Aztec myth, by the sun god Huitzilopochtli in his decisive victory over the moon and stars. The "Moors" were thus doubly marked as Aztecs. The narrative of Moors and Christians is frequently adapted in Mexican performance to reflect the trauma of indigenous defeat.

Over the door of the chapel, an arc of flowers inscribed the prayer, "Virgen de Guadalupe bendice a tu pueblo" (Virgin of Guadalupe, bless your village). Inside, above an altar buried under flowers, hung an image of the Virgin of Guadalupe painted on stone. A pious caretaker of the chapel, Margarita López, told us that the image had miraculously appeared, already painted, in 1668 at "the old bridge." At the south end of the Calzada de los Aztecas, beyond the fortified wall, an arched colonial bridge still crosses a ravine.[10] "The people of the village," Margarita explained, "bring their own household images to gain power from the miraculous image in the chapel."

When the morning performance ended, each group danced up the chapel steps to present its mask of Santiago, pale-faced and crowned with sun rays, to the empowering image of the Virgin. The mask is "a sacred object for all of us," Armando told me. "It is *una cara divina* [a divine face]." During the year, it does not reside in the chapel or the church but "passes from house to house," spending "a week or so in each home." San Pablo Ixáyotl has an almost identical mask, made in 1960. Before that, the villagers of San Pablo used to borrow a neighboring *rostro divino* (divine face). From time to time, during its patronal saint's day festival in January, San Pablo still invites Huexotla's "face" to pay a visit.[11]

Given the sacred status of the mask, it may seem surprising that a second group of *santiaguitos* could split off from the first, manufacturing their own "divine face," and that a neighboring village could copy Huexotla's mask without giving offense. But in San Luis Huexotla, sacred images and their power are recklessly multiplied. Not only were there now two masks in Huexotla—and a third in San Pablo—but divine faces and household images were able to gain power from the miraculous stone painting of the Virgin, itself a reproduction of the Guadalupe in the basilica. Divine power spreads, in this spiritual economy, by simple proximity. Moreover, although the newer group had sprung from "a kind of envy" of the older, there now appeared to be no competition for sacred power between the masks and their custodians. The older group had taken the newer group's mask to the basilica to enhance its power (cf. Figs. 4.1 above and 5.2 below).

Folk theology, it seems, has not embraced the "law of scarcity" that undergirds so many of the dominant narratives of Western theology. Regina Schwartz, in her thoughtful study, *The Curse of Cain*, has drawn attention to the insistence of the Judeo-Christian tradition that God can only bless Abel or Cain, that Isaac must choose between Jacob and Esau. A father, in this meager spiritual economy, cannot bless both his sons. But the Virgin of Guadalupe, despite clerical monopoly of her original image, can freely multiply her reproductions and so her power to bless the folk who value them. The "divine face" of Santiago can reproduce itself. Power gained by one mask can extend to another with no loss to the first. Folk theology, like those strands of the biblical narrative that tell of the abundant provision of manna in the wilderness or the Pentecostal outpouring of the Holy Spirit, embraces a countervailing "vision of plenitude."[12] Those who, lacking political power, know most of material scarcity like to imagine a God who is generous.

Schwartz argues that the stories of Cain and Esau have been used to promulgate a cultural law of scarcity, justifying violence against the other who threatens our possession of a limited blessing. Although Schwartz focuses primarily on ethnic hostilities, one could make the case that hierarchical visions of power also invoke the law of scarcity, resisting generosity and insisting that scarce blessings be allowed to trickle slowly downwards from the top. Clerical sanction of a single image and priestly control of the sacraments both fit this model. Because the folk theologians of San Luis Huexotla are not inclined to hoard divinity, they are free to reproduce the face of Santiago and so to multiply the power it represents. Their theology is in keeping with the Carnival impulse to imagine plenitude and counter to the Lenten inclination to indulge in scarcity.

Armando invited us to eat with his *cuadrilla*. Together, we marched through the village and sat down at long tables in someone's front yard, amid chickens and debris. Shy girls served us hunks of meat, tortillas, guacamole, and a fine green salsa. Armando told us that he'd danced for thirty-two years. "It's an honor to dance," he said. Nine times he'd been given the "big honor"

5.1 *Danza de los santiaguitos.* San Luis Huexotla, 1998.

of playing General Sabario. He pointed to four young boys playing nearby in Moorish costumes. "In twenty years," he said, "they'll be the generals."

After lunch, the *cuadrilla* danced briefly in the street (Fig. 5.1). Then, with the band playing cheerfully, we all marched down a dusty lane between cornfields to the home of Armando's brother, who supplied a bundle of fireworks: homemade rockets mounted on cornstalks. As we marched back to the chapel, he lit several with a cigarette, launching them from his hand. I joined several men to urinate behind a wall. My wife paid a peso to a village entrepreneur who was marketing his outdoor privy. He was a Baptist. "The dances do not please God," he said sourly. "They're pagan."

The evening performance, lasting about five hours, was officially structured around three choreographed battles. "The Moors win the first," Armando explained. "Santiago wins the second. The Christians win the last." But the Christian victory was not, in fact, the last. A final confrontation yielded a conciliatory success for Santiago.

As the dance got under way, the Christians faced one another in two parallel lines at one end of the stage; the Moors did the same at the other.[13] Two simple wooden chairs, one at each end, represented thrones. The *angelito,* feather-winged and tinsel-haloed, sat sucking a lollipop at the foot of the Christian throne (Fig. 5.2). The first battle was preceded by lengthy embas-

5.2   Little angel. San Luis Huexotla, 1998.

sies and vaunting speeches from both sides, interspersed with lively dance tunes that would have graced a German beer hall.[14]

Some episodes were comic. When the Moors captured the Christian ambassador, they blindfolded him, rendering him unconscious, and then, to a slow march, made repeated unsuccessful efforts to kill him (Fig. 5.3). Again and again, Sabario swirled his scimitar and plunged it deep into the captive's belly, leaping in the air to thrust it further home (in fact, slipping it beside the victim's thigh). Frustrated, Sabario listened to the Christian's heart and made a pumping motion with his hand to signal that the heart still beat. He plucked a hair from the ambassador's head and sliced it, testing the sharpness of his scimitar. To the same end, he gently ran his thumb along the blade, shaking his hand in sudden pain to show that even so slight a touch had cut him. He beckoned other Moors to help him dispatch the captive and pushed them angrily away when they, too, failed. Nothing fazed the unconscious ambassador except the inadvertent tickling of the sword thrusts. It was hard for him not to laugh. Although this was one of the longest scenes of the dance-drama, it was not called for by the script. It seems to have been included for its comic value, for the dramatic opportunities it affords the actor playing Sabario, and for its portrayal of the Christian ambassador as both "humiliated" and divinely protected.[15]

Later, the Christian King and the Monarca Musulmana (also known as Pontius Pilate after the villain of the Easter story) sat opposite each other on chairs placed center stage. While the Christian King pontificated, his Moorish counterpart nodded in contemptuous mockery of agreement, made signs to indicate the Christian King was crazy, and finally rested his feet on the Christian's knees and pretended to doze off. This led to the first battle, a sudden rush of Moors against Christians and a brief clash of swords that ended with the Christians dropping to their knees in token of death. The Moors formed two lines that advanced repeatedly into captured Christian territory, dancing cheerfully around the rows of kneeling Christians.

Then the mask of Santiago was brought out and ceremonially strapped with a bandanna to the head of the dancer acting the part of the Christian King. Transformed, he stood. The corona of sun rays, atop a golden disk and mirrored helmet, dominated the European features of the face, rendering this figure both the patron saint of Spain and an incarnation of the sun. Brandish-

5.3 General Sabario (Armando Espinosa) threatens the Christian Ambassador. San Luis Huexotla, 1998.

ing his sword and holding out his cross, Santiago advanced majestically, to the music of a slow march, towards the Moors. It was a moment of intense dramatic power.

His march impeded by a Moorish banner held across the stage, Santiago gestured powerfully with sword and cross. The banner did not yield. Returning to the Christian ranks, Santiago ritually waved his sword and cross over the Christian ambassador. The latter rose from his knees, restored to life. Together, saint and soldier advanced on the Moorish flag. Blocked once more, they returned to raise the Christian General Ramiro from the dead. Thereafter, each impeded advance was followed by a triple resurrection, adding yet another rank of three to the advancing Christians. Even supported by a fully revived Christian army, Santiago did not subdue the Moorish flag. I take this to be his choice rather than his failure. His victory in this second battle consisted not of Moorish defeat but of Christian restoration.

Three Christians then returned the mask of Santiago to the chapel, presenting it to the Virgin and leaving it in a position of honor before the altar. On the other stage, the Santiago of the second group was still raising the dead. His mask had been fitted with colored lightbulbs that blinked on and off, connected by a long black cord to an offstage power source. Food stalls at street level sold bread, meat, and fresh corn on sticks. Across the street from the chapel, a young Moorish soldier from the first group took advantage of the lull in the dramatic action to try his skill at a commercial video game.

The third battle consisted of a series of stylized clashes between Moors and Christians, swords flashing in aerial choreography above the dancers' heads, feet leaping to a merry tune. Although they fought well, the Moors lost. The Christian King tried to impose conversion on each defeated Moor, thrusting his small wooden cross in the crouching Moor's face. When the Moor averted his eyes, the Christian lifted his victim's chin, demanding that he pay attention to the cross. Each Moor turned away, resisting forced conversion.

Angered by the succession of defeats, the Muslim Monarch and Sabario slew the Moors by pairs as they slunk shamefaced back to camp. The executions gave rise to comedy as each Moor, pinned to the floor, kicked his legs in exaggerated death throes. Sabario and the Monarch then took their turn against the Christians but were defeated. The Monarch's death was marked by the loud explosion of a firecracker on the far side of the stage. Smoke wafted from beneath the boards. Concerned for the dancers' safety, the Christian King paused to hammer home a loose nail in the floorboards with the butt of a machete. Sometime during this third battle, the *angelito*'s mother took him, screaming, home. Maybe it was past his bedtime; maybe she was finally embarrassed by his disheveled wings and dirty robe.

With the Moors thus dead and unconverted, the mask of Santiago was retrieved from the chapel and the Christian King again transformed into the saint. Face beaming, flanked by the Christian ambassador and General Ramiro, Santiago slowly advanced to the center of the stage. In San Pablo, this climactic moment coincided with sunset so that "the last rays of the setting sun were reflected in the divine face,"[16] but in Huexotla it was by then already dark. Two Christians brought Santiago the slumped corpse of the Muslim Monarch. Just as he had done previously with the dead Christians, so now Santiago ritually waved his sword and cross over the Muslim Monarch. The dead Moor revived and, at last, willingly kissed the cross. The process was repeated with General Sabario and Prince Malikadel; then, three by three, with all the fallen Moors. Each trio of resurrected Moors fell in behind the saint, received amid his Christian followers. When all had been restored, the mixed army of Christians and converted Moors slowly marched the full length of the stage to the Muslim Monarch's throne. Gently, with the tip of his sword, Santiago tipped the chair backwards. A child caught it as it fell and laid it quietly down.

The conflict was over. Armando called for a polka. The band struck up. Moors and Christians joined together in a dance of loud and effervescent joy at Santiago's final triumph of irenic restoration. The sense of dramatic resolution was sudden, palpable, and happy. Afterwards, the dancers paid a last visit to the Virgin. As they left the chapel, still bearing the mask of Santiago, I spoke to Armando.

"Santiago is the sun, isn't he?" I asked.

He smiled. "Yes," he said.

Was the entrepreneurial Baptist right, then, in saying that the dance is pagan? Do the dance's visual references to sun, moon, and stars and its repeated theme of death and resurrection recall an ancient (and probably bloody) seasonal fertility rite in honor of the sun? I think not, preferring the more straightforward explanation that the dance's many deaths reflect the violent history of Mexico and that its resurrections manifest the tendency of folk performers to construct a world in which the injustices of history and daily life can be reversed. Just as the people of Sariñena embrace a vision of *convivencia* rather than of conquest in their play of Moors and Christians, and the people of Loíza invoke a diminutive Santiago to resist triumphalism, so, I believe, the *santiaguitos* of San Luis Huexotla enact in their dance a challenge to the European narrative of armed conversion.

They do so in a comic mode, allowing the performance to engage in a good-humored dialogue with the script and the traditional narrative that shapes it. The script dignifies the Christian ambassador; the performance makes us laugh at his predicament. The text has the Christian King lecture his Muslim counterpart; the performance has the latter register his boredom. The traditional narrative has Santiago intervene to slay the Moors; the Huexotla performance has him revive both Spaniards and Aztecs. The script ends with the forced subordination of the heathen; the performance ends with a communal polka. Thus, as Jáuregui observes, the "non-verbal languages" of costume, action, music, and dance challenge the view of history inscribed in the written text.[17] It is fitting that the first performance of the day is without words. Only when the embodied voice of dissent has been performed without interruption may prescribed speech enter into subordinate dialogue with it.

Although the comic vision of the dance repudiates the violence of the conquest, it does not reject the Catholicism that came with it. The dancers in San Luis Huexotla are both Indian and Catholic. They embrace Catholicism without denying their indigenous heritage. They acknowledge their indigenous heritage without ceasing to be Catholics. Gabriela Urquiza Vázquez is right when she says that Huexotla's *danza de los santiaguitos* is "the folkloric expression of an extraordinary syncretism" but wrong, I believe, when she sees in that syncretism a "reduction" from the high goals of the "didactic religious plays" first taught to the villagers by Franciscan friars.[18] The syncretism of the dance was not evidence of a Christianity tainted with "paganism" but a window onto the discerning Christian vision of the dance. The dance, I believe, embodies a profoundly moving meditation, from an indigenous Catholic perspective, on the nature of religious conversion.

The Christians in the dance are first defeated by the Moors (as were the Spaniards by the Mexica). When the Christians at last conquer their opponents, they are unable to convert them. The defeated soldiers resolutely turn their faces from the proffered cross. The written text may imply compliance at this point, but the gestures that accompany its performance signal resistance.[19] Thus the action of the dance repudiates the claims of forced conversion. Not only is such conversion wrong; it is, in any true or lasting sense, impossible.

Santiago's ability to convert the Moors flows not so much from his saintly rank as from his conciliatory approach. In a radical departure from every Spanish version of his story, Huexotla's Santiago neglects to lead the Christian troops to victory. Respecting the barrier of the Moorish flag, he retreats and then revives both fallen Moors and fallen Christians. Afterwards he is able to convert the Moors (or Aztecs), precisely because he presents himself as one already strangely familiar to them. His face may be Spanish, but his corona reflects the devotion to sun, moon, and stars woven into his converts' capes. When Latrobe, during his visit to Huexotla in 1834, bought "an ugly monster of an idol," he noted that it went "under the high-sounding name of Huitzilopoc[h]tli," the Aztec god of the sun.[20] Santiago in the dance bears traces of both Christian saint and Aztec sun god.

Moreover, this ambivalent figure of divine power wears a cross on top of his corona and induces the Moors to kiss a hand-held cross. It is a commonplace of the religious history of the Americas that the Christian symbol of the cross was initially read by many Indians as a sacred sign of the sun's grandeur extending to all four points of the compass. According to one report from the early days of Catholic Huexotla, the friars were puzzled by the popularity of one of the altars in the parish church. Eventually, it was discovered that "the ingenious [Indian] builders had carved in the decorative border of the altar their cosmogonic sign [of the four cardinal directions], in the form of a cross, thus appropriating for their own gods the altar of the conquering gods."[21]

Santiago succeeds because he approaches his potential converts with familiar symbols that allow them to embrace the new religion without relinquishing the potent symbols of the old. The formal syncretism of the dance is thus not accidental but essential to its performance, for the dance proclaims the impossibility of conversion by force to a religion that offers no familiar reference points. On the contrary, the dance suggests, genuine conversion takes place only when the new religion adapts itself to the world into which it travels and in which it hopes to gain adherents.

This insight may be anathema to the theological purist, but it shares with the central Christian narrative of the Incarnation the acknowledgment that there can be no such thing as a Christianity that is not already acculturated. Christians do not tell of a God who became a kind of generalized human being, hovering vaguely and transcendently above the particularities of human life. They proclaim instead a God who became a human being bounded in every way by the particularities of his own time and place. His skin color, his language, his food, his songs, his dances, all identified Jesus of Nazareth as a Jew living under enforced Roman colonization. The same was true of those who first put their faith in him. Christianity expressed itself initially in subaltern (and dissident) Jewish cultural and religious symbols.

In time, Christians also learned to express themselves in symbols and

rituals drawn from the dominant Hellenic and Roman cultural vocabular-
ies. Northern European Christianity added symbols from its own regional
(and pagan) past. And so it has continued as the church, too often backed
by force of arms, has taken its message to Asia, Africa, and the Americas.
The missionary enterprises of the church have always struggled—often with
little success—against the temptation to confuse their own cultural forms
with a fictional essence of Christianity. Despite this, new Christians have
almost everywhere found ways of expressing their faith in symbols drawn
from their own heritage as well as from the alien culture of the missionary
church. Christians need not be embarrassed by this inevitable process of hy-
bridization. According to their own founding narrative, God set ample precedent by becoming human—both transcendent God and brown-eyed Jewish
male—at a specific time and place.

San Luis Huexotla's *danza de los santiaguitos,* if I am reading it correctly,
both articulates and exemplifies such a theology of cross-cultural conversion. Rejecting a law of scarcity that insists on a choice between two cultures, it prefers a law of plenitude that allows God's blessings—and those
that God blesses—to embrace both cultures. The "divine face" of Santiago,
according to this indigenous Catholic perspective, deploys signs from both
European Christianity and Aztec sun worship to express the benevolent
power of God to awaken the soul and—the Christian's ultimate hope—to
raise the dead. Santiago's majestic advances along the stage, giving new life
both to Christians and to Moors, were to my eyes both profoundly moving
and profoundly Christian.

If it still bothers the Baptist entrepreneur that signs from a once pagan
vocabulary contaminate the Christian image, he should remember that the
sacred sign of the sun, like that of the cross, is not exclusive to the Mexica
religion. The blessing entrusted to Aaron and his sons for delivery to the
Israelites imagined the divine face as a kind of brilliant sun: "The Lord make
his face shine upon you and be gracious to you; the Lord turn his face toward
you and give you peace" (Numbers 6:25–26). The Psalmist compared God to
"a sun" (Psalm 84:11), and the author of the Book of Revelation wrote of the
glorified Christ, "His face was like the sun shining in all its brilliance" (1:16).
The "divine face" of the sun worn by Santiago bridges the gap between the
old religion and the new. So does the cross he offers. To kiss the cross held out
by such a saint is to become Catholic without ceasing to be Indian. It is, the
dance suggests, the way of genuine conversion to indigenous Catholicism.

Festive syncretism is not, therefore, something to be feared by the Christian theologian or romanticized by the historian of folk theater. For the

former, it can point to a law of divine plenitude so often absent from the theology of the powerful. For the latter, it may signal the location of a hidden transcript that, far from bearing faint traces of archaic rites, embodies the vital meaning of the event for its present folk performers. And so my sixth heuristic principle is this: the folk theology of a fiesta is more likely to reside in its mixed, syncretic, or inclusive elements than in those elements that aim at purity and fail. One can apply this in Spain: San Antolín was more interesting than Christ the King in Sariñena; it was in the mutual dependence of sacred and profane in Vilafranca that the folk theology of the fiesta displayed itself. But the principle is even more helpful in Hispanic America. Both at the basilica of Guadalupe and in San Luis Huexotla, "mixed" dances performed by Catholic Indians offered a far more vibrant folk theology than either "indigenous" dances performed by urban mestizos or an image of the Virgin that never strayed from sacred space controlled by clergy. Folk theology uses mixed forms to speak to a culture that is itself unavoidably hybrid.

But if our suspicious Baptist is still unable to shake the conviction that his village's dance is indelibly tainted by paganism, he should perhaps consider the hybrid nature of his own practices. Is it his Christian faith or the pervasive influence of North American free-market capitalism that drives him to sell the use of his privy during the fiesta? Or has he been misled by American televangelists and their Mexican converts into thinking that Christianity and capitalism are one and the same? In any case, I beg to differ with his curt judgment on the *danza de los santiaguitos*. The dance, for me, embodies a folk theology of divine generosity, rebirth, and joyous reconciliation that is far more compatible with a God whose face shines and who decides to become human than is the parsimonious rental of a privy.

WE HAVE NOW completed our tour of patronal saints' day festivals. Before moving on to the feast of Corpus Christi, it may be helpful to bring together in one place the six heuristic principles that I have scattered through Part One. I make no claim for their universality or comprehensive scope; I note only that they have helped me better understand the fiestas I describe in this book.

First, I have found James Scott's distinction between public and hidden transcripts to be of great value, allowing me better to identify "the manifold strategies by which subordinate groups manage to insinuate their resistance, in disguised forms, into the public transcript."[22] Religious festivals are rarely, as official records may misleadingly suggest, monological displays of power. Rather, they are enacted dialogues, implicit negotiations between dominant and subordinate groups, between the hierarchical powers of the church (or state) and the unwritten but no less articulate power of the street. Scott provides me with the language to describe this dialogue.

Second, the hidden transcript—and hence the full complexity of meaning—of a fiesta is legible in performance even in the absence of verbal corroboration. Careful historical and social scholarship will guard against false readings and may point to hidden transcripts. So, too, may conversations with performers and other members of the festive community, but it is the performance itself that must be read with the greatest care and accorded the greatest authority. Readings of the performance that lack verbal corroboration may be mistaken, but readings of the fiesta that rely solely on verbal authority will be almost certainly be sadly lopsided.

Third, fiestas afford a fertile opportunity for the insinuation of a hidden transcript of folk theology into the public transcript of formal Catholic devotion. Such folk theology is neither quaint nor unsophisticated; nor is it a diluted version of the dogmatic theology of the church. Rather, I have found it a fresh source of theological reflection, a fruitful corrective to the authoritative voices—mediated through clerical controls—of sacred text, reason, and ecclesiastical tradition.

Fourth, official explanations that locate the origin of a fiesta in the distant past, especially when backed by the authority of uncontested scholarship, are best treated with considerable suspicion. Such explanations rhetorically banish injustice and its needed remedy to the past, thereby obscuring the much more vibrant—and potentially threatening—social and theological commentaries enacted by the present fiesta. The conjunction of scholarship and local authority can be a formidable barrier to the fiesta's hidden transcript.

Fifth, large-scale urban fiestas tend to be the most susceptible to this kind of official and scholarly obfuscation. An urban public transcript whose rhetoric privileges indigenous, "primitive," ancient, or exotic peoples often conceals a hidden transcript of social and economic control by the powerful, indulges a frustrated middle-class fantasy of "noble savagery," and further marginalizes the living descendants of indigenous or enslaved peoples. Since those on the lower rungs of the social scale have many ways of insinuating a hidden transcript of resistance even into so complex and romanticized a public transcript, such large-scale urban fiestas tend to be the most contested.

Sixth, attention to the hybrid or syncretic character of fiestas is essential to their full appreciation. A syncretic multiplication of sacred images and a cross-fertilization of symbols from different religious traditions may signal the location of the fiesta's hidden transcript. Moreover, the folk theology of the fiesta will employ such fecund hybridity to articulate a carnivalesque principle of divine inclusion and plenitude in direct opposition to the Lenten principle of exclusion and scarcity invoked by the powerful.

Applying these principles to days of patron saints and virgins, we have found strenuous resistance to civil and ecclesiastical hierarchies of power. We have seen a resolute insistence that God neither endorses nor imitates such hierarchies but instead dwells happily (if not in a regnant Christ, then in the more affable images of local saints and virgins) even with the least of his people. We have observed a refusal of fastidious asceticism in favor of a hearty enjoyment of food, drink, song, dance, romance, and pyrotechnics, an enjoyment of the physical world sanctioned by the benevolent presence of those images of saints and virgins. And we have noted sometimes an imagined community that extends not only to the most marginalized of Catholics, but even to Moors, dragons, and the demonized (if not finally to demons). We turn now to the festival of Corpus Christi to see whether folk theater and folk theology can maintain this stance in the context of a festival whose clerical origins were so firmly triumphalist.

PART TWO

Corpus Christi

6.
Dancing under Friendly Fire
(CATALONIA)

IN 1565 THE Coventry Draper's Guild paid an anonymous pyrotechnician fourpence for "setting the worlds on fire." Three worlds, one at each performance, were consumed during the Doomsday play that the guild staged at the close of the city's Corpus Christi cycle.[1] In late medieval Coventry, the world ended not with a whimper but with a spectacular bang.

The story of how the festival of Corpus Christi developed into a time when worlds went up in flames is important both to the history of theater and to the understanding of folk theology. Since Corpus Christi grew out of the older patronal saints' day festivals, the story also links the first two parts of this book. In Part Two, we travel to Corpus Christi festivals in the foothills of the Pyrenees, the quixotic plains of La Mancha, and the high Peruvian Andes.

Festive days of saints and virgins are almost as old as the church. Beginning, as early as the second century, with the commemoration of martyrs on the several anniversaries of their deaths and adding, in due course, festivals in honor of the Virgin Mary, popular Christianity had developed by the sixth century a whole array of local saints' days, wonder-working shrines and relics, and images invested with numinous power.[2] Part of the early appeal of the martyrs was their reputed ability to "reach across the crevasse of uncertainty" that opened up before the Christian at death and to extend from the other side a "human gesture of acceptance."[3] The feast of Corpus Christi both incorporated and opposed the cult of the saints.

First promulgated by the bishop of Liège in 1246 and established as a universal feast by papal decree in 1264, Corpus Christi officially celebrates the belief that the eucharistic bread contains the real presence of Christ. The doctrine of transubstantiation, developed over the previous four centuries, had concentrated the scattered channels of sacred power in priestly hands by declaring the bread of the mass to be the holy relic par excellence. Other ment. In Coventry, worlds were ignited. The Barcelona procession had its share of pyrotechnic demons. But performance is a tricky medium and the intentions of its official sponsors often go awry. "Hell," it turned out, "was everybody's favorite part of the . . . presentations." A monstrous hellmouth, spewing forth devils, smoke, flames, and noise, was far more entertaining than the dignified singing of angels or a pompous procession of clergy. Devils were irredeemably vulgar, too, having a propensity for flatulence and foul language. "Boisterous hell scenes" thus "became comic relief to the more solemn goings-on." Moreover, since any Last Judgment staged by European folk performers inevitably damned "great folk like kings, queens, bishops, and rich merchants," this, too, "was a crowd-pleaser."[10]

Although still the formal highlight of the procession, the host beneath its baldachin, together with its escort of civic and ecclesiastical leaders, was eclipsed by the more spectacular elements of the festivities. Not all were infernal. In Barcelona, the opening battle between angels and devils armed with swords, the stilt-walkers who played the giants Goliath and Christopher, the pyrotechnic dragons that attacked Saints Margaret and George (the latter on horseback), the devils that tempted two saints and the impenitent thief on the cross, the eight Christian knights on hobbyhorses who fought twenty-four Turkish infantry in the street during the pageant of Saint Sebastian, the bestiary of papier-mâché animals, and, bringing up the rear, "two wild men carrying a bar to hold back the people" would all have surpassed the static host in festive audience appeal. By the late sixteenth century, clergy throughout Spain were objecting vigorously to the "disorder and confusion" caused by the intrusion of so many "profane" elements into a procession devoted to "the Holy Sacrament." Even worse, they said, the masked figures and the dancers were invading the sacred space of the church and interrupting the liturgy.[11]

In northern Europe, the Protestant Reformation put an end to the Corpus Christi procession and its attendant drama. In Catholic Spain, despite intermittent clerical objections and the efforts of various rulers to tame it or to bend it to their own uses, the pageantry of Corpus Christi continues to thrive in one form or another. When the Bourbon monarchy, in the eighteenth century, tried to purge the Spanish Corpus Christi procession of its "bad taste," many of the "profane" elements migrated to patronal saints days festivals. In 1772 a royal decree prohibited the appearance of giants and dragons in Madrid; in 1780 a more comprehensive decree extended the ban to all the popular apparatus of the Corpus Christi procession throughout the country.[12] In Vilafranca del Penedès, traditional Corpus Christi dragons and devils simply changed venue, moving to the procession of Saint Felix soon after he was named co-patron of the town in 1776. It is an ironic testimony to the resilience of folk theology that the feast designed to surpass and domesticate the cult of the saints eventually supplied the most elaborate festive iconography for the cult's many local celebrations.

In the twentieth century, Franco took a different approach to the feast of Corpus Christi: he promoted it as an emblem of Spanish identity and Catholic triumphalism.[13] Cities loyal to Franco, such as Toledo, maintained elaborate religious processions even after his death. Others, like Manresa, quietly boycotted the procession. In a few places, the profane *entremesos* and their infernal fire held their ground, banished the sacred host from the streets, and seized control of the festival of Corpus Christi. In Berga (Barcelona), in the foothills of the Pyrenees, the last procession of the sacrament took place in 1970.[14] Devils, fire-breathing mules, giants, Turks, and hobbyhorses now hold sole sway. The festival is known as the Patum, after the rhythmic striking of the big *tabal* (bass drum). My son Matthew and I were there in 1996, two months before his fifteenth birthday.

Arriving at Berga's town hall on the Wednesday morning of Corpus Christi week, we found four giants waiting in the foyer. Elegant kings and queens, they wore rich robes draped over towering wooden frames and boasted finely sculpted papier-mâché heads. Shortly before midday, they moved out into the sunshine of the Plaça Sant Pere. A man on a stepladder adjusted their clothing. At noon, the *passada dels gegants* (promenade of the giants) set off through the town, led by the *tabaler* (drummer), dressed in colorful seventeenth-century livery.[15] The giants followed, towering above a surging crowd of pilgrims. Then came the *cobla* (band) and, behind it, ranks of youngsters, arms linked, singing and dancing. At the far point of the *passada,* the *geganters* (those who play the giants) stepped out of their enormous masks and set them temporarily on the sidewalk. Adults disappeared into Cal Tonillo (Tony's Place) for shots of *barreja,* a potent mix of muscatel wine and anise liqueur drunk only during the Patum. Children outside the bar took turns striking the drum. Afterwards, we headed back, the band playing, the crowd dancing happily, and the giants whirling from time to time like enormous dignified dervishes.

From the mid-nineteenth century until the late twentieth century, Berga's elite claimed that the Patum had its origins in a local Christian victory over invading Moors and that all its parts could be read accordingly.[16] The *passada dels gegants* was thought to signify "the submission of the sons of Mohammed to the God of the Eucharist, imposed by the conquerors."[17] But literate

6.1 Giants. Berga, 1996.

theory, as is often the case, ignored popular performance. The giants parade as heroes, not as prisoners (Fig. 6.1).

On Wednesday evening the first *passacarrers* (promenade through the streets) began in the Plaça Sant Pere. Officially, it honored the municipal authorities by performing outside their homes, but between times it was a six-hour roaming street party with theater and fireworks. In front, the *tabaler* led a group of young men and women, each bearing a *maça* (mace or pole) that ended in a metal drum with a painted devil's face on each side. Fixed to the top of the drum was a *fuet*, a slow-burning firework about eighteen inches long. Inside the drum were pebbles. When the procession paused, the bearers cleared a narrow space in the midst of the crowd and leaped in disorderly strides from one end to the other. The pebbles rattled in the drums and the *fuets* trailed sparks over the heads of the onlookers, many of whom lined up to take a turn jumping with the *maces*. I asked whether the painted devils were good or bad.

"Neither good nor bad," I was told. "Just devils."

Next came the *guites* (bad-tempered ones), two long-necked monsters, each "with the body of a mule, the head of a dragon, and the neck of a giraffe."[18] A huge torso, made of green cloth stretched over a wooden frame, sprouted a long pole that was sheathed in green cloth and topped with a fierce black mask. The jaws of each beast contained a metal holder for three *fuets*. Supported by two men within and several more outside, the larger *guita* reached high into balconies to spray fire over elevated spectators. The smaller, more mobile *guita* chased pedestrians, trapping its victims against a wall or in a doorway and spraying them with fire. Behind the *guites* came a pair of giants. Although the giants invoked an atmosphere of friendly celebration, the fire of the *maces* and the *guites* seemed to threaten danger. I worried lest Matthew be scarred by dragon fire.

Thursday was Corpus Christi day. In the morning, the four giants and the *àliga* (eagle) were carried into the square. Families posed in front of them; children peeked under the giants' skirts. Shortly before 11:00 A.M., a dignified cortege passed from the town hall, across the corner of the square, and up the steep stone steps into the church: the *tabaler*, the *cobla*, a man with a silver *mace* denoting the authority of the town hall, two embarrassed boys in wings and blond wigs representing Saint Michael and an unnamed angel, eight young festival queens, and a gaggle of soberly dressed dignitaries. The group entered the church doors through an honor guard of eight devils holding *maces*. Inside, the bishop of Solsona presided over the Corpus Christi mass.

As noon approached, the Plaça Sant Pere, its compact dimensions made to seem even smaller by the five-story buildings that surround it, grew dense with people. Those in the square wore floppy cotton hats and long-sleeved shirts, scored with prestigious burn marks from previous years, to protect against falling sparks. Others found vantage points on balconies, the church steps, or behind the *barana*, a waist-high stone wall shielding the rising street in front of the church from the drop to the square.

When the mass was over, the sober cortege returned from the church to the town hall, escorted through what was now a narrow passageway lined by representatives of the Patum: devils, dwarfs, hobbyhorses, *guites*, and giants. The bishop of Solsona, no longer in clerical vestments, walked with the mayor. As a young priest, barely out of his teens, he had danced in the square.[19] Now he sits next to the mayor in the town hall balcony. The eccentric guard of devils, mythical beasts, and monsters simultaneously honored the representatives of church and state and confined them within the margins of their own authority. Whereas priests had once excluded Corpus Christi maskers from the church, the maskers now denied ecclesiastical and secular officials access to the public square. The streets of Berga during Corpus Christi belong to the Patum.

At noon the music struck up.[20] Strong men pushed back against the crowd to clear a brief and narrow passage from the town hall to the center of the square, where more pressure cleared a small circle of space. Four Christian knights on skirted hobbyhorses and four Turkish foot soldiers jostled through the crowd. The Turks formed an inner circle that skipped counterclockwise, while the hobbyhorses formed an outer circle that galloped clockwise. When the music reached its cadence, each Turk struck the wooden block in the hand of the nearest knight with his scimitar. After the third repetition, the knights drew their daggers, some tossing them in the air and catching them again. Three Turks knelt in submission. The fourth Turk escaped into the crowd, pursued but never caught by the fourth hobbyhorse.[21] I take this escape to be a mild subversion of the official rhetoric of Christian victory enacted by the dance. The challenge is echoed by the direction of the opposing circles, for counterclockwise is the favored direction of the Patum, and it is the Turks rather than the Christians who are privileged to take it.

The second *entremès* was also a mock combat, pitting the diminutive Saint Michael and his companion angel against eight devils dressed in red and green felt suits and horned papier-mâché masks (Fig. 6.2). The devils' handlers pushed back the crowd. The *tabaler*, standing in a small balcony of his own, beat his drum: Pa-TUM, Pa-TUM (Fig. 6.3). The band, seated on high bleachers beside the church steps, began to play. The devils, each carrying a *maça* filled with pebbles and topped with a slow firework, leaped in gangling steps from one end of the cleared space to the other. The angels skipped delicately to and fro across the devils' path, avoiding contact with their adversaries. Eventually, as each devil's firework reached its concluding charge and exploded, he lay down, feigning death. Only then did the angels finish him off with token thrusts of lance and sword. When all the devils were vanquished, the *salt* (jump) was over. Once again, the official rhetoric of Christian victory was called into question, this time by the clear advantage in terms of aesthetics, size, courage, and vitality that the devils maintained until the end of the *salt*.

There was no pretense of Christian resistance to the *guites* that followed (Fig. 6.4). The large *guita* attacked spectators watching from the *barana*. One of the animal's handlers jumped onto the wall and, holding the mule's giraffe-like neck, ran up and down the length of the wall, forcing the spectators to retreat to avoid the sparks and then surge back to regain their vantage point. The small *guita* suddenly dropped its neck and spun on the spot, showering onlookers with sparks. One year, I was told, it had climbed the staircase inside the town hall to reappear on the balcony to the consternation of the mayor's guests. But not everyone was afraid of the beast. In the square, chil-

6.2   Saint Michael (with shield), angel, and *maces*. Berga, 1996.

dren were holding their hats out to it to attract the burn marks that confer status. Each *guita*, when its *fuets* finally exploded, shuddered vigorously.[22]

The pace slowed temporarily with the dance of the eagle, a rotund and regal papier-mâché effigy worn from the waist up by a single carrier who looked out through a grille in the bird's chest. Now an emblem of Catalan independence, it is for many the most beloved of Berga's *entremesos*. The eagle began its dance by bowing first towards the church and then towards the town hall. The gesture may be read as deferential but is more likely a warning to the twin powers of church and state not to exceed their due authority. The eagle's dance, I was told, denotes the struggle for freedom. The first steps of the dance were constrained, as if the eagle were chained to a single spot. Then the pace of the music quickened and the eagle skipped from side to side, each time increasing the breadth of its movement. Finally, liberated, it set off in a counterclockwise rush around the square, ending by

6.3 *Tabaler*. Berga, 1996.

spinning on itself, while spectators and handlers dropped to the ground to avoid being struck by the eagle's tail. In a legendary blow for freedom, its spinning tail is reputed to have "killed a soldier once."[23]

There followed cheerful dances by the *nans vells* (old dwarfs), *gegants* (giants), and *nans nous* (new dwarfs). The old dwarfs played castanets. The giants danced an elegant waltz, finally defying vertigo by spinning in place, skirts swirling. The music of the new dwarfs, the merriest of all the Patum's dance tunes, set the crowd to clapping loudly. The noon performance ended with the *tirabol*, a massed counterclockwise jump around the square. While the band played, small groups of spectators, arm in arm, combined to form a human whirlpool in the square. The *guites* joined the fray, the fireworks clamped between their jaws scattering trails of smoke and orange sparks, and, in one corner, two of the giants spun in place. Had anyone fallen, the momentum of the *tirabol* would have brought others tumbling down on top of them.

That night, between 9:30 P.M. and 3:00 A.M., the whole process from the Turks and hobbyhorses to the new dwarfs was repeated four times, with the addition, at the end of the second and fourth cycles, of the *plens* (full [devils]). For the first two cycles, Matthew and I watched from the town hall balcony. Not only the steps of the *entremesos*, but the patterns of the sur-rounding crowd were clearer from that height. Concentric circles formed around the Turks and hobbyhorses. Heads blossomed with red hats when the *maces* jumped. The *maces* were carried not by devils but by unmasked men and women in street clothes. The crowd pressed inwards, while the handlers yelled, gesticulated, pushed, and hurled themselves at the crowd to clear a space for the dancers.

For a moment it seemed as if it were all nothing more than an exercise in crowd control. But the crowd had its own internal restraints and didn't toler-ate transgression. When, on this fine night, a man in a long raincoat singled himself out by holding a black umbrella high above his head and wander-ing briefly into the middle of the dancing Turks and hobbyhorses, the crowd whistled. When he obtruded even more abrasively by walking up and down amid the fiery *maces*, the crowd voiced its objection more strenuously. Then, foolishly, the man challenged the *guites*. As the larger beast's handler ran its neck up and down the *barana*, driving back the crowd, the man with the umbrella stood on top of the wall, blocking the way. The handler knocked him backwards into the retreating crowd. Three times, the man climbed

6.4 *Guites*. Berga, 1996.

back up and three times the large *guita* toppled him. Finally, the little *guita* came up behind the *barana*. The two monsters trapped the intruder between them, spraying sparks directly onto the exposed skin of his face and neck. The crowd cheered. The challenger vainly tried to protect himself with his now battered umbrella. Finally, the *guites* left him alone. He mounted the wall once more, jumped into the square below, fell, picked himself up, and retreated. We didn't see him again. I expect he was drunk.

Although so prolonged an exposure to the fire must have stung him, it is clear from Matthew's detailed videotape of the incident that the *guites*' victim was not burned. Even when sprayed at close range against the flesh, the fire of the Patum causes no damage. *Patumaires* (those who take part in the Patum) talk affectionately of the caress of the fire; it's meant to look more threatening than it is. The appearance of danger and imminent disorder is as much a stage effect as any other. But real disruption of the festive order is not tolerated. Just as some unscripted virtuoso piece of acrobatics by one of the *castellers* in Vilafranca would have endangered the tower, so the man with the umbrella endangered the Patum by his drunken individualism. Crowd and performers, as one, opposed him.

After this disruption, we enjoyed the calmer dances of the eagle, dwarfs, and giants. Then, after the second cycle, a fresh anticipation filled the square. Silently, more than a hundred masked dancers filed up a steep alley from their subterranean dressing room to the square. They were dressed, like the devils of the midday *maces*, in red and green felt suits. A protective wreath of packed green vines circled the neck and a tuft of vines was tied to their tails. Every devil wore three *fuets* on each of the mask's two horns and two more *fuets* on his tail. The *plens* positioned themselves throughout the densely packed crowd. At a signal, all the lights went out, plunging the square momentarily into pitch blackness. The *plens*' companions lit the *fuets* of their respective devils, creating pockets of sparkling light. The band struck up a fast, repeated tune. The drum provided its own insistent rhythm. The *plens* and the entire crowd began to jump counterclockwise around the square in a burning whirlpool of fire. Clouds of smoke roiled up the chimney of the square, dropping black ashes on those of us in balconies. The *fuets* began to burst, a few at first and then many together, drowning the music in a barrage of explosions. As the last firecracker burst, we were again in total darkness before the floodlights lit up the square and the music stopped.

Berga's archivist, Xavier Pedrals, told me that at the beginning of the twentieth century there were thirty-two priests and many monks in Berga. Now there are four priests and no monks. On the other hand, he added, there were only eight *plens* back then. Now, one hundred twenty *plens* appear at a time. And since a different person wears the costume on each of the four occasions they appear, nearly five hundred people play *plens* each year. The balance has shifted between the devils and the clergy.

After the first round of *plens*, we yielded our seats on the balcony to other guests of the mayor and spent the rest of the night on the church steps. When the *maces* reappeared, I noticed that the second angel was played by an unshaven, gum-chewing man. The costume and wig were far too small for the burly actor, who mocked the official rhetoric of angelic power by exaggerating the role's effeminacy. When the *plens* came out again, Matthew wanted to go down into the square. We edged closer, but I wasn't ready yet to entrust him to the fire. A lengthy *tirabol*, repeated twenty times or more, gradually brought the night's activities to a close. Reluctantly, despite the hour, small groups spun off and wandered slowly home, arm in arm, through the town's narrow cobbled streets.

On Friday morning, I bought Matthew a red floppy cotton hat. At midday we watched the *patum infantil*, a children's version of the daytime Patum, complete with smaller *maces* and *guites*. Matthew baptized his hat with tamer fire. That evening, we saw two complete cycles of the *patum infantil*, ending with the junior *plens*. The children danced with remarkable precision and skill. Not only is the *patum infantil* an effective socialization of the town's youngsters into the most important communal ritual of the year. It also reinforces the message I was only slowly grasping: you need not fear the fire.

On Saturday evening, we joined friends for the second *passacarrers*, stopping in a crowded bar for food and drink before rejoining the action a hundred yards along the street. The promenade was in no hurry. Later, we paused to watch an exuberant display of fireworks explode from the castle walls above the town. At Cal Tonillo, we drank *barreja*. Matthew, after a small sip of the potent liquor, settled for a soft drink. At about 1:30 A.M., while a final informal *tirabol* swirled in the Plaça Sant Pere, Matthew and I walked slowly back to our hotel.

On Sunday, Thursday's program was repeated. At the midday Patum, when friends invited Matthew to join the team carrying the smaller *guita*, I relented. I was beginning to trust the fire. Matthew came back afterwards, his heart pumping, and admitted that the fear of stumbling and being trampled was greater than the fear of being burned. He was thrilled.

In the evening, we watched the *plens* being dressed in the old stables below the Plaça Sant Pere. Noyes invites her readers to imagine the experience from a participant's perspective: "The stable is approached by a long narrow stair that descends between two buildings on the plaza. A line begins to form there an hour or two before the *salt de plens*, and you approach, step by step, the low door. Inside, you climb in darkness to the upper level, where a face looks over a half-door—the porter of hell. He murmurs something to voices behind, and, after a pause, gives you a devil suit and a mask." From there, you go down more stairs to "an unfinished dirt floor completely submerged in vidalba [vines]," which are "crawling with snails and striped beetles." You pull on your suit and kneel down. "One of the dressers puts on your boxwood wreath, wraps your ears and forehead tightly in white bandages, then places the mask over your face. Then begins a tying and a tightening, a poking of itchy vidalba in all your exposed places."

Once the dressers are agreed that you are sufficiently protected, your companion "takes you to the outer stable, where they tie more *fuets* on your tail and twist it up in vidalba. Now, wound about like a corpse or swaddled like a newborn and almost blind inside the mask, you are taken by the arm and led back up the long stair to the *plaça*." When the music starts, "you begin to jump for your life, the crowd pressing, the sparks falling on your hands and inside your mask. You hear explosions above your head; the texture of the *plaça* changes beneath your feet; a second of open space and air is too quickly resubmerged in smoke and crowd for you to catch your breath."[24]

Jaume Farràs describes this "final scene of the Patum" as "a deluge of fire, a veritable infernal orgy."[25] By now, Matthew and I had grown accustomed to the fire and we danced with the crowd, pressing in on the *plens*. Afterwards, we assured ourselves we had not been afraid. If I understand it correctly, the folk theological goal of the Patum is to inoculate participants against the fear of fire. It's not just a matter of physical fear. To emerge unhurt from the scattered sparks of diabolic *maces*, from the more direct assault of monstrous *guites*, and from the final "infernal orgy" of the *plens*, wearing ample evidence of having played with fire, is to have challenged hell unscathed. Better—or worse—it is to have made friends with hell.

This folk theological challenge and accommodation may be understood at several levels. There is, first, the matter of resistance to earthly powers. The threat of hellfire has all too often been invoked by Christian authorities not for salvific purposes but to promote subordinate obedience. That may have been its purpose all along. "Postmortem sanctions," a recent historian of the early development of the doctrine of hell observes, "became more dire as internal sanctions became more necessary."[26] In Spain, the eternal consequences of heresy justified the political unity imposed by the Inquisition.

For Catalans, the conjunction of conservative Catholicism and a dictatorial state is a more recent trauma. Under Franco, to embrace hell was to resist the regime. The sentiment lingers. "The exaltation of hell," Noyes was told, requires "the conquest of fear," but to dance beneath the friendly fire of the Patum confers "absolute freedom."[27]

As part of their rejection of a Catholicism sullied by its close association with Franco, many in Berga like to think they take part in an ancient pagan ritual. The conservative Catholic allegory of the Patum as a celebration of Christian victory over Moors and Turks has been replaced with an equally potent allegory of seasonal ritual. The Patum is no longer read forward from the Turks and hobbyhorses but backwards from the *plens,* who are reinterpreted as "vegetal deities" unjustly demonized by the church. From centuries of Christian overgrowth, according to Farràs, "an ancient ceremony of natural regeneration" has reemerged.[28]

Such an allegory may be needed for a while to dispel the taint of Franco's triumphalist Catholicism, but it would be a mistake to read the "exaltation of hell" only in political or neopagan terms. To do so would be to miss the contribution of the Patum to Christian folk theology. We can approach that contribution by way of a simple observation: if the *patumaires* truly believed they were in danger of hell, they wouldn't stage the Patum as they do. What my son and I took part in was not an act of desperate bravado—a bold defiance of inevitable damnation—or a reckless capitulation to the forces of evil; it was a joyous communal celebration of freedom. Hell is exalted in the Patum not as a force whose power is to be embraced or feared; it is held up in order to expose its impotence. Hell cannot hurt the *patumaires,* for they have seen through it. It's nothing but a bogeyman, a Wizard of Oz, a bad-tempered mule of cloth and sticks.

Such confidence can, of course, be expressed by someone who regards all religion, Christianity included, as a hoax. Some of the *patumaires* may fall into this category. But it can also be expressed from within Christianity. In 1321 Frederick the Undaunted, margrave of Thuringia, attended a performance of a play based on the biblical parable of the wise and foolish virgins (Matthew 25:1–13). Despite the tearful intercession of the Virgin Mary, an unrelenting Jesus condemned the foolish virgins to hell, a decision roundly applauded by Lucifer and Beelzebub. When the play ended with no sign of divine mercy, Frederick stormed angrily away, objecting, "What is the Christian faith if God is not moved to pity even by the prayers of the Virgin and all the saints?"[29]

He had a point. Why, in so many churches, are warnings of damnation

issued to those who have already embraced the Christian faith? If the intercession of the Virgin and the saints (or of Christ in his role as mediator) is
effective, why imply from the pulpit, the altar rail, or the religious stage that
it may be ineffective after all? If the Christian gospel is truly good news,
why burden those who have believed it with persistent threats of bad news?
The Patum's folk theology refuses infernal intimidation and proclaims good
news in pyrotechnic mode.

But the Patum goes further, refusing to restrict impunity to Christians. Its
exaltation of the impotence of hell is not dependent on the preliminary exclusion or defeat of Turks, Moors, or pagans. As in Vilafranca and Medianía,
the festive vision is inclusive. The only villain was the intruder with the
black umbrella; and even he was tamed and temporarily excluded but not
consumed by fire. The fire burns no one.

Some theologians would recoil from the implied heresy, but Karl Barth
(a great and reasonably cautious theologian) once wondered whether God's
promise to "reconcile all things to himself" (Colossians 1:20) might actually
mean what it appears to say. "This much is certain," he wrote, "that we have
no theological right to set any sort of limits to the loving-kindness of God
which appeared in Jesus Christ."[30] The world, he dared to hope, might end
with neither a bang nor a whimper but with a universal cry of joy. The Patum
couches its hope more tentatively, asserting only—against two millennia of
clerical threats—that the fire burns no one. But it celebrates its freedom from
fear with a great communal festival. I am glad my son and I at last joined in.

Demons and dragon. Vilafranca del Penedès, 1995.

A *conchero* tunes his instrument. Basilica de Guadalupe, 1998.

Saint Michael (with shield) angel, and *maces*. Berga, 1996.

Santiago (Armando Espinosa).
Basílica de Guadalupe, 1998.

Pecado. Camuñas, 1997.

Machu. Cusco, 2001.

Txatxos. Lantz, 2001.

Q'apaq Negro overseer. Cusco, 2001.

Satan in smoke. Oruro, 2000.

Masked Gilles. Binche, 1999.

Fancy mas queen. Port of Spain, 1996.

Devil. Oruro, 2000.

7.
A Confraternity of Jews
(CASTILE–LA MANCHA)

ON A BITTERLY COLD first Sunday of Lent, 12 February 1486, seven hundred fifty *conversos* (Jewish converts to Christianity) "went in procession . . . bareheaded and unshod" through the streets of Toledo, then the capital of Spain. "Howling loudly and weeping and tearing out their hair," according to a contemporary account, the penitent *conversos*—both men and women— stumbled "through the streets along which the Corpus Christi procession goes, until they came to the cathedral." Their humiliation was watched by "a great number of spectators." After a mass and sermon in the cathedral, each prisoner publicly acknowledged "all the things in which he had judaized [relapsed into Jewish practices]." The *conversos* were then condemned "to go in procession for [the] six Fridays [of Lent], disciplining their body with scourges of hempcord, barebacked, unshod, and bareheaded." The final demeaning procession would take place on Good Friday. Stripped for life of many civil privileges, the *conversos* were warned that "if they fell into the same error again, . . . they would be condemned to the fire."[1]

Human power is sometimes loath to withhold the pain of punitive fire until the afterlife. Over the sixteen years that followed Toledo's first *auto de fe* (act of faith) in February 1486, some two hundred fifty people were burned in person in the city. Twice that number were burned in effigy.[2] Although the number of executions declined over the years, the Holy Office of the Inquisition continued for several centuries to employ the pyre to suppress dissent. Established in 1480, at a time when Ferdinand and Isabella were obsessed with reducing to unity the kingdoms consolidated by their marriage, the Spanish Inquisition was not finally abolished until 1834. Although its reach later extended to *moriscos* (Moorish converts to Christianity), Lutherans, and others suspected of heresy, its initial and enduring purpose was to rid the church of Jewish influence. Especially after Spanish Jews were given the forced choice of conversion or expulsion in 1492, *conversos* were widely suspected of being Christians in public and Jews in private.

No city was more affected by the Inquisition than Toledo. Despite its earlier reputation as a model of religious tolerance and *convivencia,* the ancient cathedral city was home to an active tribunal of the Spanish Inquisition from 1485 until the late eighteenth century and was, in 1756, the site of the last Spanish *auto de fe*.[3] It is still the site of one of the largest and most conservative Corpus Christi processions in Spain. Toledo's "majestic" procession, in which "military and religious orders parade with great pomp before a monstrance carved in some of the first gold brought back from the Americas," still, for some observers, "reeks of the Inquisition."[4]

Fifty miles southeast of the city of Toledo, a small town of some three thousand inhabitants annually stages its own very different Corpus Christi festival. Officially, the celebrations in Camuñas enact an orthodox *auto sacramental,* or morality play, in which grace and virtue triumph over sin.[5] Unofficially, the fiesta offers a scathing indictment of the memory of the Inquisition and its persecution of *conversos*. Its ambiguity has not gone unnoticed by the authorities. Prohibited by the national Republican government between 1931 and 1939 because of its religious nature, Camuñas's Corpus Christi festival was conversely banned by the archbishop of Toledo from 1947 to 1959 for its "idolatrous character."[6]

In May 1997 I spent Corpus Christi in Camuñas. The landscape preserves the fictional memory of Don Quixote and the fortified remains of militant religion. From my hotel window in nearby Consuegra, I could see whitewashed windmills on a southern ridge rising from the plains of La Mancha. Beside the windmills stood a ruined castle, once owned, along with the town itself, by the Castilian priorate of the military order of the Knights Hospitaller of Saint John.

On the Wednesday evening of Corpus Christi week, I watched two dozen Sins run up the hill behind Camuñas's parish church. At the main door, they formed a guard through which an equal number of Dancers entered the building. Two linked halves of the single Confraternity of the Holy Sacrament, the *pecados* (Sins) and *danzantes* (Dancers) meet separately throughout the year, joining forces for Corpus Christi. The *danzantes* wore white cotton trousers colorfully embroidered at the calves, white shirts beneath black jackets, and red papier-mâché masks with long noses. Most carried tambourines. One played a drum; another, a pair of *porras.* The latter, unique to Camuñas, consists of a short wooden scepter and an elongated castanet. Striking the scepter with the castanet produces an insistent, slightly hollow

7.1   Sins scrape the cobbles outside the church. Camuñas, 1997.

rhythm. A cross-dressed man, known as the *madama*, wore a light brown skirt and played castanets (see Fig. 7.4 below).

The *pecados* followed. Hanging at their waists were red papier-mâché masks, distinguished from those of the *danzantes* by their horns (partially concealed by colored ribbons and rosettes) and by their small noses. The Sins carried long wooden staffs and wore demonic colors: black trousers and red cummerbunds. While the congregation filled the pews, the *pecados* made their way to the altar, and the *danzantes*, footsteps and percussion echoing, briefly danced around the church before settling by the altar. A priest conducted mass. Afterwards, the Sins donned their masks and formed a guard outside the church door. The *danzantes*, preceded by a religious banner and followed by a crucifix wreathed in flowers, danced out backwards so as not to dishonor the church. The *pecados* issued a low ululation from behind their masks and dragged their staffs over the cobbled ground (Fig. 7.1). The gesture and the sound implied disgruntled threat.

A tour of the town followed. The *pecados* ran ahead, so that the *danzantes* and the crucifix had to pass repeatedly between two rows of scraping, ululating Sins. Periodically, the *danzantes* also formed a corridor, extending

7.2 *Pecado mayor* in pig mask. Camuñas, 1997.

outward from the flowered cross. The Sins lined up in single file, some distance away, facing the crucifix. One by one, they launched themselves with
an arm movement that suggested a furtive flapping of wings, ran with short
quick steps between the Dancers, slowed before the cross, executed a small
jump, stopped, knelt, unmasked, and walked away. This episode, collectively
known as the *carrera* (run), suggests a failed challenge and, perhaps, submission on the part of the Sins to religious authority.

Three *pecados* wore distinctive costumes. The first, the *pecailla* (little
sin), wore a brown cape sewn with a white Maltese cross. The second, the
pecado mayor (great sin), wore a black cape, sewn with three white Maltese crosses, and a black papier-mâché mask with an elongated pig's snout
(Fig. 7.2). A third, maintaining order in the midst of the line, was the *correa,*
so named after the leather strap with which he imposes discipline during
private meetings of the confraternity. The *correa* wore a red cape with three
white Maltese crosses (Fig. 7.3).

The crosses recall the dominating presence of the Knights of Saint John,
later known as the Knights of Malta, in Consuegra. Authorized by a papal
bull of 1183, the military order exercised a kind of feudal lordship over

the region for several centuries. Only in 1557 was Camuñas granted a royal charter as a town in its own right, independent of Consuegra.[7] The Great Sin's mask recalls a different kind of suppression. It bears a striking resemblance to an iron scold's bridle, shaped like a pig's head, that was used in seventeenth-century Germany "to punish those who, by their words, had transgressed against prevailing conventions." An internal spike secured the victim's tongue.[8] Antoinette Molinié believes the Spanish Inquisition may have used a similar device to punish "heretical" *conversos*, whose derisive nickname—deriving in part from their refusal to eat pork—was *marranos* (pigs).[9] The leather strap, too, may recall the Inquisition, which commonly sentenced its victims to public flogging.[10] Thus all three signs—cross, mask, and strap—denote the ecclesiastic use of force to compel submission.

After each *carrera*, a householder offered us candies, nuts, and *zurra* (a mixture of white wine, lemonade, and sugar). At one stop, Gabriel Romero told me proudly that the papier-mâché mask he wore as the *pecailla* was one hundred fifty years old. Over the decades, it had received several coats of new paint. As we talked further, he told me that the *danzantes* were all "*judíos*

7.3 *Pecado mayor, pecailla,* and *correa,* Camuñas, 1997.

[Jews]." He pointed to the long noses of their masks as evidence (see Fig. 7.4). He added that many *conversos* had settled in the area and that the *danzantes* represented the Jews' conversion to Christianity. (I lack figures for Camuñas, but in fifteenth-century Máqueda, northwest of Toledo, there were 281 Jewish families to only 50 Christian.)[11] The pious young woman who bore the processional crucifix offered a more distanced reading. The *danzantes*, she said, were Old Testament Jews dancing before the Ark of the Covenant while awaiting the Messiah. The captain of the *danzantes* disagreed. He preferred to find his identity in the morality play: the Dancers represented Virtues opposing the Sins.

On Thursday morning, the Dancers were honored participants in the Corpus Christi mass. The Sins remained outside, their masks perched atop their heads. At key moments, on a signal from a spotter inside the church, one of the *pecados* fired a rifle in the air. Each time, the *pecados* lowered their masks, repeated their characteristic ululation, and dragged their staffs over the cobbles in what Consolación González Casarrubios calls a "display of anger" over their exclusion.[12]

Afterwards, the two groups formed up in the elongated square to the east of the church. An outdoor altar stood against the church wall. Behind the altar were huge cardboard cutouts of a chalice and a monstrance; in front, the ground was strewn with fragrant herbs. Beating an insistent rhythm, the *danzantes* formed a corridor in front of the altar. From the far end of the square, the *pecados* launched their *carrera*, the implicit challenge of each individual charge collapsing at the foot of the altar as masked ululating run gave way to unmasked silent genuflection.

Then the Sins yielded the length of the square to the *danzantes* for a dance known as *tejer el cordón* (weave the thread). The twenty-four Dancers formed two parallel lines. To a rhythm unmoderated by melody, the *madama* began to dance. Skirt swirling, high-stepping, he wove his way down between the two rows, up behind the right flank, down between the rows again, and up behind the left flank. Each time he completed this figure-of-eight, the senior remaining Dancer joined in behind him until, after twenty-four gradually diminishing figures-of-eight, all the Dancers were following in a line behind the *madama*. Then the entire series was repeated, with the senior remaining Dancer peeling off to his original position at the completion of each figure so that, after twenty-four more gradually broadening figures-of-eight, the original formation was restored. The entire dance lasted about twenty minutes, requiring considerable stamina on the part of the *madama*, who danced energetically throughout.

7.4 Dancers in long-nosed masks, led by the *madama*, dance ahead of the host in the Corpus Christi procession. Camuñas, 1997.

Before its ban in 1948, the dance had always been performed inside the church. After the dance's restoration in 1960, it moved outside to accommodate a larger audience.[13] Locally, it is believed to be an ancient dance adapted to a Christian purpose in the sixteenth or seventeenth century.[14] Indirect confirmation that the dance is at least that old may come from a similar figure, known as "thread" (or, later, "thread the needle"), that can be documented in the English morris dance from the late sixteenth century. This, too, involved a cross-dressed dancer, known in the English tradition as Maid Marian, who wove his way among the other male dancers.[15] There was, in the sixteenth century, considerable cultural exchange (most famously in royal spouses) between the courts of England and Spain. The origins of both dances, however, are more likely to be courtly than pagan.[16]

Once the dance (and another round of the *carrera*) were over, the Corpus Christi procession began a lengthy tour of the town. The Sins led the way, lining the street from time to time to let the Dancers (Fig. 7.4), still bracketed by the banner and the garlanded crucifix, pass between them. A priest beneath a baldachin conveyed the sacred monstrance. When the procession halted at small private altars, the priest prayed and wafted incense; the *peca-dos* knelt before running the *carrera* again. As the procession returned at last to its starting point, the Sins rushed up the hill to hoot and drag their sticks while the Dancers entered the church. The latter danced around the two outside aisles and down the nave, ending unmasked and kneeling in front of the altar. I watched from the choir loft. After prayer and a jovial word from the priest, the *danzantes* and the congregation left. The formal procession was over, but an informal parade of Sins and Dancers round the town continued for some time.

Interpretations of the day's ritual in Camuñas vary. Those who advance the allegorical explanation argue that the *madama* represents divine grace, the senior *danzantes* represent the theological virtues, and the remaining *danzantes* are the souls of men being saved by grace and virtue. This theory is of recent vintage. Articulated most fully in a book published in 1985 by Pedro Yugo Santacruz, it seems to have been developed in the 1950s as an effective means of persuading the ecclesiastical authorities to lift their ban.[17]

Of greater (albeit still uncertain) antiquity is the identification of the *danzantes* as Jews. Although Camuñas's incomplete archives attest to the existence of the Confraternity of the Holy Sacrament by 1770, early details of its festive celebrations are lacking. Many documents, stored in Consuegra, were destroyed in a flood in 1891.[18] Some sixty miles southwest of Camuñas, however, in the town of Puertollano, a Corpus Christi dance was banned in 1763 on the grounds that it was organized by a "confraternity of Jews." Puertollano's archives speak of the dancers with contempt, but the brief description of the dance suggests that it may have been similar to the one that survives in Camuñas: "Executing a sort of dance, both dancing and leaping, they enter the church at the moment when his majesty [i.e., the consecrated bread] is displayed, and, even worse, some of them are dressed as women."[19] A document in the Camuñas archives, from 1927, refers to the town's "confraternities of Jews and Sins." No mention is made of Virtues. Nor is any word of Virtues found in various accounts of the festival published between 1948 and 1974.[20] "If you ask the Dancers who they are," Martín Brugarola wrote in 1948, "they'll tell you they are Jews."[21] The Captain of the Dancers may now prefer the virtuous allegorical reading, but it is one that lacks the patina of age.

All this leads to some startling (if never quite explicitly stated) conclusions. If the *danzantes* are Jews, then the *pecados* are Christians. Moreover, their red and black costumes and concealed horns designate the Christian

Sins as hypocritical demons. The pig-snout mask on the *pecado mayor* may suggest that it was the Christians, rather than the Jews, who deserved to be punished by the Inquisition; and that the Inquisition itself ranks as the Spanish Church's "great sin." It is the Jewish Dancers, rather than the Christian Sins, who are admitted to the parish church; and it is the Jews who, in their opposition to the Sins, represent the Virtues. This is not quite what one expects of a traditional Corpus Christi dance, let alone of a ritual that claims to be a folk variation on an *auto sacramental.* Nevertheless, its suggestion that the *conversos,* whom the Inquisition persecuted, may have been virtuous servants of the Christian God while those who persecuted them in the name of Christ were sinful hypocrites in the service of the Devil is one that is fully supported by the events of the *día de los tiznaos* (day of the blackened ones), which on Friday intervenes between the two elegant Corpus Christi processions. Gabriel told me that it was the *día de los tiznaos* that drew the archiepiscopal ban.

Dressed not in their processional costumes and masks but in old street clothes, the *pecados* appeared at about 11:00 A.M. on Friday. Several had blackened faces. Four novices, young men prepared for admission to the Sins' half of the confraternity, had cheeks marked with sooty crosses. The Sins wandered in a group from house to house, drinking, eating, and playing practical jokes. One pretended to put a firecracker in a companion's coat pocket and then ran away with his fingers in his ears. The friend panicked briefly, trying to extinguish a nonexistent firework. Another handed round a plate of dog food as if it were a palatable snack; someone inadvertently tasted it. There were limits to the fun. When the Sins put one of their number in a trash can and rolled him down the street, a woman yelled at them from a balcony and insisted they return the can to its proper place. The Sins complied.

After a couple of hours, they decorated a metal farm cart with greenery and loaded it with a damp bale of straw, to which they set not fire but smoke. The cart resembled those once used to carry heretics to execution.[22] The *correa,* ordinarily responsible for discipline, was crowned with a white paper miter marked with a cross, recalling both an episcopal miter and the white conical hat worn by victims of the Inquisition. Thus dressed, the *correa* was designated Santo Paparroa, a name that readily suggests a parody of the pope, the Holy Father of Rome (*santo Papa de Roma*).[23] Santo Paparroa was loaded onto the cart and, armed only with a furled umbrella with which to beat the straw when it burst into flames, was wheeled through the streets of Camuñas. It was a rough ride. The Sins rocked the cart vigorously. They bumped it down a flight of steps. When Santo Paparroa tried to escape, they quickly recaptured him, reinstalling him in smoking ignominy.

About 1:30 P.M. the irreverent parade reached the Plaza del Arenal, where a scaffold or gallows (horca) had been erected on a permanent concrete dais. It bore a striking resemblance to the gallows of the Inquisition.[24] The cart was shaken violently from side to side and then upended in the center of the square, strewing pope and straw on the pavement. For a while, youngsters and Sins threw buckets of water at the smoke, one another, pretty girls, and the crowd in general. Then a dramatic rite of initiation began.

One by one, to an ominously slow drumbeat, each of the novices was carried across the square. Along the way, he was covered with straw, drenched with water, and forced to drink large quantities of zurra through a funnel. (Inquisitors frequently subjected their victims to a similar "water torture." One graphic illustration of the period shows a torturer pouring water through a funnel into the mouth of a bound and naked woman while a clerical secretary dispassionately records the proceedings.)[25] Eventually, clutching a makeshift straw cross, the novice was deposited at the foot of the scaffold. As he tried to climb the ladder, he was beaten with a short-handled broom from above by the pecailla and held from below by older members of the confraternity who shouted, "¡No suba! ¡No suba!" (Don't go up! Don't go up!).

Finally, the novice was allowed to climb to the top of the scaffold, where he sat astride a plank between two older men: the Confessor and the Judge. The novice handed his cross to the Confessor, who tossed it contemptuously to the ground. Placing a noose around the novice's neck, the Confessor launched an interrogation, asking the novice such simple catechetical questions as "Do you believe in God?" and "Do you believe in the Trinity?" Holding the novice's head, the Confessor shook it from side to side after each question, so that the novice was forced to answer with a heretical negative. His interrogation over, the novice turned to face the Judge. Holding an open umbrella as a parody of a baldachin and wearing a toy pink pig's snout that linked him to the Great Sin of the Christians, the Judge pronounced sentence. The noose was raised, a rifle fired, the novice was sprayed with water, and the procedure began again with the next applicant.

Some in Camuñas claim this is a rite of purification, but most admit that it's a parody of the Inquisition and that, along with the dance and the carrera, it enacts some kind of collective memory of the tribunal's treatment of conversos. Jewish traditions in this part of Castile–La Mancha were "particularly ancient and rich."[26] Even this admission, however, does not resolve the matter of interpretation. To this question, the community as a whole was to return in a public forum on Saturday night.

In the meantime, I spent most of the day in Toledo. I wandered through the old Jewish quarter. I stood in synagogues that had been given to military-religious orders after the expulsion of Jews and now served as museums. I explored the cathedral, built between 1227 and 1493 on the site of the Moorish Great Mosque, which had itself replaced a Visigothic church. I stood on the walls of the Alcázar, a sixteenth-century fortress still regarded by those who remember Franco fondly as a monument to its Nationalist defenders during the Civil War. And I sipped port at an open-air café in the triangular Plaza de Zocodover, where the victims of the Inquisition had been burned. Ancient, brightly colored tapestries hung from the surrounding balconies in preparation for Sunday's Corpus Christi procession. (In 1991 the secular Spanish government decreed that Corpus Christi should no longer be celebrated on Thursday but only on the following Sunday. Unlike Berga and Camuñas, Toledo grudgingly complied.)

In the evening, Toledo permitted itself a little secular fun. Giants, big-heads, and the town's distinctive *tarasca* paraded through the city's narrow streets. One of the eighteenth-century giants is identified as El Cid, champion of Spanish Catholicism and victor over the Moors of Valencia. The *tarasca* is a wheeled dragon. It breathes no fire but is ridden by a diminutive doll, deliberately recalling the Whore of Babylon with whom "the kings of the earth committed adultery," for she, too, in the apocalyptic vision of John of Patmos, sat astride a monstrous beast (Revelation 17:2–3). The doll is named Ana Bolena after Henry VIII of England's second wife. Henry's first wife, divorced in favor of Anne Boleyn, was the Spanish princess Catherine of Aragon.

Toledo's parade was tame compared to Berga's *passacarrers.* Not only was the dragon wheeled; so were the five large giants. Only the smaller giants were borne by men within, and of them, just one made any attempt at a dance. From time to time, Anne Boleyn whirled atop the dragon, propelled by some internal mechanism. There were no fireworks, no attacks on the crowd. The dragon and giants would parade again the next day, well ahead of the much larger and more solemn Corpus Christi procession. An essay in the official Corpus Christi program of 1955 ascribed a low Catalan pedigree to the "monstrous figures and the giants," which had historically mixed "superstition with religion" in Toledo's Corpus Christi celebrations. "Now," it added, "these monstrous figures have been abandoned" and only the *tarasca* still "comes out from time to time on the eve of Corpus Christi."[27] The "monstrous figures" are once again allowed out in public, but they are well behaved and offer little competition to the religious procession.

I returned to Camuñas in time for the Third Annual Conference on Corpus Christi, which began well after dark in the town's Cultural Center. The room was packed. The first speaker delivered a conventional history of the feast of Corpus Christi in general and a standard allegorical reading of Camuñas's fiesta in particular. Antoinette Molinié, a French scholar who has written several articles on Corpus Christi in Camuñas, was the second speaker; she grounded the festival in the regional history of the *conversos*. In the time of Ferdinand and Isabella, she told us, there had been many Jews in the eastern part of La Mancha who had publicly converted to Christianity while continuing to practice their Judaism at home. Nowhere, she said, had the *conversos* been subject to more rigorous persecution than here. Consuegra, of which Camuñas was then a subsidiary, is specifically named in the records, as are local families repeatedly persecuted by the Inquisition. She showed us a photograph of the German pig's head bridle. No one in the audience had seen it before, but all agreed that something very like this must have been the original of the papier-mâché mask worn by the *pecado mayor*.

In light of all this, Molinié suggested that the ritual of the *horca* was a means of ridding the novices of any remaining traces of Judaism before they could be admitted to the confraternity of Sins. She compared it to the rite of baptism in the early church, which, she said, washed the Christian clean of all traces of ancestral Judaism. And she suggested that it retained the memory of the historical expulsion of the Jews from Spain.[28] This seemed to me to privilege official religious history over the enacted signs of folk performance. What I had seen in Camuñas suggested a very different stance towards the region's Jewish heritage. The identification of Christians as Sins and Jews as Virtues, the ready acceptance of the Jewish Dancers into the church and the exclusion of the Christian Sins, the explicit parody of pope and Inquisition, and, especially, the evident injustice of the Confessor's interrogation had persuaded me that the *horca* was not a ritual expulsion of the remnants of Judaism but a protest against the past mistreatment of *conversos*.

Molinié also suggested that the dramatic roots of Camuñas's annual confrontation between good and evil might be found in the tradition of mock battles between Moors and Christians. Perhaps the Christians had become the Knights of Malta and the Jews had replaced the Moors.[29] The absence of any signs of battle inclines me to think otherwise. In any case, it is only the public transcript of the *moros y cristianos* that enacts the expulsion of the

Moors; the hidden transcript imagines a world in which traditional enemies finally live together in difference. If elements of Camuñas's Corpus Christi festival could be shown to have their roots in the *moros y cristianos*, it would strengthen my conviction that the people of Camuñas (unconsciously perhaps) are defending rather than expelling their Jewish ancestors.

It is the Corpus Christi procession in Toledo rather than the folk dance and parodic ritual in Camuñas that celebrates the suppression of otherness and the triumph of religious uniformity. When the Solemn Procession of the Most Holy Body of Christ left Toledo's cathedral on Sunday morning, it was led by the *guardia civil* (national guard). There were no demons and dragons to clear the streets. In a concession to pageantry, the guards rode horses and wore colorful nineteenth-century uniforms, but they were still responsible, as the official program frankly put it, for "making the multitude stay on the sidewalk."[30]

After the "kettledrummers of the most excellent city government" and the "gala band of the national guard" came a ceremonial verger in a white wig and the gold-plated processional cross of the cathedral, a fifteenth-century gift from Alfonso V of Portugal to the archbishop of Toledo. Twenty-four religious groups followed: confraternities, chivalric orders devoted to religious ends, massed representatives of the city's youth groups, nuns, regular clergy from the five orders of monks and friars remaining in Toledo, and the cathedral clergy. The numbers were intended to impress. The Confraternity of the Most Holy Christ of Calvary, for example, boasted five hundred members and eight hundred "sympathizers." Interspersed between the groups were treasured objects of historical and religious significance, including the Cross of Cardinal Pedro González de Mendoza. The official program reminded onlookers that this "was the first Christian symbol to stand on the watchtower of the Alhambra after the Catholic Monarchs [Ferdinand and Isabella] conquered the city of Granada."[31] Granada fell in 1492, the last bastion of Moorish sovereignty on the Iberian Peninsula.

Then came a group of "little pages," boys and girls in white wigs and multicolored Baroque uniforms, who scattered rose petals in front of the consecrated Host. The monstrance itself is a source of great pride in Toledo. More than eight feet high, it contains—in addition to a single wafer of sacramental bread—77 pounds of pure gold and 403 pounds of silver, not to mention "an infinity of gems, pearls, and enamel."[32] After the monstrance came the most powerful representatives of church and state: the archbishop of Toledo—primate of all Spain—and the most important civil and military authorities of Castile–La Mancha, the city of Toledo, and the province of

Toledo. Representatives of the University of Castile–La Mancha followed. Closing out the procession—ensuring crowd control at the end as the national guard had at the beginning—were the armed forces of the city's Military Academy. Franco studied at the academy as a young man.

No folk elements disrupted this display of ecclesiastical, civil, and military power. The well-behaved giants and *tarasca* had passed a full hour ahead of the procession. The crowd kept its subordinate place on the sidewalks, gazing at but not participating in the display of divine and human power. Only by belonging to an organization that had found and kept its place in the appointed hierarchies of power could a citizen take part in the procession. Just so, in other centuries, had crowds lined the streets of Toledo to watch the victims of the Inquisition, weeping, walk the Corpus Christi processional route to penance in the cathedral or conflagration in the Plaza de Zocodover.[33]

As for me, I was not in Toledo on Sunday morning. I read about the celebrations later, having chosen to remain in Camuñas, where Thursday's festivities were repeated. Once again the Jewish Virtues were the guests of honor at the mass, while demonic Christian Sins remained outside, impotently threatening with their hooting and their scraping of the cobbles. One by one, running, the Sins attacked the modest monstrance or the flowered crucifix, their challenge ending in a genuflection. The Jewish Dancers danced their celebration of the grace of God. A convivial folk theology prevailed.

At this distance in time—in the absence of archival evidence—it is impossible to tell whether the dissenting voices of Camuñas's Corpus Christi festival originated in the creativity of a true "confraternity of Jews" or whether a *cofradía* of old Christians chose to protest the treatment of their *converso* neighbors by the Inquisition. I am convinced, however, that the annual celebration in Camuñas testifies to a strand of popular resistance in the history of Corpus Christi that deserves to be heard alongside the more powerful voices of the official rites of church and state in Toledo.

8.
Saint Sebastian and the Blue-eyed Blacks
(PERU)

FOR A FEW HOURS on Thursday morning, Corpus Christi in Cusco resembles its haughty peninsular cousin in Toledo more than it does its exuberant kin in Berga and Camuñas. But shortly after noon, the solemn pomp gives way to multiple patronal saints day festivals. Fifteen images of saints and virgins take to the streets, accompanied by dancers whose mockery of colonial pretensions invokes the spirit of Carnival. The miscegenation of festive traditions befits the celebration's multiple ethnic referents, invoking the several heritages of Spain, the Incas, the rural Indians of the Amazon and the Andes, and the urban mestizos who make up the majority of the festival's participants. And this is just one day in a week of Corpus Christi activities that run concurrently with the massive civic parades that precede the reconstructed Inca solstice festival of Inti Raymi (Sun Festival). I was in Cusco for Corpus Christi and Inti Raymi in June 2001.

Early on Thursday morning, the interior of the cathedral being under repair, an outdoor altar was placed at the top of the steps overlooking the spacious Plaza de Armas. Behind the altar and to its sides, in a sweeping arc of sanctity, were arrayed the images of fifteen saints, from San Antonio Abad and his pig[1] at one end to the Virgen de Belén (Virgin of Bethlehem) at the other. Waiting in the street, in front and to the right of the cathedral, was the wheeled, eighteenth-century silver *carroza* (carriage) that would bear the consecrated host. Its ornate domed monstrance, made with 365 pounds of gold and silver, stands more than eight feet high and rests on a wheeled silver platform draped in velvet. In front, its wings spread, is a finely wrought silver pelican that feeds its young from a self-inflicted chest wound, red with more than twenty rubies.[2] The bird is an ancient symbol of Christ's sacrifice.

At the foot of the steps stood an honor guard of uniformed schoolchildren. Higher up, to the right of the altar, sat representatives of the military and civil government. To the left were nuns and other privileged religious.

Behind the altar were dozens of empty seats, filled at 10:00 A.M. by robed clergy who filed out from the cathedral's west door. The seating was arranged so that the altar and its surrounding dignitaries were shaded by the cathedral while the rest of us, who stood in the square itself, faced the full strength of the Andean sun. Vendors sold paper visors to those who had no shady hats.

The mass gestured in the direction of inclusiveness. The music was contemporary and invited congregational singing. A blind boy, who had memorized the epistle for the day, stood behind the lectern and "read" from a Bible he couldn't see. The archbishop of Cusco crossed from his throne behind the altar and embraced the boy. But, a few minutes later, the archbishop began his sermon by acknowledging, in careful order of rank, all the clerical, military, and civic dignitaries in attendance. Only then did he greet his "brothers and sisters" across the street. When the consecrated bread was distributed, there was barely enough time for the priests to place wafers on the tongues of those beside the altar, the privileged schoolchildren, and a few elderly worshipers who struggled to the front of the crowd.

After the mass, the archbishop walked below a baldachin to his seat aboard the *carroza*. Pushed by burly young men concealed within, the carriage took a slow hour to make its pious circuit of the square. Two long lines of priests preceded it; leaders of confraternities, some in indigenous Andean dress, followed. Loudspeakers blared devotions. Some members of the crowd threw flower petals at the passing *carroza*. A Cusqueña friend, Ana Miranda Jiménez, admitted to me that she found this part of Corpus Christi boring.

High in the Peruvian Andes, Cusco was the capital of the Inca Empire until Francisco Pizarro and his army of Spanish adventurers arrived in 1533.[3] Although, for ease of communication with other Spanish colonies, Pizarro established a new capital on the coast at Lima, Cusco retained the prestige of its Inca past. In 1572 Viceroy Francisco de Toledo consolidated the power of the Spanish crown over the mountainous Inca Empire with the capture and execution, in Cusco's Plaza de Armas, of the last fugitive Inca ruler, Túpac Amaru I.[4] A year later, declaring Corpus Christi "the principal festival and procession of the year," the viceroy summoned "all the Indians" of the city's several parishes to help with preparations and ordered every Spanish-led trade guild to "bring out its dance or play." The texts of the plays were to be "examined" by an ecclesiastical judge.[5] The colonial festival was intended, at least in part, as a dramatization of the triumph of Spanish Catholicism over Inca paganism.

The Spaniards were helped in this regard by the temporal coincidence of the imported Catholic festival with the Inca festival of Inti Raymi and, more generally, with the widespread harvest festivals that marked the reappearance of the Plciades and the end of the Andean agricultural cycle.[6] Also influential was the occasional feast of Q'apaq Hucha (Great Guilt). Celebrated at times of real or perceived danger, it involved the portage of religious images to Cusco from the empire's holy sites, a great festival of drinking and dancing in the main square, displays of group identity and social ranking, and, after several days of celebrations, the return of the statues to their respective temples. Q'apaq Hucha sometimes coincided with Inti Raymi.[7]

Encouraged by the Spanish authorities, indigenous elements migrated to Corpus Christi. In 1551 or 1552 the cathedral choirmaster "composed a part-song . . . for the feast of Corpus Christi, in perfect imitation of the Inca singing." He drew his inspiration from Inca plough songs in which the repeated word *hailli* (victory [over the soil]) marked the rhythmic raising and dropping of the foot-ploughs. "Eight mestizo boys . . . appeared in Indian dress, each with a plough in his hand, and acted the song and *hailli* of the Indians in the procession, the whole choir joining in the chorus."[8] The boys were schoolfellows of Garcilaso de la Vega, who later recalled the Corpus Christi celebrations of his youth. Large numbers of Indian "nobility," he wrote, entered the city with "all the decorations, ornaments, and devices that they used in the time of the Inca kings for their great festivals." Some wore the wings of condors, while "others had strange devices and dresses of gold and silver foil, . . . or appeared as monsters with horrifying masks." Other Indians, "vassals" of Spanish *caballeros,* carried the images of Christian saints on *andas* (litters) as they had once ceremonially carried *mallquis* (mummy bundles) holding the mummified remains of Inca rulers.[9]

In 1620, concerned that the festival "had declined from its earlier splendor," Cusco's *corregidor* (royal administrator) ordered all the Indian parishes and settlements within thirty-five miles of the city to bring their "dances and *invenciones* [dramatic spectacles]" to town for Corpus Christi.[10] Indigenous nobility in the costumes of Inca kings walked ahead of the images of Catholic saints, while rural Indians performed their native dances. The canopy-covered bishop, bearing a small, sun-shaped monstrance, brought up the privileged rear of the procession. This juxtaposition of traditions, Carolyn Dean has argued, was not just the inevitable syncretism of colonial popular religion but an essential sign of Catholic triumph. The native participants in the Corpus Christi procession represented "the people over whom Christians had triumphed." They were the visible spoils of successful evangelism and the embodied signs of ethnic subordination.[11]

But few festivals, especially in the contested public space of a major city, are ever quite that simple. By recalling their royal ancestry, the assimilated Inca nobility asserted present rank. Other indigenous groups used Corpus Christi to recall their own triumphs. Passing the cathedral in 1555, the Cañari chief Francisco Chilche deliberately provoked the watching Inca nobles by displaying "a model of an Indian head which he held by the hair." During the rebellion of Manco II in 1536, Chilche had defeated and beheaded an Inca warrior in single combat.[12] Yet other Indians danced in 1615 as "savage" Amazonian Chunchos, a practice that predated the arrival of the Spaniards and still endures.[13] In 1835 José María Blanco reported that a dance of "half-naked" Chunchos "with feathers in their hair" was one of "the most common dances of the Indians . . . , especially on the day of Corpus Christi."[14] It still is. Contesting both Spanish and (more recently) mestizo domination, it is one of several windows onto an alternative view of Andean society embodied in the festival.

In 1700 the more informal procession on the octave of Corpus Christi was interrupted by a pitched battle between members of rival parishes armed with slings and stones. Competition over the relative splendor of several groups of "masked Indian dancers, dressed as Spaniards," appears to have prompted the disruption. Such dances were banned the following year.[15] Perhaps the authorities welcomed the chance to suppress the dance because it "mocked Spaniards and Spanish culture."[16] After the Great Rebellion of Túpac Amaru II (1780–1782), Spanish officials also tried to eradicate vestiges of native dance and dress. What had once been a sign of subordination was now a threat. Neither ban had much success.[17]

Popular exuberance also worked against a simple endorsement of official hierarchy. Sometime in the 1680s, students tied an animal tail to the cape of the *corregidor* so that it wagged behind him as he carried the processional Corpus Christi standard. The bishop, who was at odds with the *corregidor*, protected the students.[18] David Cahill remarks, "The Corpus celebration in Cusco integrated and reinforced social gradations in the structure of its processional arrangements even while a carnivalesque element eroded, however ephemerally, the obeisance and obsequiousness that necessarily accompanied such barriers."[19]

The written record does not survive alone. A series of sixteen anonymous paintings (ca. 1674–1680), which once hung in the parish church of Santa Ana at the northern entrance to Cusco, bear visual testimony to the tensions, aspirations, and cultural confusion of Cusco's Corpus Christi procession.[20] Led by parish leaders dressed as Inca kings and followed by clergy in ornate vestments, carved images of saints and virgins pass tiered altars and balconies draped with colorful tapestries. Ranks of monks walk on finely woven carpets beneath triumphal arches. The well-to-do watch from balconies, while less privileged spectators with Indian, European, African, Jewish, and mestizo features line the streets. "Some are restrained and attentive; others gossip, smoke, eat, and indulge in horseplay."[21] Yet others sell their wares: a black woman hawks pancakes from a basket, and a boy with a peashooter fires at "a man selling wooden horses [caballitos de palo]."[22]

Although the iconography of the saints and altars is largely European, some bear signs of their Peruvian setting. On an altar representing the Last Supper, the meal set before Christ and the disciples appears to be—as it is in Marcos Zapata's painting of the Last Supper that still hangs in the cathedral—the Andean specialty of roast guinea pig. Among the several smaller saints carried through the streets is an image of Rose of Lima, canonized in 1671. The warrior angels on the altars, like so many of their kin in Andean canvases of the period, wear elaborate feather headdresses. And in the tree to which the martyred Saint Sebastian is tied perch half a dozen exotic birds. Sebastian's parrots—like the Chunchos—still appear, opening in their incongruity their own small window onto the hidden transcript of the festival.

In one respect, the paintings overreach themselves. Five portray the saints on elaborate wheeled carros (floats), similar to those then in use in some peninsular Corpus Christi processions. But the depicted carros reflect imagined grandeur rather than Cusqueño practice. Then, as now, Cusco's saints were shouldered on andas (litters) by male parishioners.[23] In other respects, the paintings hint at internal tensions. In one, honoring the corregidor of the period, a boy with a peashooter fires beyond the margins of the painting at the unseen bishop who follows.[24] Inca solar pectorals worn by parish leaders in some paintings enjoy an ambivalent relationship with the sun-shaped monstrance carried by the bishop in others.[25] Which reflects the glory of the other? And in the last (and largest) canvas of the series, Inca costumes disappear altogether, replaced by the resplendent robed and feathered uniforms of a Cañari military corps, whose members dominate the painting. Many Cañari lived in Santa Ana parish; one of their leaders is thought to have commissioned this painting.[26]

The festival continued to reflect social tensions and their suppression. In 1788, after the rebellion of Túpac Amaru II, Ignacio de Castro affirmed the restoration of colonial order in his account of Cusco's extravagantly prosperous and aggressively harmonious Corpus Christi. "In the streets and squares the most sumptuous altars of extraordinary elevation and harmonious structure" were erected, "embellished with rich displays of precious metals, valuable jewels, and rare furnishings." Triumphal arches "of equal cost" straddled beautifully carpeted streets. "All the parishes" processed "with the images of their patron saints on *andas*, some made of embossed silver, others finely carved and gilded, [and all] adorned with artificial flowers of gold, silver, and silk." "Magnificent" dances, "admitted by ancient custom into this triumphal pomp," followed the impressive *carroza*. The dancers' "liveries," stripped of their former feathers, were made "entirely of embossed silver trimmed with variously colored jewels" and were "renewed each year." Not everything was to Castro's taste, however. He complained bitterly that "so holy a day" should be preceded by "a night of excessive license."[27]

Cusco's colonial Corpus Christi celebrations were a vibrant mix of Spanish Catholic triumphalism, popular devotion, hierarchical display, subordinate dissent, solemn ritual, carnivalesque exuberance, Inca reenactment, ethnic caricature, parish rivalry, civic pride, mercantile opportunity, and heterogeneous crowds. "Nowhere in Latin America did Corpus Christi achieve as much renown as in Cusco."[28] Although the relative proportions have shifted over time, the basic ingredients remain the same.

The mass and the solemn procession of the *carroza* do not now come first, either in temporal sequence or in popular acclaim. The religious festivities begin a day earlier with the more lively *entrada* (entry) of the saints. I spent the first part of Wednesday morning in the parish church of San Pedro, where two groups of men were carefully dressing the images of Saint Peter and the Virgin of the Purification (or Candlemas). The sixteenth-century processional statue of Peter, made (all but the head and hands) of lightweight wood paste,[29] had been tied securely to his litter by ropes looped around his waist and over his white cassock. He awaited his papal robes. The more elaborate Virgen Purificada, carved in polychrome cedar, was already robed in finely wrought purple. She stood on a three-tiered embossed silver litter. Behind her, the archangel Gabriel thrust his spear into the mouth of a blue dragon's head, whose wooden nostrils bled red paint. A doll-sized *angelito* in petticoats and purple velvet dress hung further back, attached by a long wire that in procession allowed him to bob up and down. An older man studiously polished Gabriel's silver helmet.

From San Pedro, I made my way to the Plaza de San Francisco, where a fruit and vegetable market was in full swing. In the square itself and in the street outside the nearby Church of Santa Clara, the first of the fully dressed saints assembled. The Virgen de los Remedios (Virgin of the Remedies), at a mere three feet high the smallest of the images, was the first to arrive (Fig. 8.1). Elevated on an ornate silver litter and shaded by a circular

8.1   Virgin of the Remedies. Cusco, 2001.

pink canopy (held loosely by a single wooden hand so that it wiggled as she walked), she, too, shared her stage with an archangel, a dragon, and an undulating *angelito*. Like all the images, the Virgin and her company were ornamented, dressed, and carried so as to maximize the impression of lifelike movement. Loose-fitting clothes, Gabriel's long wig, the bouncing parasol and *angelito*, and the rolling walk of the bearers all conspired to enliven the sculpture. Processional sculptures are created to be viewed in motion.[30]

San Jerónimo (Jerome), nearly seven feet tall, dignified and dazzling in his flowing red cardinal's cape and broad-brimmed hat (see Fig. 8.5, below), swept next into the square, surrounded by multiple standard-bearers, crowds of parishioners, a brass band, a line of men blowing conch trumpets, and two dance troupes.[31] Those dancing the *contradanza*—an elegant parody of a European square dance—wore multicolored beaded jackets and pale wire-mesh masks with blue eyes and black mustaches.[32] In the iconography of Andean dances, pale skin, blue eyes, and mustaches are a sign of mixed blood. The Q'apaq Qolla dancers wore stylized *monteras* (flat fringed hats), from which ribbons, beads, and silver coins dangled. Their knitted white wool masks (*waq'ollos*), resembling ski masks with holes for the eyes and mouth, sported black mustaches, red lips, and eyes outlined in blue. The Qollas impersonated llama drivers and other rural merchants of mixed Spanish and Aymara heritage from the high altiplano to the southeast of Cusco, a region known to the Incas as Qollasuyu. The adjective *q'apaq* (wealthy or elegant) acknowledged the profit they derive from trade within the Spanish monetary system.[33] Saint Jerome and his entourage had traveled fifteen kilometers on foot that morning from his parish church.

Saint Sebastian arrived a few minutes later, having traveled just seven kilometers. Cusqueños speak of a race between Jerome and Sebastian to the center of Cusco, but the legendary rivalry seems to be grounded not in present practice but in the pre-Hispanic identities of the two parishes. San Jerónimo was settled by Orco Indians and San Sebastián by Ayamarca Indians, both expelled from the site of Cusco by the twelfth-century arrival of the Incas. Family and street names in the two villages still bear witness to the original tribal identities.[34]

I watched sixty *cargadores* (porters) strain under Sebastian's weight. Draped in a rich gold and purple cloth, with the solid gold and silver arrows of his martyrdom piercing his arms and chest, the seventeenth-century processional statue was tied to a tree whose spreading foliage crowned his head (Fig. 8.2). At each of the four corners of his golden litter sat a carved bust of a bare-breasted woman with a painted feather headdress (Fig. 8.3). The women seemed an odd accoutrement for a Christian martyr, but they are markers, like the parrots and the Chunchos, of an alternate narrative of conquest enacted by the parishioners of San Sebastián. Sebastian was preceded by a dance troupe called Q'apaq Chuncho (wealthy Chunchos). Two lines of Chunchos in tall feather headdresses (see Fig. 8.7 below) were led by a pair of "Catholic kings" in silver crowns. On each crown was a small cross.[35] Warriors brandished wooden spears (*chontas*) and kings clutched swords, but all wore the now-familiar pink wire-mesh masks with blue eyes and mustaches. *Mestizaje* (mixed ancestry) was clearly a common theme of the Corpus Christi dances.

Chunchos bear many meanings in the iconography of Andean dance. Most simply, they represent the "uncivilized" Indians of the rain forest. Rural highland Quechua, however, claim the Chunchos as their ancestors, linking them to the legendary Ñaupa Machu (ancient old ones) who peopled the Andes in the time of moonlight before the sun came. Those who were not turned into stone by the sun escaped his petrifying rays in the darkness of the jungle.[36] Another strand of oral Andean tradition maintains that the last Inca escaped unharmed into the rain forests, whence Inkarrí (King Inca) will

8.2   Saint Sebastian. Cusco, 2001.

return to establish the utopian rule of those who speak only Quechua. Some believe that the dance of the Chunchos enacts this hope.[37]

In some fiestas, Chunchos defeat Qollas in ritual battle. Robert Randall sees the annual victory of the unmasked and therefore pure-blooded Q'ara Chunchos (poor Chunchos) at the high mountain festival of the Christ of Qoyllur Rit'i as a symbolic victory of the Indian way of traditional religion and agriculture over the Spanish or mestizo way of trade and finance.[38] Gisela Cánepa Koch takes the victory of the masked and therefore blue-eyed Q'apaq Chunchos in Paucartambo's festival of Our Lady of Carmel as a claim of legitimacy by the town's Quechua mestizos. By adopting the dominant Spanish language and accepting the prosperity that comes with trade, they have not abandoned but taken on the civilizing role of Inkarrí.[39] The Q'apaq Chuncho of San Sebastián, danced by Indians but led by "Catholic kings," would appear to insist on the possibility of combining an indigenous identity, a Catholic faith, and an economic goal.

The Q'apaq Chuncho dancers were accompanied by several *ukukus* (bears), armed with whips and dressed in white ski masks and loose black woolen "furs." "Half-bear and half-man," they represented "the blurring of

8.3   Saint Sebastian: detail of native women. Cusco, 2001.

the boundaries between the animal and the human worlds."[40] The *ukukus* served as both clowns and marshals, mocking solemnities, cracking "obscene jokes in a falsetto voice,"[41] and generally disrupting the Chunchos' dance even as they ensured its overall progress. Straddling the boundaries of animal and human, wild and orderly, they brought with them the healing powers of the high *apus* (sacred places): several *ukukus* carried large roped blocks of therapeutic ice, retrieved in pilgrimage the previous week from the glacial regions of the Christ of Qoyllur Rit'i.[42] According to Catherine Allen, the bear's "paradoxical combination of awkwardness and power," which typically leads to his defeat in Quechua storytelling, expresses the experience of "a rural class of conquered people in a highly stratified colonial society."[43] Harvesting the sacred power of the *apus* and awaiting the redemption of Inkarrí, the rural Quechua yet feels out of place in the dominant mestizo world. The bear represents his fear of defeat, the Chunchos his hope of victory.

Following Sebastian and his dancers, the giant Saint Christopher lurched into the square, bearing the Christ Child on his shoulder and using a palm tree as a staff. The tallest and heaviest of all the saints, Cristóbal is hard to control and frequently threatens to veer off onto the sidewalk, scattering on-lookers. To add to the prestige of his bearers, a boulder is concealed beneath the ruffled lace "river" at his feet. Saints Ann and Barbara arrived together. Several virgins followed.

As the assembled saints and virgins awaited the formal start of the *en-trada*, San Sebastián's *ukukus* cleared a space and began to play between two watching lines of Chunchos. Pairs of *ukukus* took turns engaging in whipping battles. Afterwards, they ran at one another, first knocking each other to the ground and then leaping headfirst onto what became a cross-stacked pile of bodies. Finally, they stood in two facing lines and began a brief parody of the Chunchos' dance, trying vainly to clash their whips as if they were swords or spears, muddling complex dance routines, and veering off into the audience in their dizziness. Drum and trumpet played a ragged tune.

The *entrada* began at about 1:30 P.M. From the arch of Santa Clara at the southwest corner of the square, the fifteen saints and their entourages pro-cessed directly down the arcaded Calle Mantas, along one side of the Plaza de Armas, and up the steps into the Church of El Triunfo beside the cathedral, a distance of about four hundred yards that took the entire procession two hours to cover. Brass bands played loudly, firecrackers exploded in clouds of smoke, and parish officials bore colorful standards, while the swaying mo-tion of the bearers animated the saints and all their waving flowers, wigs, robes, tassels, flags, and *angelitos.*

The saints traveled in their traditional order. San Antonio Abad, San Jeró-nimo, San Cristóbal, and San Sebastián led the way. As Sebastian passed us, a neighbor in the crowd drew my attention to a live, green parrot perched in the foliage of the martyr's tree.[44] Carved (and lovingly painted) bare-breasted women, live parrots, and wild, dancing Chunchos are not part of the tra-ditional European iconography of Saint Sebastian. A cheaply printed "his-tory of the saints," sold everywhere in Cusco during Corpus Christi, told the official story of Sebastian as a captain in the Roman army who was mar-tyred under the Emperor Diocletian, ca. 288, by a firing squad of archers. But the booklet also admitted to "another version," according to which Sebas-tian was "filled with arrows by the heretical Indians of the forest." In at least one Quechua dictionary, *hereje* (heretic) is given as a Spanish synonym for *ch'unchu* (Chuncho).[45]

Santa Barbara and Santa Ana followed. The warrior Santiago, with a life-sized Moor spreadeagled beneath his horse's raised front hoofs, was led by

8.4   Q'apaq Negro dancers. Cusco, 2001.

a corps of uniformed soldiers. San Blas (Blaise), a bishop, gathered sculpted choirboys at his feet. Saint Peter, now fully dressed, was followed by Saint Joseph, who looked down lovingly at Jesus. Standing amid a selection of simple, store-bought toys, young Jesus held Joseph's fatherly hand and gazed back confidently.

Five virgins brought up the rear. The seventeenth-century Virgen de la Natividad (Virgin of the Nativity), whose face is dark enough to prompt speculation as to whether she is of mixed blood or merely a *chola* (Hispani-cized Indian),[46] was accompanied by a line of conch trumpeters, in chorus sounding like the monotone wail of a tugboat siren. Trumpeters and bearers were dressed in woven, multicolored Andean waistcoats and *ch'ullus* (coni-cal woolen hats with earflaps). So, atypically, was the *angelito* jouncing be-hind her.

Ahead of the Virgin danced a Q'apaq Negro troupe (Fig. 8.4). The dancers wore masks with exaggerated African features: thick red lips, broad white grin, bulbous nose, and black skin. Their hands were covered with black gloves. Each dancer carried in his right hand a black wooden fist on a red stick, while his left hand was tied by a loose silver chain to his waist. Bro-caded hats and breastplates over white shirts and skirts of dangling colored bandannas completed the costume. Q'apaq Negro dancers recall the black slaves who worked in the colonial silver mines of Paucartambo. Leading the troupe was a *caporal* (overseer), who kept time with a *matraca* (wooden rattle). Five musicians, with an accordion, a violin, a pair of *quenas* (Andean flutes), and a drum, played a plaintive dance tune.[47]

The slaves' black masks had blue eyes. The mask of the *caporal*, who wore a blue, beaded cap with a tiny silver cross sewn into its brow, also had black skin, but his features were European. Not only were his eyes blue, but he had a narrow nose, thin lips, and golden eyebrows, mustache, and trim goatee (see Fig. 8.8 below). The designation *q'apaq*, or wealthy, was ironic: the only black to profit from the mining was the overseer. Moreover, the masks erased the racial boundaries by which such privilege was justified: the Spanish overseer had black skin, while the African slaves had blue eyes. Blue-eyed blacks joined Chunchos, parrots, and bare-breasted women as markers of a hidden transcript.

After the Virgin of the Nativity came the Virgen de los Remedios, pretty in pink; the purified Virgin of Candlemas, a golden candlestick in hand; the Virgen de Belén, the oldest image in the procession, dating from around 1560; and the Virgin of the Immaculate Conception, known because of her beauty as La Linda (the Pretty One).

Their normal Corpus Christi lodging in the cathedral under repair, all but one of the saints and virgins ended their day in the adjacent Iglesia del Triunfo. The Virgin of the Remedies went home to the Church of Santa Catalina, less than fifty yards away. While the last of the virgins were passing through the square, the Qollas of San Jerónimo formed two facing lines in front of the cathedral. Several ran the gauntlet of the others' whips. The crowd applauded. A cross-dressed man, known as the Imilla (young woman), danced in a red wool skirt, a white lace blouse, and a black silk mask that concealed its wearer's features but had none of its own. In the ritual battles at Paucartambo and Qoyllur Rit'i, the victorious Chunchos capture the Imilla, signifying the hope that they rather than the Qolla traders will reproduce.[48] No such battle took place in Cusco. Instead the Qollas, behaving like *ukukus*, launched themselves into a cross-stacked pile of bodies. The Imilla stood briefly on top. As the Qollas peeled off, the dancer at the bottom of the pile played dead. His "corpse," placed on a wooden toy cart, was wheeled away, a parody perhaps of the procession of the martyred saints on their litters. Cusqueños appreciate the "carnivalesque dimension" of the Qollas.[49]

The saints and virgins came out again the next morning for the Corpus Christi mass. After the sedate progress of the *carroza*, they left their posts behind the outdoor altar and enjoyed a more boisterous circuit of the plaza (Fig. 8.5).[50] I noticed two new versions of the *contradanza*. One, ac-

8.5   Saint Jerome completes his circuit of the Plaza de Armas while the Virgins wait their turn. Cusco, 2001.

companying San Antonio Abad, included both men and women and was known as Qoyacha (little queen). The men wore the standard pale-faced wire-mesh masks; the women wore broad-brimmed hats hung with ankle-length colored ribbons.[51] San Jerónimo's all-male *contradanza* group had added two *machukuna* (old men or ancestors), an adult who directed the troupe and a younger apprentice. Each *machu's* painted papier-mâché mask was distinguished by pink coloring, blue eyes, a dangling blond horsehair mustache, and an enormous phallic nose. The nose reflected the generative role of the ancestors, mocked the pretensions to good breeding of the upper-class mestizo engaged in a fashionable European dance, and linked the overbearing mestizo to those ancestors who, acting malevolently toward the living, are known as *machukuna*.[52]

By late afternoon, the last of the saints and virgins had returned to their lodging in the Triunfo. Stories abound in Cusco of their overnight escapades behind closed doors.[53] I left them to it, wandering off to the food stalls in the Calle Saphi to eat *chiri-uchu* (cold spicy), a traditional Corpus Christi dish of stewed chicken, spiced pork sausage, alpaca jerky, fresh cheese, fish roe, seaweed, sweet fried bread, toasted maize, hot peppers, and roast *cuy* (guinea pig).

The archbishop, clergy, and *carroza* did not appear again. Their role, so central in the official record of the colonial Corpus Christi, is now confined to Thursday morning. The saints and virgins were only partially eclipsed. Remaining indoors until the octave of Corpus Christi a week later, they received daily crowds of visitors. Despite their colonial origins and European narratives, the saints have secured their popularity by taking on unique local identities and preferring (like their devotees) street parties, flirtation, and overnight gossip to clerical propriety.

The saints' dancers also retired from view for the week, to be replaced by troupes from schools, clubs, and senior centers for the civic celebrations leading up to Inti Raymi. Some performed the saints' masked dances, dramatizing mixed heritage (from Spaniard to bear), but most preferred dances that claimed an exclusively indigenous origin. The most popular were *qhaswas* or *carnavales*, peasant Carnival dances that involved "celebration of community, fertility, and happiness among the rural population."[54] The young dancers carried scythes or hoes and wore large ornamental disks of harvested crops on their backs. Couples flirted with each other's partners. Other dances celebrated weaving, herding, or hunting; invoked native warriors; or imitated Inca dress and ritual.

Mestizo imitation of native agricultural dances in Cusco is as old as the plough song composed by one of the first cathedral choirmasters. Since the 1920s, such dances have been promoted by urban middle-class Cusqueños who envision a continuity between a romanticized native rural present, to whose harsh realities they are immune, and a mythologized Inca past, to which they wish to lay claim.[55] Unlike the *danzas de los aztecas* at the basilica de Guadalupe, they are the fruit of careful research into living indigenous traditions, paying a genuine, albeit somewhat self-indulgent, homage to their sources. At their best, in the raucous streets of Corpus Christi week, cheered by crowds of partisan supporters, they show a remarkable energy and power.

On Friday morning, by special invitation of a young performer, I saw "indigenous" dances in a two-hour schoolyard show by kindergartners. On Monday, I spent four hours in the Plaza de Armas watching an energetic primary school parade. Some of the older students, including a group of Inca stilt-dancers, were remarkably skilled. The dance parade was followed by a bevy of allegorical floats with Inca themes. The highlight was a motorized float bearing a mummified Inca ruler, followed by a long line of *mallquis*

8.6   Bundled mummy. Cusco, 2001.

on shouldered litters (Fig. 8.6). No doubt the bundled mummies were fake, but the skulls that peeked from within the woven blanket shrouds were real. Some scholars believe that the willingness of native parishioners to carry Catholic saints in procession was due to their familiarity with the portage of mummified rulers.[56] Rumor circulates in Cusco that secretly preserved Inca mummies were once concealed within the hollow Corpus Christi saints.

On Tuesday, another four-hour parade showed secondary schools and colleges in dazzling choreographic variety. Exuberant harvest dances sublimated sexual energy. Aymara hunters wore the carcasses of wild ducks on their backs. The extended yellow sleeves of the *qhaswa kio* dancers turned arms into banners. Generic *danzaq* (dancers), in pale-faced, wire-mesh masks and rainbow-colored leggings, wove ribbons round a portable maypole. Young men in gray woolen masks played old men with walking sticks. In the *danza Mishaguas,* named after a jungle river north of Cusco, two boys in shorts, black paint, and monkey tails loped away from native hunters in grass skirts. Teachers fed the monkey-boys bananas. Meanwhile, massed schoolgirls in uniform ran from one side of the square to another, cheering, waving banners, and hurling clouds of confetti as their dancing classmates passed. After the colleges came the senior centers, fewer in number and inclined to the more sedate *contradanzas*.

Late Wednesday afternoon, yet another parade filled the Plaza de Armas, featuring more than one hundred sixty dance troupes from a single institution that enrolls students from primary to graduate school: the Colegio Inca Garcilaso de la Vega. I had seen most of the dances before, but a few were new: a dance of ironmongers in blackface, a *danza saqra* (devil dance) with demonic animal masks,[57] and a troupe of dancing condors with beaked masks and wings. After nightfall, carnivalesque elements multiplied. Two *ukukus* danced along the street with a blond American girl they'd plucked from the crowd. Releasing her, they kissed her on the cheek and acted lovestruck. Some of the Imillas flaunted their cross-dressed character, exaggerating both the masculinity of the dancer and the femininity of the role. One group of students carried a parody of Saint Sebastian: a litter bearing a cardboard tree and a young man in shorts. As the litter lurched along the street, the "saint" repeatedly fell off.

Just as colonial Corpus Christi in Cusco can be said to have dramatized the triumph of Spanish Catholicism over indigenous paganism, so the city's modern Inti Raymi might be said to dramatize the reverse. The week of civic parades danced homage to a romanticized Inca past and indigenous present, slipping occasionally into satire of the saints confined indoors. At the end of the week, the restaging of Inti Raymi in the Inca ruins of Qorikancha and Saqsayhuaman would cap this triumph. But nothing is quite that simple in a large-scale urban festival. The saints received daily visitors, and nuns in woven ponchos were visible reminders that many of the schools were run by Catholic orders. Moreover, while the embodied rhetoric of the parades subordinated the hierarchical vision of colonial Spanish Catholicism to a more egalitarian vision of Cusco grounded in a shared Inca heritage, all was not in fact shared equally. Rural Indians did not participate in their own representation. Those who were present sold crafts on the sidewalk or posed (for a small fee) for tourists' photographs. It was the middle-class mestizos who ran the civic show. The suburban Indians of San Sebastián and San Jerónimo, whose ancestors had been expelled by the real Incas, had discreetly reminded us of this appropriation in their dances of mestizo Chunchos, Qollas, blacks, and big-nosed country-dance directors. That some of the mestizo students imitated these parodies of mestizos imitating non-Cusqueños only compounded the complexity of the fiesta's multiple layers of contestation.

The saints reappeared late on Thursday afternoon, the octave of Corpus Christi, accompanied by their brass bands but not by their dancers. Some of the lighter saints and virgins, the latter with their petticoats and parasols, seemed almost to be dancing themselves, so rhythmic was the rolling gait of their *cargadores*. As Saint Sebastian passed, I could see he now had two live parrots in his branches. When I asked about his birds and bare-breasted women, my friend Ana told me a more elaborate version of the martyr's local story. Sebastian, she said, was a Spanish soldier, seduced by Indian women and filled with arrows by their men. The portage of Saint Sebastian through Cusco, I realized, invited two responses. The pious, attending to the public transcript, could contemplate the sufferings of a Christian martyr, while others, attending to the embodied hidden transcript, could rejoice in the irony of a "civilized" conquistador too weak to resist the lures of "uncivilized" women or the primitive weapons of their men.

As night fell, most of the saints again climbed the steps to the Church of El Triunfo, but Saints Barbara and Ana scurried off towards the latter's parish church and the Virgin of the Remedies slipped down the street to her home in the Church of Santa Catalina. Jerome prepared to pass the night in the Church of Santo Domingo, whose clergy had for many years exercised jurisdiction over the parish of San Jerónimo.[58] Before he left, the other saints and virgins bade him good-bye. Each in turn faced Jerome, took several steps forward, and bowed, an effect created by the genuflection of the front rows of *cargadores*. This gesture was repeated three times and then Jerome followed suit. The brass bands played.

On Friday morning, the departure of the saints resumed. Their dispersal made it impossible for a single spectator to follow all the action. Attracted by the number of his dance troupes, I spent the day with Saint Sebastian. An escort of Chunchos marched on either side of the saint as he left the church, running ahead soon afterwards to lead his homeward progress (Fig. 8.7). The Chunchos performed a lively square dance: the two crowned kings and each of six pairs of feathered warriors came to the middle, clashed weapons, and skipped back between the advancing rows of dancers to rejoin them at the rear, eventually returning to their original formation. Behind them, four pairs of *ukukus* did the same, clashing whips rather than swords or lances. Despite their conflicting headgear, the Catholic kings and "infidel" Chunchos never confronted one another. They were not at war.

Behind the Chunchos came the Qoyacha. The dozen young women in velvet dresses and ribboned hats seemed out of place amid the predominantly male masked dances. Perhaps, like the captured Imilla of the ritual battles, they represented the reproductive future of the village. Perhaps they simply wanted a chance to dance with the men ahead of the saint.

8.7   Q'apaq Chuncho dancers. Cusco, 2001.

Then came a Q'apaq Negro troupe, dancing in two lines of six with the *caporal*, blond mustache and goatee painted on his black mask, leading the way (Fig. 8.8). A *maqt'a* (boy), a smaller figure with the character of a *cholo* servant or buffoon, danced out of formation, wearing a devil mask. The *maqt'a* of the Q'apaq Qolla troupe, which followed, wore the role's traditional mask. With its exaggerated hooked nose and prominent cheekbones, it caricatured typical Indian features, but it still had blue eyes.[59] Each of the sixteen Qollas wore behind his waist a stuffed baby llama and twisted in his raised fingers a strand of llama wool. Dancing at the rear of the group was the cross-dressed Imilla.

Finally, immediately before the standard-bearers and the saint, came a troupe of Majeños. Their name derives from the prosperous muleteers of Majes (Arequipa), who used to import alcoholic drinks to the Cusco region.[60] Sporting the same grinning, big-nosed, blue-eyed masks as the *machu-kuna* of the *contradanza*, the Majeños wore broad-brimmed straw sombreros and carried beer bottles from which they pretended to drink. With every other step, choreographed as a drunken stagger, they opened their dark leather jackets to display well-fed paunches. Two *patrones* (bosses) and their

8.8   Q'apaq Negro overseer. Cusco, 2001.

damas (women), the latter played by women in blue-eyed masks and white *chola* stovepipe hats, danced between the two rows of eight muleteers. The Majeños represented prosperous but drunken mestizo traders. The role of their subordinate but often subversively mischievous pair of *maqt'as* was to share obscene jokes with the crowd and to make fun of the bosses.[61]

At midday, we stopped by the roadside for a meal. I had spent much of the morning watching the Q'apaq Negro dancers; now their *caporal* invited me to join them for lunch. Women served us chicken, maize, and boiled potatoes, which we washed down with home-brewed *chicha* (maize beer), *trago* (cane alcohol), and bottled beer. The dancers' masks, beaded hats, and wooden fists lay in a semicircle on the ground. I asked one of the men about the mask's blue eyes. He told me many of the blacks in Cusco used to have blue eyes because of their mixed blood. After lunch, the band played lively dance tunes. The grassy roadside brooked no generational division: young men danced happily with grandmothers.

In the late afternoon, our leisurely progress reached the parish of San Sebastián, where the saint, given a place of honor in the village schoolyard, was engulfed in offerings of flowers and food. Schoolchildren showered him with yellow petals. In a vast adjacent open field, the army of dancers and friends settled down in the warmth of the late afternoon sun on the straw-colored grass. Andean hillsides formed a stunning backdrop to the bucolic scene. I drank another beer with the Q'apaq Negro troupe and watched them dance. A few yards away, the Chunchos and *ukukus*, too, went through their routine. Some older women warned me it was all over bar the heavy drinking. The saint would enter the parish church, but after dark the dance troupes and their followers would retire to their respective *locales* (club rooms) to get drunk. I said my good-byes and caught a bus back to the center of Cusco.

Superficially, the meaning of the day was clear. The procession and its dancers honored the patron saint. Since the day was ruled by folk theology rather than by clerical restraint, the celebrations included communal eating, drinking, and dancing. But there was more to it than that. All the masked dances represented ethnic groups to which the dancers themselves did not belong: Chunchos, blacks, Aymara traders, and pale-skinned muleteers from Majes. Arguably the only ethnic self-portraits were the self-deprecating but subversive *maqt'as* and, if Allen is right, the clumsy but powerful *ukukus*. The blue eyes added mestizos and Spaniards to the ethnic cast. Thus was dramatized the minority sense of drowning in others.

Dominant pretensions to superiority were mocked. Claims of racial purity were belied by the omnipresent blue eyes. The arrogance of prosperous mestizos was undercut by the black skin of the blond *caporal* and the drunken boasting of the paunched Majeños. The blue-eyed masks of otherness also revealed a silent scorn of the middle-class Cusqueño claim to a romanticized indigenous heritage. In the character of the *maqt'a* and the *ukuku*, the natives of San Sebastián offered a less romantic portrait of what it is like to be Indian in an economy dominated by mestizos.

As an alternative to present inequalities, they offered a utopian vision of their own in their processional enactment of the local story of the saint. The copious foliage, the parrots, and the bare-breasted women in feathered crowns placed Sebastian in the Peruvian jungle rather than the Roman Empire, a setting reinforced by his escort of dancing Chunchos. In this context, the dying soldier pierced by arrows became an ignominiously defeated Spanish soldier rather than a heroic Christian martyr. The victorious Chunchos, who in triumph led him bound and captive through the streets of Cusco, were not savages but symbols of resistance to external domination. Since the dancers were Catholics, the Chunchos were led by Christian kings. Their resistance was directed not at Catholicism itself but at the external dominance so often entangled with it.

The other dancers found a place in this narrative of Saint Sebastian through their references to outside exploitation. The chains of the Q'apaq Negro dancers recalled the cruelty of Spanish greed, while the pot-bellied Majeños represented external commercial exploitation. The Qollas, habitually defeated by Chunchos in ritual battle, represented the eventual downfall of all who take advantage of those for whom the Chunchos stand. The descendants of the first Ayamarca settlers of San Sebastián had outlasted both the Incas and the Spaniards who had once displaced them. Majeño muleteers and Aymara llama drivers, too, had now become redundant. Why shouldn't all external exploitation go the way of Sebastian the feeble Spanish soldier? The parishioners of San Sebastián would not always need to represent themselves as *maqt'as*. Articulated in procession, not in words, this utopian vision countered both the traditional European triumphalism of Corpus Christi and the justifiable anxieties of an indigenous minority in a world dominated by others.

Several of the departed saints would have their own local Corpus celebrations in the weeks ahead,[62] but Cusco's shared Corpus Christi was now all but over. In its waning, Inti Raymi ruled. The next day (Saturday) saw the longest civic parade of all. Beginning at 10:00 A.M. and ending long past midnight, countless representatives of government departments, businesses, civic clubs, and surrounding villages filed through the Plaza de Armas.

Interspersed with reiterations of almost every dance I had already seen, both "mestizo" and "indigenous," were squadrons of office workers in ponchos, street sweepers in bright orange uniforms, middle-class "Incas" waving colored banners, and, most eye-catching of all, a group of bare-breasted young "Indian" women with feathers on their heads and live pythons round their necks. The order of parade was fiercely egalitarian. Decided in advance by lot, it aspired to no coherent narrative. Around midmorning, the last of the statues to leave the Triunfo—San Pedro and the Virgin of Candlemas— fought their way upstream through the oncoming parade before embarking on their homeward promenade.

Sunday, 24 June, was the day of Inti Raymi. Because the movable feast of Corpus Christi can fall anytime between 20 May and 23 June, the date of the modern Inti Raymi has been fixed not on the actual solstice (21 June) but on the first date that always follows Corpus Christi. First staged in 1944, the modern Inti Raymi is not a reconstruction but an "evocation"[63] of the Inca festival, consciously designed by its prosperous Cusqueño backers to evoke a noble indigenous past and to stimulate tourism. It has succeeded in both regards. Acknowledging its spectacular scale, its commercial goals, and its delusions of authentic grandeur, I think of it as "Cecil B. DeMille does the Incas."

The first act took place at about 9:00 A.M. in Qorikancha, the ancient Inca ceremonial center that has reemerged, after several earthquakes, from beneath the colonial Convent of Santo Domingo. Hundreds of young men and women in matching Inca costumes jogged in single file from the top of the stone Inca walls to the grassy space beneath. From his vantage point atop the walls, an actor representing the Inca ruler addressed them in ponderous Quechua. The crowd, dense with foreign tourists, applauded. A parade through the cobbled streets to the Plaza de Armas followed. Soldiers with painted cardboard shields and weapons, princesses with offerings of corn and potatoes, and amateur musicians playing flutes and drums preceded the Inca, who was carried (like the Corpus Christi saints) on a litter. The actors had been chosen for their "authentic" Indian features. The costumes were of the kind that parents prepare for a school play.

I caught a taxi to the ruins of Saqsayhuaman, the defensive fortress overlooking Cusco, where the parade would eventually arrive on foot. Seats on the bleachers were available for a substantial fee, but I preferred to sit with the packed nonpaying crowds on the overlooking rocks, where I found a cramped space amid the many who had arrived much earlier. Over several rows of heads, I could see the hills opposite but only the far side of the playing area below. Waiting, we made friends with one another, shared food, and suffered pins and needles.

Around 2:00 P.M., the vanguard of the spectacle appeared. Hundreds of extras waved uniformly colored banners on the hills opposite. Then the Inca arrived, dismounted his litter, and, surrounded by his priests and counselors, ascended a wooden platform—painted to look like a stone temple—in the center of the playing area. The action, punctuated by episodes of mass choreography on the grass surrounding the platform, slowly unfolded in inaudible Quechua. A llama was sacrificed. A priest held up the palpitating heart. After a couple of hours, spectators with numbed limbs began to drift away. No doubt it was good for the economy and for the romanticized self-image of middle-class Cusco, but I found it tedious. My sympathies lay with the masked dancers of San Sebastián, who, with their blue-eyed Chuncho masks, had satirized the Cusqueño longing to be both upper class and Indian.

PART THREE
Carnivals

9.
A Scattering of Ants
(GALICIA)

ON 12 MARCH 1445 the Faculty of Theology at the University of Paris issued a letter to the bishops and chapters of France, deploring clerical behavior during seasonal festivities: "Priests and clerks may be seen wearing masks and monstrous visages at the hours of office. They dance in the choir dressed as women, panders, or minstrels. They sing wanton songs. They eat black puddings at the horn of the altar while the celebrant is saying mass. They play at dice there. They cense with stinking smoke from the soles of old shoes. They run and leap through the church, without a blush at their own shame. Finally they drive about the town and its theaters in shabby traps and carts; and rouse the laughter of their fellows and the bystanders in infamous performances, with indecent gestures and verses scurrilous and unchaste."[1]

The season of these shenanigans was not Carnival but Christmas. Long before Carnival first began to be reported with any frequency in fourteenth-century Europe, the twelve days of Christmas (26 December to 6 January) had been the season when "the world was turned upside down."[2] Yet the popular view of Carnival, endorsed by those who promote the feast no less than by those who would suppress it, declares it heir to pre-Christian seasonal rites, a "last pagan fling before . . . the penitential rigors" of Lent.[3] One version of this theory, first advanced positively by Renaissance humanists and negatively by church reformers, links Carnival to the urban Greek and Roman rites of Bacchanalia and Saturnalia. Another, first proposed by nineteenth-century Romantic folklorists, supposes Carnival to derive from ancient rural fertility rites of spring. Neither is now given much scholarly credence. The modern Carnival, a careful historian of the feast insists, has "no documentable connection with ancient festivities."[4]

The theory of Carnival's pagan opposition to Christian Lent survives because it serves a wide range of contemporary needs. Those who forbid Carnival's mockery of the powerful, who claim the prestige of great antiquity for its local manifestation, who oppose it to a politicized Christian triumphal-ism, or who treat it as a liminal opportunity to shed customary inhibitions all employ the narrative of pagan origins. A good case can be made, however, for the argument that Carnival developed within the Christian community from the topsy-turvydom of Christmas.

Throughout medieval and early modern Europe, Christmas was a time for festive reversals of status. As early as the ninth century, a mock patriarch was elected in Constantinople, burlesquing the Eucharist and riding through the city streets on an ass.[5] And as late as Innocents' Day (28 December) 1685, in the Franciscan church of Antibes, lay brothers and servants "put on the vestments inside out, held the books upside down, . . . wore spectacles with rounds of orange peel instead of glasses, . . . blew the ashes from the censers on each other's face and hands, and instead of the proper liturgy chanted confused and inarticulate gibberish."[6]

Cross-dressing, masking as animals, wafting foul-smelling incense, and electing burlesque bishops, popes, and patriarchs mocked conventional hu-man pretensions. So did the introduction of an ass into the church, in com-memoration of the holy family's flight into Egypt, and the braying of the priest, choir, and congregation during mass.[7] Flinging dirt was another popu-lar activity. The bishop of Exeter reprimanded "ministers" and "boys" in the parish of Ottery St. Mary for "disfiguring . . . vestments and other furnish-ings of the church . . . by the spattering of filthy mud" during Christmas services. The congregation, less fastidious, "dissolved into disorderly laugh-ter and illicit mirth."[8] French deacons "dragged through the streets carts full of excrement [ordures], which they enjoyed throwing at the crowd that gathered around them."[9]

The Feast of Fools, a name variously given to all or part of the Christ-mas liturgical revels, has been most thoroughly documented in France, but it was known from England to Bohemia to the Iberian Peninsula.[10] E. K. Cham-bers, who did more than anyone else to assemble the historical record of the Feast of Fools, judged it dismissively as "an ebullition of the natural lout be-neath the cassock,"[11] but John Southworth has astutely observed that "the message" delivered by the Feast of Fools was "a spiritual one." Far from being a mere parody of conventional liturgy, the Feast of Fools "deserves respect as a genuine expression of liturgical drama," for it is a "literal acting-out of the Magnificat."[12]

Since at least the sixth century, Mary's canticle of joy has been sung every evening in the Roman church during Vespers. Sanctified for liturgical use by its professed Marian authorship, the song smuggles into the orderly ritual of the church an unexpectedly subversive message, for it rejoices in a God whose inclination is to topple human power structures and to raise the downtrodden to a position of honor and feasting. Ornate ceremonial traditionally obscured the burden of the words: the Magnificat was sung more slowly than the preceding psalms while the celebrant performed an elaborate censing of the altar. Once a year, however, in medieval Europe, the lower clergy insisted that the topsy-turvy implications of the canticle and of the Incarnation that it announced be acknowledged and enacted.

"The signal for the carnivalesque celebrations and parodies of the liturgy to begin"[13] was the canticle's central phrase, "Deposuit potentes de sede et exaltavit humiles" (He has put down the mighty from their seat and has exalted the humble). In the cathedral of Notre Dame in Paris, at the second Vespers of the Feast of the Circumcision (1 January), the choir repeated the *Deposuit* with such prolonged exuberance that the bishop had to insist in 1199 that the verse be sung no more than five times.[14] In the cathedral of Lleida, the Magnificat of the Feast of Saint John the Evangelist (27 December) signaled the start of the boy bishop's rule: "It was understood that [the singing of the *Deposuit*] inaugurated the rule of the humble rather than the powerful; what happened next was childish uproar and hullabaloo."[15]

The Feast of Fools, with its explicit justification in the Magnificat, noisily proclaimed the Christian basis for festive roles of reversal. Although pre-Christian practices may have contributed some of the festive iconography, much of it—the ass, the stinking parodies of incense, the clerical gibberish, and even cross-dressed men mocking priestly garb—found sufficient justification in the Christmas story or the liturgy. Eamon Duffy writes, "A perfectly good Christian justification could be offered for these popular observances, however close to the bone their elements of parody and misrule brought them. Christ's utterances about children and the Kingdom of Heaven, Isaiah's prophecy that a little child shall lead them [Isaiah 11:6], and the theme of inversion and the world turned upside-down found in texts like the 'Magnificat' could all be invoked in their defense."[16] The good news of Christ's birth, deftly collapsing hierarchies, needed no support from pagan ritual to be the cause of seasonal hilarity.

The Feast of Fools was understandably popular with the laity.[17] Not only did townsfolk come to watch the shenanigans within the church, but "the spirit of irreverence" proved "contagious" and spread to the secular arena. "The bishop of fools and his entourage of boisterous subdeacons, vicars, and chaplains" frequently led mock processions through the city, performing "irreverent or scatological drama in makeshift theaters and carts" along the way.[18] In Troyes, in 1444, when the bishop tried to prevent the feast, the clergy defiantly consecrated the archbishop of fools in the town square.[19] In sixteenth-century Lille, on the Feast of the Innocents, boys in disguises "ran through the streets throwing ashes at one another, singing dissolute songs, and hitting people."[20]

The feast spread not only spatially into the streets but also temporally towards Lent. In an anonymous French poem from the late thirteenth century, *The Battle of Lent and Fleshliness*, two feudal barons mobilize their troops. The unpopular Lent marshals only fishy followers, while the popular Fleshliness musters meat, sauces, and rich desserts. The two battle indecisively "until Christmas comes to the aid of Fleshliness and assures him the victory."[21] In January 1443, in Norwich, the aptly named John Gladman, "having his horse trapped with tin foil and other nice disguisy things," was, in token of the "mirth" proper to the season, "crowned as King of Christmas." He was followed through the city streets by a rider draped in herring skins, his horse "trapped with oyster shells," who represented the ensuing "sadness" of Lent.[22] In both cases, it was not yet Carnival but still Christmas that resisted Lent. Just as "the whole period from Christmas to Lent must have been considered a festive period in Norwich," so it was in many other parts of Europe.[23]

The church finally suppressed the ecclesiastical Feast of Fools, but its secular counterparts survived. The well-documented story of the Mère Folle (Foolish Mother) of Dijon illustrates such a shift of venue.[24] When, in 1435, the Council of Basel anathematized the Feast of Fools, the duke of Burgundy announced his intention to continue "the noble feast of joyous fools" in the private chapel of his palace in Dijon.[25] By 1553, when an act of the Parliament of Dijon added secular weight to the ecclesiastical ban, abolishing the Feast of Fools in all areas under its control, the chapel's company of fools had taken to the streets, extending its celebrations to Carnival and other civic festivities. Several hundred uniformed fools regularly marched through the city streets, *marotte* (fool's scepter) in hand. Elegant horse-drawn wagons followed, on which members of the company performed plays designed "to correct the bad habits of society" through faithful (and comic) public imitation. Husbands who beat their wives were special targets, being mounted in person or in effigy on the back of an ass and led through the town by "a troupe of fools disguised in hideous masks and fantastic costumes." The company was known by the name of its leader, the Mère Folle, no longer a bishop of fools but now a cross-dressed "prince of Mardi-Gras."[26]

Dijon's Mère Folle and other such groups were known generically as abbeys of misrule or *sociétés joyeuses* (merry companies). The Feast of Fools was not their only precedent. Rural France had long fostered companies of young bachelors known as *abbayes de la jeunesse* (youth abbeys). Each "abbey" annually elected, often at the Christmas season, one of its number as "king" or "abbot." He and his followers were responsible for the year's seasonal festivities and occasional horseplay. The latter included practical jokes at weddings—the medieval equivalent of tying tin cans and condoms to the newlyweds' car—and charivari, which punished violations of the conventional norms of marriage by exposing "lawbreakers" to public laughter. The condemned were often paraded through the village riding backwards on an ass.[27] Records of youth abbeys can be found, from the twelfth century on, "throughout rural Europe in Switzerland, Germany, Italy, Hungary, Rumania, and perhaps England and Scotland and Spain."[28]

The charivari, unlike the Feast of Fools, had a repressive aspect.[29] Designed to enforce rather than to subvert customary norms, its adoption by the urban abbeys of misrule was part of a process of civic domestication. The city authorities had "found a way to parry" the excesses of the secular feast of fools "by placing [the merry companies] under the supervision of trustworthy burghers, obliging them to follow the example of the hierarchical structure that existed in the guilds, corporations, and the various other corporate bodies organized among the population."[30] But the temptation to subversion could not always be resisted. In 1630, the Mère Folle was implicated in an antiroyalist riot. The abbey lingered for another thirty years until its final suppression in 1660, after which "public merry-making took refuge in the joyous masquerades of Carnival," for which Dijon was still well known in the nineteenth century.[31]

The historical development of European Carnival is, of course, much more complex than a few pages of condensed narrative or the single example of the Mère Folle can demonstrate. Unlike Corpus Christi, whose beginnings can be traced to specific ecclesiastical decrees, the story of Carnival tends to be one of subsequent prohibitions rather than of inaugural authorizations and is thus much harder to reconstruct. A complete and cogent history of Carnival has yet to be written. Nevertheless, I am persuaded that the popular belief that Carnival preserves pre-Christian rites has less to commend it than the argument that Carnival is rooted in the antihierarchical and antiascetic faith that God became human flesh. Coupled with the universal human inclination to make mischief, Christmas, I believe, bred Carnival.

Carnival festivities in many parts of the world still span the weeks between Christmas and Lent. Although the season's major public revelries now cluster at its conclusion rather than at its beginning, this has less to do with pagan roots than with the gradual appropriation of Christmas by the bourgeoisie and with the natural tendency of civic authorities to confine public masking and subversive revelry to as short a time as possible before their traditional terminus of Lent. Redefining disruptive roles of reversal as a last pagan outburst before Lent rather than as a legitimate response to the birth of Christ made them much easier to regulate and suppress.

In Part Three, we travel to rural Carnivals in Galicia and the Spanish Pyrenees, to a small-town Carnival in Belgium, to a vast and sprawling urban Carnival in the Caribbean, and—by way of returning to our starting point in patronal saints days—to a Carnival in the Bolivian Andes devoted to the Virgin of Candlemas. The purpose of our journey is not to marshal these festivals as collective witnesses for Carnival's Christian roots but to enjoy them as sophisticated pieces of communal theater, each with its own more immediate historical origins. Nevertheless, I will continue to draw attention to the varied ways in which individual festivals engage in negotiation with the official beliefs and behaviors of the church. Like the Feast of Fools, Carnival deflates pretensions and fattens stomachs, proposing a more radical reading of the Christian narrative than is generally heard from pulpits and altar rails. We begin with a devouring of pork and a scattering of ants.

ALL BUT THE MOST careless of those who packed the dirt square had closed the topmost buttons of their shirts. Many had added knotted bandannas and most had covered their heads. Several were in costume: one young man wore twin ponytails and painted freckles; a group of women posed as watermelons. Another figure, eight feet tall, draped with animal skins and crowned with a wild goat's head, glided silently through the crowd (Fig. 9.1). The diabolical cast of his curled horns and cloven hoofs was softened by his glass eyes and benign smile. A group of boys ran into the square, scattering handfuls of earth, but proved to be a false alarm. A quartet of bagpipers and drummers came and went. Anticipation mounted as the shadows lengthened and the evening air grew chill.

Then, at last, there was chaos. Women clutching plastic shopping bags poured into the square, strewing a mixture of dry earth and ants. People pressed against the margins of the square, slapping themselves to quell the mordant insects. A cloaked figure on a donkey passed through the confusion. Young men, wearing only bras, diapers, and close-cut, brazen hair, struck the crowd with prickly furze branches and monstrous kale stalks. Another man, bent double and cloaked in sackcloth, his face concealed behind an an-

9.1   Carnival goat mask. Laza, 1998.

tique wooden cow mask, gored frightened women. A machine on a creaking wooden cart trundled into the fray, spraying flour from a hose in the rear while men on board flung fistfuls of flour in all directions. It was all over in fifteen minutes. The crowd stilled, a rock band struck up, and couples began to dance. I was in the small Galician farming village of Laza for Carnival.[32]

Galicia, the southernmost of the Celtic lands, reaches over Portugal to touch the Atlantic in the northwest corner of Spain. Its Carnival season extends from the first chime of the New Year until Ash Wednesday. At midnight on 1 January, in Laza and the nearby town of Verín, the men who play the communities' most characteristic masked figures, known respectively as *peliqueiros* and *cigarrones,* don their belts of bells and run through the streets, ringing in the New Year.[33] Thereafter, anticipation builds. Boys make noise by blowing animal horns and drumming with sticks on gas cans hung around their necks. Practical jokes are played.[34] A battle of the sexes erupts. Young men throw bran, flour, or ashes at young women, sometimes stuffing fistfuls in mouths and down clothes. The women retaliate in kind.[35] Gendered effigies are displayed, captured, and burned.[36] In Verín, in February 1998, late at night on the Thursday before Carnival, I watched costumed women (and a few cross-dressed men) parade through the streets shouting good-naturedly, "Away with men!"

Laza's Carnival weekend began the next night with a *folión* (merry procession).[37] About eleven o'clock, under an intermittent drizzle, a small crowd gathered at the southern entrance to the village. Men and boys wore horned helmets, reminiscent of those worn by their Celtic ancestors. Two men carried cow skulls on tall poles. Others bore long straw torches. A band of bagpipers warmed up. Several revelers, anticipating by thirty-six hours the arrival of the *peliqueiros*, carried whips and wore a belt of bells. Some were already drunk. A metal container full of old tires was set ablaze and dragged behind a farm wagon towards the village center. A boisterous, torchlight parade followed, loud with the noise of bells, bagpipes, drums, whistles, and horns. Several times, as we passed beneath overhanging balconies, women poured ashes on us. We stopped at bars to drink. In the early hours of the morning, tires and torches still blazing, the parade started along a country lane towards the neighboring village of Soutelinho. By then it was raining heavily. Drenched, I abandoned the festivities, drove back to my hotel, washed the ashes out of my hair, and went to sleep.

The *peliqueiros* appeared for the first time on Sunday morning. The *peliqueiro's* distinctive wooden mask boasts a large triangular nose, pale skin, red cheeks, a black goatee, a thin mustache, and a trim beard of rabbit fur. The mask is crowned by a large tin hat, shaped like an episcopal miter or military headgear, with a wild animal painted on the front and the back covered with the *pelica* (dried animal skin) from which the masker's name derives. The *peliqueiro* wears a short brocaded jacket with military epaulets and braids, a broad cummerbund, and a leather belt bearing in the back six large tubular brass bells that yield a distinctive tintinnabulation as he runs. He carries a whip with a wooden handle and a thong made from the skin of a young bull (Fig. 9.2).[38] As worshipers left the church after Sunday morning mass, they passed between two rows of *peliqueiros*, who administered mild lashings with their whips. The *peliqueiro* is regarded as the "owner and lord of the new order established during Carnival."[39] "The people who go to church are punished for it by the *peliqueiros*."[40]

From the churchyard, the *peliqueiros* moved to the Praza Picota. This is not so much a square as an irregular confluence of narrow dirt streets, rising or falling into an open area in front of the Cafe Bar Picota. A paved terrace, extending the plaza to the south, provides the only level ground. The terrace is guarded from the drop into the street below by a stone bench and iron railing. In the square, girls in traditional dress supervised the annual

9.2 *Peliqueiros.* Laza, 1998.

distribution of *bica* (pound cake) while the *peliqueiros* lashed the backs of the participants and scantily clad young men parodied the communal feast with theatrical displays of gluttony.

Sunday evening saw a parade of satirical and, in many cases, aggressively vulgar floats. There was a blond-wigged transvestite nurse performing mock sodomy on a genuinely bare-bottomed male patient; a corpse on a stretcher; half a dozen acrobatic young men, their hair dyed brazen, wearing nothing but kneesocks, slippers, and diapers (Fig. 9.3); and the pope surrounded by a cardinal, a member of the national guard, Saddam Hussein, and (in honor of the pope's recent visit to Cuba) a kneeling Fidel Castro. From the pope's crotch a narrow hose pipe, plugged with a hollowed carrot, poured a constant flow of milky liquid into the street (Fig. 9.4). After the floats had passed, the *peliqueiros* ran to and fro in lines of as many as ten at a time, using their whips to clear a path through the crowd, ringing their bells, and turning abruptly to repeat the action in reverse. This required considerable skill, since the narrow eye slits in the mask meant that each could see only the

9.3   Satirical float: men in diapers. Laza, 1998.

back of his fellow a few inches in front but not his own feet or where he was stepping. One false step would have had a disastrous domino effect.

On Monday, I watched from a private balcony overlooking the Praza Picota. At midday a muddy tarpaulin was carried into the square and torn into rags. Those waiting in the square attacked one another with the dirty, sodden cloths. Most of the participants wore waterproof outer garments. Two men wheeled in a plastic trash bin full of mud in which the rags could be freshly soaked. Flour was later added to the mix. For two hours, anyone who entered the square was assaulted. A few rags were flung at my balcony, but most smacked against the wall behind me. A quartet of men in nurses' uniforms defended the raised sidewalk in front of the Cafe Bar Picota against all comers, and the whitewashed wall behind them quickly sprouted muddy stains. A motorized bathtub, full of liquid red clay, drove around the square, spraying water. When it stopped, muddied warriors dipped a rag in the tub, hurled it, caught another cloth, and dipped that, too, in mud (Fig. 9.5).

Afterwards, I had lunch with Antonio Salgado, a native of Laza now living in New York. His mother and sisters fed us lavish helpings of soup, cured head of pork, goat, fresh cod, red and homemade white wine, flan, pound cake, coffee, and cognac. Antonio assured me that Laza had an uninterrupted tradition of Carnival, despite the prohibition under Franco. At first Laza kept its Carnival by taking it to the surrounding mountains, but gradually Carnival was able to return to the village. Some men dressed as *peliqueiros* while others watched for the national guard. As a boy, Antonio had stood on street corners whistling a warning whenever the guards appeared. Eventually, even the *guardia civil* relaxed and the Carnival took place without restriction. In those days, Antonio said, the local economy was so poor that only five or six *peliqueiro* costumes were available. Young men worked on the railroad to save enough money to rent a costume for a couple of hours, signing up

9.4 Satirical float: the pope ejaculates, watched by Saddam Hussein, a cardinal, Fidel Castro, and other dignitaries. Laza, 1998.

9.5 Mud bath. Laza, 1998.

weeks in advance for a place on the rental schedule. So that everyone could take part, *peliqueiros* appeared throughout the Carnival. Now that everyone can afford their own costume, the *peliqueiros* all come out together "at the best times."

Late in the afternoon, I went back to the Praza Picota. A group of older men had captured a *peliqueiro* and were leading him about trussed in ropes before they took him into the bar. *Peliqueiros* are "obliged to invite whoever captures them for a glass of wine."[41] All but the most careless of those who packed the square had closed the topmost buttons of their shirts. When men and women clutching plastic bags poured into the square, strewing a mixture of dry earth and ants, members of the crowd tried to protect themselves as best they could. The ants had been gathered from the fields outside the village and doused with vinegar to make them bite more fiercely.

Vicente Risco believes that the practice of scattering ants migrated to Carnival from the feast of Corpus Christi. In nearby Allariz, where there was "in time past" a large Jewish community, two men used to walk before the monstrance in the Corpus Christi procession, scattering ants "to drive away the Jews."[42] Why ants should have been used for this purpose is unclear. Perhaps the habit migrated to Carnival because of the season's widespread consumption of pork, a food shunned by Jews. In any case, the ants are now explained in Laza as part of a general invasion of civilized space (the village square) by wild forces of nature (ants, furze branches, the violent cow mask, and the creatures on the *peliqueiros'* hats). But Antonio Muñoz reports that the villagers don't really "agree" with this "acquired and artificial interpretation." Their real motivation, he suggests, is "repetitive custom, the particular identity that [the ants] give to Laza's Carnival, and the ludic pleasure of provoking panic in the spectators."[43]

Immediately behind the ant-throwers came a figure on a donkey. The rider, so cloaked against the ants as to be of indeterminate gender, was followed by several barely dressed men carrying prickly furze branches and enormous kale stalks. In the chaos, there was hardly time to take it in, but viewed in retrospect on video, the episode recalls the iconography of Jesus' Palm Sunday entry to Jerusalem, familiar to Spaniards from Easter Week re-enactments. The branches and stalks are standard fare at this moment in Laza's Carnival, but the rider on the donkey was an innovation, perhaps suggested by the customary branches.[44] Such parodies of sacred history (or of the church's processional reenactment of sacred history) are not uncommon in Laza's Carnival. In 1992 one entry in the parade of floats displayed, to the consternation even of the folklore-friendly parish priest, a naked mock crucifixion and a grieving Virgin Mary who appeared to throw herself on the body of her crucified son "but on closer inspection was pretending to perform fellatio on Christ."[45]

The donkey and his rider passed quickly through the square, but the men with furze branches and kale stalks stayed, striking the crowd repeatedly. I caught a glimpse of another man, bent double and cloaked in sackcloth, his face concealed behind an antique wooden cow mask. The mask's horns were real, but its tongue and eyes were made of painted cloth. The cow is known as *la morena* (the dark one).[46] Traditionally, the *morena* charged frightened women, trying to hook its horns beneath their skirts, but all the women I saw wore pants and the *morena* seemed to attack onlookers of either gender indiscriminately. Some claim that the *morena's* attack signals a "rustic pagan fertility rite with a marked sexual character."[47] Simple prurient interest may be more to the point. Mariana Regalado remembers a group of older men "who talked about how exciting it was if you happened to see when the *morena* got the girl's skirt up. . . . Their eyes positively glowed with the memories."[48]

Bringing up the rear of the invasion, a machine on a creaking wooden farm wagon trundled into the fray, whirring ominously and spraying flour from a hose in the rear while, for fifteen minutes, men on board flung flour in all directions. People sheltered in hoods and doorways, surged hither and thither, and pushed against strangers in their efforts to avoid the ants, the flour, the cow, the furze, and the kale. Finally, the invaders left, a band mounted the stage at the dead end of the flour-strewn terrace, and couples began to dance. A file of *peliqueiros* ran through the dancers, executed a unison about-face at the stage, and returned, ringing their bells and flailing their whips, to the bar. I peered over the terrace railings at a pair of drunks. Neither was able to stand long enough to help the other up. Someone emptied on the drunks the last ants from a plastic bag.

Later, a large farm wagon was pulled into the square by the brazen-haired men yoked together. On board was an ample supply of bread and *cachucha* (cured head of pork).[49] Three riders cut slices and handed them down to those clamoring around the cart or threw them into the more distant crowd. Some parts of the pig's head were easily identifiable; I saw teeth on two morsels of jaw that flew over my head. Three *peliqueiros* circled the cart, ferociously whipping the backs of those who clamored for food and attacking anyone who dared to sprint across the open space dividing crowd and cart. I asked why. "To stop the crowd crushing the cart," I was told by one villager. Another said, "To clear a space around the cart," and yet another, "To maintain a bit of order in the midst of disorder." None of these explanations seemed satisfactory. Finally, the wagon left the square, the rock band struck up again, and dancing began. A ceremonial *queimada* (a potent liquor, made from fruit and coffee beans and served flaming) was distributed to the already intoxicated revelers.

Laza's Carnival closed on Tuesday evening with the *testamento do burro* (the donkey's will) and the burial of Carnival. Men in horned helmets and straw coats, reputedly worn by Celtic ancestors in this coldest of Spanish regions, led a donkey to the stage at the end of the terrace. The *peliqueiros* accompanied the entourage. The donkey's rider mounted the stage and read the animal's last will and testament, assigning its various body parts to different local and world figures according to reputation. I heard mention of the mayors of Laza and Verín and of President Clinton, but I failed to catch which of the donkey's members was left to him. The loudest cheer came when the donkey asserted the primacy of Laza's *peliqueiros* over Verín's *cigarrones*.[50]

I left before the burial of Carnival, in which church ritual and death itself are parodied, but I have seen the 1989 version of the burial on film.[51] The funeral procession, escorted by the *peliqueiros*, was led by a figure representing death, cloaked in black, carrying a scythe, and riding a donkey. A "bishop" under a canopy and several "priests" in ecclesiastical robes followed. A young man in a coffin, his face painted white and his lips and eyes outlined in black, represented Carnival. Several weeping women, dressed in black, their faces whitened with flour, accompanied the corpse. Regalado describes what happened next: "At the end of a long and obscene 'mass' (including a 'bishop' who blessed people with 'the finger'), the 'bishop' started to intone the words, *'Resuscitate, resuscitate,'* at which time the two-foot 'penis' of the 'corpse' of [Carnival] rose up, rhythmically shaking, from the coffin wherein the body lay."[52] Carnival, his eyes wide open and his tongue hanging out lasciviously, made the enormous dildo rise quickly and repeatedly by means of a wooden lever and a leather strap that he manipulated with his right hand. As the coffin was borne away on the shoulders of the pallbearers, only the erect phallus was visible from below. Carnival was alive and well, ready to rise again the following year.

Some scholars make exaggerated claims for the antiquity of Laza's Carnival, supposing it to be a prehistoric fertility rite presided over by "priestly" *peliqueiros*.[53] Others, invoking the rhetoric of a seasonal battle between pagan Carnival and Christian Lent, see the invasion of the village by ants, wild cows, *peliqueiros*, and near-naked men wielding furze branches as a dramatization of the spiritual side of human nature yielding reluctantly to carnal sensuality.[54] But an understanding of Carnival rooted in the topsy-turvydom of the Incarnation, the Magnificat, and the Feast of Fools would argue quite the opposite. Such a view would see the ridicule of false piety and clerical chastity, the mockery of human power, the celebration of the flesh, the bounteous communal consumption of food and drink, the unabashed reveling in excremental mud, and the general disruption of order as a celebration of humanity, in all its messiness, in the face of Lent's denial. The festive imitation of anarchy might be said to dramatize the temporary comic victory of Christian Carnival over the glum severity of pagan Lent.

The Jesuit scholar William Lynch wrote, "Comedy, with its antipathy to the order of things, seems anarchic (and, indeed, it does have a propensity for thieves, villains, drunkards, fools, idiots, lawbreakers and other people like the reader and the writer). But it is not all anarchic; it is only a defender of another and more human order (more muddy, more actual, more free)." Comedy reminds us, in the slippage of the man of pomp on a banana peel or the burlesque of ostentatious ceremony, not to take ourselves too seriously. And it recalls, as Lynch puts it, "the incredible relationship between mud and God," the insistence of the Christian gospel that we need not rise above our station, aspiring to a false divinity, for God in Christ has joined us in our muddy humanness.[55] Our God is down-to-earth. Laza's Carnival is arguably folk theology at its comic best.

But even comedy requires its villains. In Laza, the *peliqueiros* are the villains of the piece. Although, as markers of the village's folkloric status, they have officially acquired the heroic status of "priests" or "lords of Carnival," their actions in the dramatic narrative suggest a different role. Again and again, they charge the crowd in disciplined single file, aggressively whipping and scattering villagers who stand in the way. While careful to hurt no one in fact, they dramatically enact the brutal assault of men in uniform on rural villagers. In a powerful climax to Monday evening's drama, they impede and punish the villagers' access to the distribution of pork and bread. Opposing the vision of the Magnificat, the *peliqueiros* scatter the humble and deny the hungry good things.

They may have a specific historical referent. One theory, popular in Laza itself, has the *peliqueiros* recall the tax or rent collectors of the powerful counts of Monterrei, who controlled territory in southern Ourense and northern Portugal from the late fifteenth to the nineteenth century. The counts' abandoned castle still dominates an imposing hilltop outside Verín. Some versions of this theory suggest that the collectors wore masks to terrify the peasants and that the same masks were used by the counts' huntsmen to frighten animals. The skins of captured animals, so the story goes, adorned the backs of the masks' miters. But Xerardo Dasairas discounts this legend on the grounds that masks with narrow eye slits would have hindered hunters and collectors.[56] Federico Cocho adds that similar masks can be found elsewhere in France and Spain and are unlikely to have so exclusively local an origin.[57] By way of example, Dasairas cites masks used in Italian carnivals to celebrate the retreat of Napoleonic forces.[58]

Dasairas's illustration is apt, for Galicia was the site of strong resistance to Napoleon's armies during the early years of the Peninsular War (1808–1814). For a while, between January and March 1809, the valley of the Támega—the river that runs through Verín—saw both French and Spanish armies pass by in force. The army of Galicia, under the marquis of Romana, evacuated Ourense on 19 January and retreated south to Monterrei. From there, La Romana issued calls for fierce guerrilla attacks on the French army, under General Soult, which was advancing on Ourense from the west. Beleaguered by insurgent assaults, Soult's army reached Ourense late in February and headed slowly south to Monterrei, from which La Romana had again retreated. Soult's army stayed in Monterrei from 7 to 10 March, advancing thence to capture Chaves, just across the Portuguese border, two days later.[59] The French invaders were hated by all classes of Galicia, demonized by the powerful for their revolutionary heritage and detested by the peasantry for their violent pillage of the countryside. "Elevated to the category of meta-physical evil," the French became the objects of "eternal hatred" in Galicia.[60]

Risco first suggested a military origin for the *peliqueiros* in 1979, when he noted that their headpiece "recalls certain military morions, backed with animal skin, that were used in the eighteenth century."[61] But Laza's *peliqueiros* and Verín's *cigarrones*, with their short brocaded jackets, military epaulets, white trousers, and exaggerated bicorn hats, are perhaps better understood as caricatures of early-nineteenth-century Napoleonic officers. Even the animal skin and horsehair queue may derive from Napoleonic uni-forms.[62] The same origin may also explain nearby Xinzo de Limia's Carnival *pantallas* (masqueraders),[63] who lack only the military jackets, and the deco-rated Carnival generals of the Ulla valley of central Galicia, another area of popular resistance to Napoleonic forces. In the latter case, old hostilities are sometimes modernized. In the village of Oza, in 1982, reports of Basque ter-rorism near Spain's border with France prompted rival generals to identify themselves as Spanish and French. The Spanish ambassador told his counter-part, "The French have been, since very distant times, bad neighbors to Spain and almost always tyrants." When the French "soldiers" refused to yield, the Spanish ambassador threatened war, promising, "We'll win the battle against the French, just as our ancestors did."[64]

Perhaps it would be best to read the *peliqueiros'* aggressive stance as a shifting portrait of the villagers' attitude to violent external powers in gen-eral. The *peliqueiros'* antecedents may be older than the Peninsular War and their costumes later modified to reflect the particular trauma of Napoleonic invasion. The more recent trauma of repression under Franco may have fur-ther changed their popular identity. When I asked Antonio Salgado, "Are the *peliqueiros* good guys or bad guys?" he replied, "Always good guys." This be-nevolent view of the *peliqueiros* may have less to do with their dramatic function than with inevitable local pride in "our" maskers and with the new status of the *peliqueiros* as a symbol of resistance to Franco. The performance itself belies Antonio's characterization of them as benevolent. I suspect that the *peliqueiros* became heroes only after they had been blessed with the patina of anthropological antiquity and had successfully resisted the more recent armed threat of Franco's national guard.

If the *peliqueiros* are the villains of Laza's Carnival comedy, the church and all its rites provide the clowns. Clerical pretensions to piety and ritual power, roundly mocked by the satirical floats and the burlesque ceremonies, offer no resistance to Laza's Carnival vision of independence and plenty. It is the external secular powers, whether they be the tax collectors of Monterrei, the invading armies of Napoleon, or Franco's national guard, who are the serious historical threat.

Both religious and secular powers (clowns and villains) are in the end made subservient to Carnival. During the closing burial rite, a contingent of *peliqueiros* escorts the coffin. A mock bishop and his priests follow. The public transcript of this comic funeral pronounces Carnival dead and Lent again newborn, but the none-too-hidden transcript challenges that verdict. Carnival, enthroned in his coffin, will not be dead for long. Just as the earlier figure on the donkey surrounded by furze branches and kale stalks recalled the processional rites of Palm Sunday, so the funeral of Carnival invokes the Good Friday ritual of the burial of Christ. And, like Christ, Carnival will rise again. Laza's closing ceremony is no exhausted surrender to Lent but a bawdy vision of the resurrection of the flesh. The folk theology of Laza's Carnival enacts the hope that, despite the brutality of emperors and generals and the foolishness of clergy, Mary's millenarian vision of freedom and plenty for the poor will in the end prove justified.

10.
The Bandit and the Fat Man
(NAVARRE)

A CHILL WIND WHIPPED through the main square of Bielsa (Aragon), buffeting the crowd with refrigerated air from the nearby Pyrenean peaks. Against the cold, a bonfire burned. Presiding over the festivities was Don Cornelio Zorrilla Carnaval (Cornelius Carnival the Drunk, Esquire), a life-sized effigy of clothed straw, also known as *el muñeco* (the doll). Cornelio had been hung from the central window of the porticoed town hall early that morning, flaunting a fully erect penis and a single gilded Christmas ball. Now, on Carnival Friday night 2001, he watched over a communal meal of pork grilled over the open fire, garlicked mashed potatoes, crusty bread, and red wine. A small brass band played exuberantly.

On Saturday morning, after overnight revelry—which I missed, being asleep—a dilapidated Cornelio still hung in place, but he had been stripped of his hat, his dark glasses, his booted right foot, his dildo, and his ball. I found the last, abandoned, in a narrow, sloping street two blocks away.

At dusk, after a quiet day, the village square was invaded by a dozen horned men, known as *trangas* after the long poles they carried.[1] Their faces blackened, their shoulders cloaked in animal skins, and their legs wrapped in long woolen skirts, the *trangas* chased watching women, pinning them against walls and miming copulation. The rotation of the *trangas'* hips rang the cowbells that hung from a belt behind their waist. Other traditional masqueraders followed. *Madamas,* young women in regional dresses, shivered from the cold and intermittently danced with the long-horned *trangas* (Fig. 10.1). Three pairs of *onsos* (bears) were played by young men in sackcloth and sheepskin, their faces blackened and their backs amply padded with straw. Short, hand-held sticks served as their front legs (Fig. 10.2). While their handlers led them with long chains and beat them, the bears attempted to escape into the crowd, scattering onlookers. In a combination known as the *amantato* (mounted one), a single actor represented both a bent old woman

10.1   *Madama* and *tranga*. Bielsa, 2001.

and a man riding on her shoulders. The actor's head and torso corresponded to those of the man, his skirted legs to the lower half of the old woman. The woman's upper body and the man's legs, angled forward, were stuffed.[2] The *amantato* was accompanied by a skirted *caballé* (hobbyhorse), which shuddered whenever an onlooker stroked its phallic head. The brass band, now boasting among its members a red-cheeked grenadier, a kilted Scot, and a cross-dressed nun, played rowdily. Costumed revelers of all ages danced.

The same bawdy comedy was repeated on Sunday night, after which alcoholic punch and *torta* (lemon pound cake) were freely distributed. Then everyone repaired to the village's bare concrete social hall for a long night of dancing and drinking. At six o'clock on Monday morning, a remnant gathered in the darkened square. A bearded man in a pink tutu carried a life-sized inflatable doll. Another sported lace pajamas and a nightcap. Two women posed as mad cows. A young man climbed on another's shoulders, grabbed Cornelio's feet, and tried to jerk the doll loose from the stone facade. The porter lurched tipsily to one side. The climber dangled briefly and fell to the pavement, breaking his nose. This was not in the script. Friends ran to help. Someone produced a cell phone, summoning a car to take the injured man away.

Someone else arrived with a ladder that was too short to reach Cornelio. Two cross-dressed men wrestled with a concrete flower bed beneath the central portico, laboriously shifting it a few feet into the square, and then placed the ladder on the raised earth. A young woman brandishing scissors climbed the rungs and cut Cornelio loose. The straw effigy slumped on the cobbles beneath. A man in a white veil and wedding dress kicked Cornelio to the center of the square, where the effigy was made to copulate with the inflatable doll. With difficulty, in the gusting wind, the jilted bride set fire to Cornelio. Soon Carnival and his plastic concubine were burning merrily. The bearded ballerina strummed his guitar while the rest of us warmed ourselves by Cornelio's pyre.

No sentence was passed in this diminished ceremony of execution, but

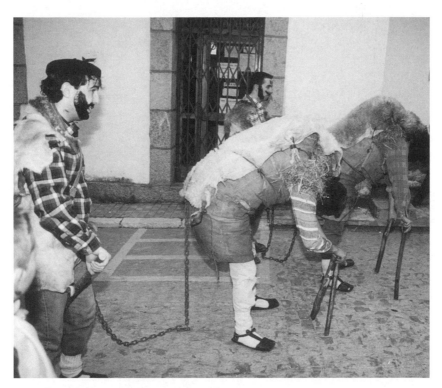

10.2   Bears and their handlers. Bielsa, 2001.

in earlier years Cornelio's judgment had been an important annual rite. I have a photocopy of the formal document, properly sealed and signed by Judge Rafael Pañart and District Attorney Angel Solans, enumerating the crimes for which Cornelio was condemned during the 1948 Carnival.[3] Charges brought by various townspeople included nocturnal seductions of both unmarried and married women, one of whom is named by her cuckolded husband; causing a fatal railroad wreck by sabotaging the tracks; extinguishing street lamps in one of the town's barrios; and stealing a donkey, a pilot's license, wedding photographs, a spare tire, one hundred pounds of imported cheese, a thousand yards of sausage, forty dozen eggs, eight cans of black pudding, and thirty-two breeding rabbits. In summary, Cornelio was found guilty of "improper conduct, both moral and social, acts of robbery, sabotage, immorality, insubordination, and disorder." The particularity of some charges suggests that specific unsolved crimes and marital grievances were being blamed on Cornelio. But "the grand scale and fabulous quantity" of the edible swag also suggests Carnival exaggeration, especially at a time when Franco was still blockading the region in retribution for its wartime resistance. (Just ten years earlier, in June 1938, the entire population of Bielsa had been evacuated and its buildings reduced to uninhabitable shells during the retreat of units of the Nationalist army across the Pyrenees to France. By 1948 most of the families had returned, but reconstruction was still incomplete.)[4]

Some scholars see Bielsa's Carnival as a seasonal fertility rite and the immolation of the well-endowed Cornelio as a sacrifice that sustains the life of cattle, crops, and community for another year.[5] So J. G. Frazer understood the many judicial cremations of Carnival effigies that he catalogued in *The Golden Bough*.[6] But one need not follow Frazer into the world of pre-Christian ritual to find a precedent for the substitutionary death of Carnival. Catholic Europe has its own more recent prototype. There is, in Bielsa, an uncanny resemblance between the posture of Cornelio on the front of the town hall and that of the crucified Christ on the wall behind the altar in the parish church. Cornelio's arms are not outstretched, but his shoulders slump and his body sags in much the same way as Christ's. Both figures hang alone on an otherwise bare wall. Whether or not the people of Bielsa are conscious of the resemblance, the one must provide at least an unconscious point of reference for the other.

The comparison between Cornelio and Christ might seem far-fetched were it not for the fact that we have already seen in Laza the tendency of Carnival not only to look backward to the topsy-turvydom of Christmas but also forward to the events of Easter week. Christ's entry to Jerusalem on Palm Sunday, his crucifixion (albeit accompanied by a Mary intent on fellatio), his burial, and the resurrection of his (fully human) flesh were all, in one year or another, the object of Laza's Carnival mimicry. Insisting that Cornelio bear all blame for the sexual adventures, thefts, sabotage, and gluttonous appetites of the people of Bielsa—fantasies and realities openly dramatized during Carnival—also looks past Lent to Easter, for it is an article of Christian faith that Christ in his dying bore "the sin of the world" (John 1:29).

The references to the Easter narrative in the Carnivals of Laza and Bielsa are indisputable, but the attitude towards that narrative is less clear. One might argue that it is the nature of Carnival to blaspheme and that the drunken execution of Cornelio in Bielsa, like the obscene burial of Carnival in Laza, is an act of deliberate mockery. But just as the laughter of the Feast of Fools was directed not at the Christmas narrative itself but at those whose hierarchies and rituals concealed its subversive implications, so the object of Carnival's religious mockery is not the Easter narrative, which joyfully asserts the resurrection of the flesh, but the antithetical (and clerically imposed) asceticism of Lent. It is not so much Jesus who is mocked in Laza as Lent's devaluation of his true humanity. Whether a similar reclamation of the carnivalesque implications of the Christian narrative is taking place in Bielsa will become clearer after we consider another Carnival I attended in 2001.

Leaving Bielsa immediately after the death of Cornelio, I drove briefly south and then, as the sun rose, west. From Pamplona, I headed north again to the tiny Basque village of Lantz, in the rolling foothills of the western Pyrenees. Until the late nineteenth century, Lantz was an important halt on the main highway from Pamplona to the French coast.[7] Now, bypassed, it sits at the end of a winding country lane. The village is laid out in an oval: two parallel streets of about a hundred yards apiece, joined at the southern end by a short loop of paved street and at the northern end by a winding, muddy cart track. Halfway along the oval, a small square joins the *posada* (no longer an inn but a rudimentary town hall serving food and drink) on one street to the open pelota court on the other. By 1:00 P.M., a sizable crowd had gathered in the center of the village.

The attic dressing room on the third floor of the *posada*, illuminated only by natural light coming through the unglazed windows, was open to visitors. The rough floorboards were sturdy but bare. One corner was deep in straw. By the time I arrived, a bizarre cast of characters was already in costume: the *ziripot* (fatso), a ceremonial fat man in sacking hugely stuffed with straw (see

Fig. 10.3 below);[8] the *zaldiko* (little horse), a simple hobbyhorse, made of a wooden hand-held frame, with a flat wooden head and a horsehair tail but no skirts (see Fig. 10.7 below); and two dozen *txatxos* (lads) in various brightly colored costumes, conical hats, and gauze masks, or, as one observer put it, "masks without faces" (see Fig. 10.6 below).[9] (*Txatxos* is an abbreviation of the Castilian *muchachos*, which, like the synonymous Basque *mutillak*, ordinarily means "young men." But, as Caro Baroja points out, *mutillak*—and therefore perhaps *txatxos*—"sometimes refers to demons.")[10] Leaning against the central beam was Miel Otxin, a stuffed cruciform effigy, nine feet tall, wearing a smiling papier-mâché mask and dressed in blue trousers, red cummerbund, flowered shirt, and a multicolored conical paper hat. One forked, inverted branch provided the skeleton of his trunk and legs. Another branch, affixed at right angles, supported his outstretched arms (Fig. 10.4).[11]

Allowing the audience into the dressing room was a part of the drama, building a sense of entry into an alien world. When another group of *txatxos*, already dressed and faceless, bounded whooping up the stairs into the dusty attic, the audience was quickly ushered out. As we stumbled two floors down and out into the sunshine, the doors of the town hall closed behind us. A dog barked. Then, from within, we heard the clang of struck metal and the menace of inhuman groaning. Gathered behind the barred doors, the cast was invoking the threat of an infernal outpouring.

After several minutes of clamor, the doors opened slightly to release a dozen *arotzak* (blacksmiths), men clothed from head to foot in loose sackcloth, partially overlaid with animal skins or wickerwork, their faces hidden (see Fig. 10.5 below). All wielded long wooden pitchforks to prod the crowd back against the houses lining the street. Some carried wicker baskets. Others hefted metal tubs of boiling water, whose steam rising into the cold air conjured up the smoke of hell. Growling, the cloaked figures shuffled down the street, shunting photographers aside, clearing the street for the procession to follow. At the southern end of the village, they established a temporary forge, where they beat an anvil.

The doors of the *posada* opened again. *Txatxos* ran out, some with shorter wooden pitchforks, others with brooms, prodding, whacking, driving us back against the walls. At first I flinched or scurried away, but a few blows reminded me that, like Berga's *guites* and Laza's *peliqueiros*, the *txatxos* were enacting violence, not inflicting pain. Some seized young women and bore them off over their shoulders but set them safely down some yards away. The *zaldiko* galloped to and fro in the midst of the *txatxos*, only to be seized, shod, and released by the blacksmiths as it passed their anvil. Behind the

10.3   Musicians and *ziripot*. Lantz, 2001.

txatxos waddled the *ziripot*, supporting himself with a long stick (Fig. 10.3).
The hobbyhorse was the fat man's foe, repeatedly charging and knocking
him over. Felled, the *ziripot* lay helpless, like an overturned turtle, until
his handler helped him up. Then came Miel Otxin, unwaveringly cheerful, the only character whose face (albeit painted on a mask) had features
neither blurred by gauze nor hidden by sackcloth. Carried upright, gripped
by handles embedded in his calves, his groin resting on his bearer's head, he
smiled down at us (Fig. 10.4). Two musicians followed, one playing a lively
tune on the *txistu* (Basque pipe) and tabor, the other adding rhythm on a
small kettledrum.[12] Behind them, like religious pilgrims at the close of a procession, walked the crowd.

    While the procession continued on its counterclockwise circuit of the vil-
lage, the blacksmiths ambled up the now deserted street to its northern end.
The color of their costumes matched the mud in the street and the pastel
brown stone of the partially whitewashed houses (Fig. 10.5). I waited with
them. After a while, the procession appeared again in the distance, winding
its way along a muddy track between low stone walls. Miel Otxin, bringing up the rear, was a silhouetted cross against the sky. Reaching the open

10.4   Miel Otxin. Lantz, 2001.

space at the juncture of street and track, the *txatxos* again assaulted spectators while the *zaldiko* charged and upended the *ziripot*. The blacksmiths seized and shod the horse. A young Spaniard described the scene for me with a single apt English word: "Higgledy-piggledy."

On reaching the *posada*, the procession cut through the square to the open pelota court. There, with the jovial Miel Otxin standing upright in the center—held quietly by two senior *txatxos*—the other *txatxos* and the *zaldiko* performed an elegant circle dance (*zortzikoa*).[13] With this, the mood of the Carnival drama changed from threat to harmony, from rough disorder to elegant order. The demon *txatxos* were transformed into charming dancers (Fig. 10.6). For ten minutes, the tamed but still motley crew danced counterclockwise round the court, arms raised, hips swirling, footwork swift and deft. Afterwards, the crowd dispersed, Miel Otxin was carried back to his attic, and the dancers quickly changed out of costume.

As a piece of abstract theater, the first day of Lantz's Carnival had worked splendidly. Anticipation had been built deliberately in the dressing room and by the cacophony behind barred doors. The mysterious *arotzak* with their pitchforks and steaming cauldrons had inspired a kind of eerie terror, yielding to the mischievous (and marginally less frightening) violence of the *txatxos*. The running combat between the fat man and the hobbyhorse had teetered between ancient mystery and comic violence. The benevolent smile of the giant Miel Otxin and the cheerful music at the rear of the procession had promised an alternative to the terror that began it. The concluding dance had fulfilled that promise, dissolving terror into simple beauty in a resolution that I found aesthetically persuasive.

The same was true on Tuesday. Arriving earlier, I saw a group of *txatxos* emerge from their communal lunch in the *posada*'s second-floor dining room and perform, still in everyday clothes, an indoor version of the circle dance. I spent an hour in the attic watching the slow construction of the swollen *ziripot* around the meager body of the young actor. Sackcloth stuffed with straw encased him. The final touch, a straw hat and a white muslin mask, erased his face. The *zaldiko*, his features also concealed by a white cloth, practiced his prancing gallop to and fro across the attic and then attacked the finished *ziripot* (Fig. 10.7). The *txatxos* dressed more quickly. Some wore women's clothes. The circuit of the village followed the same route as it had the day before, chaos leading harmony and ending with conflict resolved in the circle dance round Miel Otxin. A light snow fell.

10.5 Blacksmiths. Lantz, 2001.

10.6 *Txatxos.* Lantz, 2001.

By that night, when I returned for the third and final performance, the snow was falling heavily. Rural police monitored the narrow road leading into the village. The number of visitors was such that late arrivals had to park a mile away. When the procession began, darkness intensified the threat of the blacksmiths and the *txatxos,* but the melody of the pipe and drum resisted fear. There was a new character: a small boy in white, an open book in his hands, walked quietly behind Miel Otxin. Someone held an open umbrella over his head. José María Iribarren reported in 1944 that "two boys disguised as women, in white costumes," used to walk "very seriously" behind Miel Otxin, "each reading [silently] from a book." Later, they would "pretend to read the story of [Christ's] Passion" to the prisoner. Iribarren assumed that the two "women" represented the grieving "family of the giant accompanying him to the place of execution."[14]

After a complete circuit of the damp village, instead of cutting through the square to the pelota court, the procession continued past the *posada.* The "pilgrims" in the rear had already abandoned the procession to find vantage points around the court. Suddenly, Miel Otxin turned and, in a display of virtuoso portage by his bearer, ran at full speed back up the street and through the square to the court, pursued by a pair of *txatxos.* I followed, arriving at the court just in time to see Miel Otxin confronted by a man with a shotgun. Two shots rang out and the giant effigy fell face forward to the wet pavement. Although I had expected the execution, its abruptness was a shock. The *txatxos* stripped, beheaded, disemboweled, and set fire to the fallen Miel Otxin. Then, as the unclothed body of straw burned, they performed their peaceful circle dance around the flames. Snow fell heavily, glittering white in the firelit darkness. It was a strangely moving resolution to the two days of Carnival drama.

Lantz's Carnival may be enjoyed as a brilliantly conceived and executed communal work of abstract theater, dramatizing the nature of conflict and the sacrificial cost of resolution. But scholars have wanted to find in it a more specific meaning. Violet Alford gives it a vegetal reading, seeing it as a rite intended to "bring bumper harvests to the maize-fields of Lantz."[15] Iribarren suggests a reference to more recent history (or legend). "The giant," he writes, "is named Miel Otxin, in memory of a famous bandit who, according to tradition, committed many misdeeds in this part of the mountains."[16] In keeping with this reading, the *ziripot* is "the valiant hero who volunteered to capture the bandit."[17] The legends of banditry are still current. In the attic dressing room, I was told that the captured bandit Miel Otxin would be led in triumph through the streets.

I suspect that, as is the case elsewhere, Lantz's public transcript of victory over banditry conceals a hidden transcript of Carnival sympathy with

10.7   *Zaldiko* and felled *ziripot*. Lantz, 2001.

those who redistribute power and property. In Bielsa, Cornelio is something of a minor bandit and a rake. In Vilafranca, the bandit Joan de Serralonga is a hero of the patronal saint's day procession. In Mexico, during the Carnival at Huejotzingo (Puebla), the popular bandit Agustín Lorenzo annually elopes with a wealthy landowner's daughter and throws money to the crowd.[18] Whatever the villagers may tell outsiders, Lantz's performance presents Miel Otxin not as a villain but as a smiling folk hero.

Juan Garmendia Larrañaga links Miel Otxin less to a bandit than to Saint Pansard (Saint Paunch) or Zampantzar, the corpulent patron saint of Carnival in France and the Basque Country. An effigy of Zampantzar is burned at the close of several Basque Carnivals.[19] In a tradition dating back at least to late-fifteenth-century Abbeys of Misrule, Pansard has fought Lent in Carnival plays, enrolling good food and drink as his allies against the Lenten army of ashes and misery. The charges brought against Pansard—theft, seduction, and gluttony—establish him as close kin of Cornelio and other Carnival bandits.[20] Lantz's rotund *ziripot* can also trace his ancestry to Saint Pansard. A pair of almost identical figures take part in the nearby Carnival of Zaldundo (Alava), where they are identified unequivocally as *zampantzas*.[21] Nothing in the action in Lantz suggests that the *ziripot* has captured Miel Otxin. On the contrary, the bandit and the fat man together represent the social upheaval and gluttonous appetite of Carnival, the one resisting hierarchies of power and the other the ascetic restrictions of Lent.

The unusually spare construction of the *zaldiko* and its repeated attacks on the *ziripot* make better sense in this context. The skinny hobbyhorse, stripped of its usual voluminous skirt, recalls the meager diet of Lent. In traditional dramatizations of the battle between Carnival and Lent, the latter often rides a scrawny horse.[22] At the front of the parade, the horse's forced submission to the gloomy blacksmiths enacts the constant reimposition of hierarchical order. If Lent is to succeed, wildness must be domesticated. In Lantz, the hobbyhorse is shod. In Basque Carnivals in France, he is castrated.[23]

Lantz's Carnival procession thus stretches between the two poles of Carnival and Lent, the point of contact being the confrontation between the aggressive hobbyhorse and the genial fat man. With this insight, the full scope of the hidden transcript begins to emerge. For the Lenten vanguard of the procession is peopled by demonic *txatxos* and infernal *arotzak*, while its Carnival rear is dominated by a cruciform effigy unavoidably reminiscent of a processional crucifix. The hostile figure of the Lenten hobbyhorse launches its attacks on the Carnival fat man from the realms of hell. The fat man walks in the shadow of the cross. Contrary to all official rhetoric, the folk theologians of Lantz enact a battle between diabolic Lent and Christian Carnival.

This heady realignment of the seasonal battle is reinforced (and its theological implications extended) by the striking structural similarities between Lantz's Carnival parade and the familiar Corpus Christi and patronal saints' day processions. Barcelona's fifteenth-century Corpus Christi procession and Vilafranca del Penedès's twentieth-century patronal saint's day procession—two fully developed examples of the genre—both begin with a mob of devils clearing the streets and threatening the crowds. The *arotzak* and *txatxos* play this role in Lantz. Vilafranca's devils are followed by a collection of figures, largely borrowed from Barcelona's Corpus Christi repertoire, that bridge the gap between the profane beginning of the procession and its sacred end: a bestiary of eagles and hobbyhorses, a collection of grotesques (giants, dwarfs, and big-heads), and troupes of human dancers and acrobats. Lantz, both smaller in size and more narrowly focused on the battle between Carnival and Lent, has just two such figures: the hobbyhorse and the fat man.

The hobbyhorse is a frequent participant in both Corpus Christi and patronal saints' day festivities. Locally, a *zaldiko* of more conventional skirted design has taken part in Pamplona's festival of San Fermín (more famous for its running of the bulls) since at least 1598.[24] Although less common, the fat man also appears in such contexts. Two *cabezudos* (big-heads) named Padre Pando (Father Fat-and-Slow) and Madre Papahuevos (Mother Egg-Gulper) joined Seville's Corpus Christi procession in the early eighteenth century. A drawing from 1747 shows the pair wearing voluminous cloaks that render them obese rather than big-headed.[25] Cervantes's pot-bellied Sancho Panza, whose name proclaims his close kinship to Saint Pansard, rode with his Lenten master, Don Quijote, in a procession in Zaragoza in October 1614 celebrating the beatification of Saint Teresa of Avila.[26]

Corpus Christi and patronal saints' day processions stretch between the poles of sacred and profane. Beginning with devils and fireworks, they end with an image of the patron saint or with the host in an elaborate monstrance. Lantz's Carnival parade is similarly constructed: Miel Otxin, his cruciform design recalling the posture of the crucified Christ, occupies the sacred final place. But Miel Otxin differs from his more conventionally religious equivalents. Neither overshadowed by a costly monstrance nor surrounded by dignitaries, he remains free of clerical power. He may have been captured, but one has the sense that he yielded voluntarily and could, if he wished, break free at any moment. Larger than life, he dominates the parade. Moreover, alone of all the Carnival characters in Lantz, he has a face. Instead of a diminutive saint or a faceless sacramental wafer, Lantz parades a smiling giant.

The boy in white confirms the sacred status of the processional rear. While the umbrella held above him may have been nothing more than protection against the snow, it suggested to me a parody of the baldachin under which priest and monstrance walk in the Corpus Christi procession. (We have already seen an umbrella used for similar effect by the Judge in Camuñas's mock inquisition.) The boy reminded me not of a female mourner—although he may have had dual referents—but of the priest in white vestments who accompanies the host in the Corpus Christi procession. The crowd of pilgrims follows.

The resemblance of Lantz's Carnival parade to Corpus Christi and patronal saints' day processions further illuminates its hidden transcript, for it superimposes the poles of sacred and profane on those of Carnival and Lent. Lent is again placed in the profane vanguard of the procession and Carnival in the sacred rear. The parade thus challenges the demonization of Carnival, reclaiming the earlier link between Carnival and the incarnational topsy-turvydom of Christmas. The parade also points forward to Easter. Not only does Miel Otxin visually recall the crucified Christ, but the effigy's positional equivalence to the statue of the martyred saint or the sacramental body of Christ reinforces this link. So does the sense of voluntary captivity and the reading of the story of the Passion. (I did not hear the latter, but I may have missed it in the confusion immediately before the execution.)

Miel Otxin is not the bloody Christ of church art, a tortured victim modeling for subordinate devotees the proper submission of the poor to pain and injustice. Such obedience in Lantz's Carnival is imposed on a wild horse by gloomy, diabolic blacksmiths. Miel Otxin is instead a good-natured bandit, redistributing private property and befriending the gluttonous *ziripot*, happy (like the Jesus of the gospels) to "eat and drink with . . . sinners" (Luke 5:30). When, like the Jesus of the Easter narrative, the captured Miel Otxin is paraded by demonic forces, neither he nor the *ziripot* fights back. Instead, Miel Otxin offers himself, as one observer puts it, as "the scapegoat that bears all of the communities' failings and sins."[27]

The Carnivals of Lantz and Bielsa may well be parodies of sacred rites. But, like the censing of old shoe leather during the Feast of Fools, they are parodies that lend themselves to a serious theological reading. They mock ritual in order to retrieve meaning. The Christmas stench of smoking leather parodied the elaborate censing of the altar during the singing of the Magnificat, exposing the dissonance between a song of divine reversal and a ritual of human pomp. Lantz's Carnival borrows the iconography of religious processions in order to transpose the official values of Carnival and Lent, demonizing the latter and making the former once again a Christian feast.

Just as in Sariñena Antolín's enjoyment of communal song and dance reclaims the implications of the doctrine of the Incarnation, so in Lantz and Bielsa the cheerful immolation of a substitutionary effigy reclaims the clarity of divine forgiveness. Cornelio and Miel Otxin reenact the substitutionary sacrifice of Christ in a kind of carnivalesque folk mass, conducted— without need or benefit of clergy—by the community itself. The Carnival effigies affirm human fleshliness against the squeamishness of Lent; and, rather than threaten condemnation for those frailties and excesses to which human flesh is prone, they absorb all blame. Christ/Cornelio/Miel Otxin has borne our sins. It's that simple. The community, transformed, dances its thanksgiving.

II.
Safe for the Bourgeoisie
(BELGIUM)

NOT ALL CARNIVALS engage directly with the Christian narrative and its seasonal rituals, but most invoke the opposing theory of Carnival's link to pre-Christian rites. The motives for doing so vary. Spanish rural Carnivals invoke pagan antiquity as a sign of their moral distance from Franco's Catholic triumphalism and as a proof of age and status. The great urban Carnivals of the Caribbean, such as that of Port of Spain (Trinidad), appropriate the precedent of classical Bacchanalia as a license for present excess. Some northern European Carnivals incline more to bourgeois respectability than to dissipation or religious challenge. Eschewing all but the mildest social satire and keeping transgressive behavior well in bounds, they reinforce rather than contest the prevailing standards of morality and status. In the small Belgian town of Binche, where I spent the last Carnival of the old millennium (1999), pre-Christian antiquity is invoked not as a marker of rebellion but as a measure of local integrity and a repudiation of earlier theories of Spanish courtly influence.

On Carnival Sunday morning, I parked my car along a snowy side street at the edge of town and joined a group of cross-dressed men carrying pretty parasols. These *mam'zelles*, in eighteenth-century wigs and elegant dresses, danced demurely to the fairground melodies of a portable street organ. The organist's wife told me that her husband, Josselin Lebon, was one of only three or four men in all Europe who still made such *orgues de Barbarie* (Barbary organs). She also explained that women in Binche do not wear fancy dress for Carnival because they are too busy preparing meals and sewing costumes for the children and the men. She was herself expecting fifty-two guests for lunch. In a bourgeois Carnival, men dress as women without subverting gender roles.

We made our way to the Grande Place, where a cornucopia of costumes filled the square: mandarins with painted faces fresh from Chinese opera

11.1   Masquerader with painted face. Binche, 1999.

(Fig. 11.1), Tibetan monks with orange pompons hanging from their hats, fat-bottomed pairs of Telly Tubbies, and pollinating bumblebees. While some groups danced in small circles to a Barbary organ, others marched in place to the military rhythm of several snare drums and a single thudding bass drum. Crusaders, clowns, and courtiers mingled with Red Indians, a regiment of tin soldiers from Hans Christian Andersen, and aristocrats en route to a masked ball. Male cocktail waitresses flaunted hairy legs, blond wigs, and plastic breasts but otherwise behaved themselves: no transvestite flirting here. In Loíza I had seen the marginalized assert themselves and in Laza the rural poor make fun of those in power, but in Binche I saw the middle class dress up in costumes that aspired to the exotic and the silly. Masqueraders proudly posed for photographs.[1]

In the afternoon, some fifteen hundred *travestis* (masqueraders) in a dozen distinct *sociétés*—heirs to the *sociétés joyeuses*—descended from the railway station at the top of town to the Grande Place. Brass bands added a robust melody to the drums. Spectators in warm coats, three or four deep, lined the street. Some threw confetti. The parade offered very little in the way of satire and no hostile mockery. Occasional groups of masqueraders poked fun at the doping scandals of the previous year's Tour de France or at the inflation that had followed the introduction of the Euro, but none made fun of local or even specifically Belgian life.[2] There was no enacted threat of violence or obscenity. No act or costume risked offense. No one dared the anonymity of complete disguise. Faces were painted or eyes covered, but the wearing of a full mask was a privilege reserved for Binche's beloved Gilles, who would appear only on Carnival Tuesday. When the last of the masqueraders reached the Grande Place, it was already cold and dark.

Children roamed the streets on Monday, the older ones spraying plastic string from cans and playing at confetti terrorists, littering the streets and passersby with colored dots. Once it had been flour, "which damaged clothes irreparably,"[3] but thrift and cleanliness now ruled amid disorder. Plastic bags of punched paper holes were selling well. I filmed and fled from gangs of friendly paper hoodlums.

Afterwards, I sheltered from the cold inside a bar where confetti piled like paper sawdust on the floor. An older woman danced on a tabletop, then sat astride her husband's shoulders. Supported by a friend, he gamely tottered around the room. A Barbary organ played cheerfully. Later, older couples swished amid the litter to the music of a two-man band. A family of five collected fistfuls of confetti, stuffed cut paper down each other's shirts, and laughed. Father tackled daughter's boyfriend, shoveling confetti in his fallen rival's mouth; daughter plunged into the rescue, both knees pinioning her father's arms; inebriated mother intervened and toppled; son shoved paper down his sister's pants; and so till all were rolling, laughing, on the floor, stuttering, spluttering, scattering confetti. The band played on. When the boyfriend threw confetti at a friend of mine, she leaped the table in a single bound and fell on him. I went after her. Carnival broke through middle-class decorum. We were seven tipsy revelers.

In the late afternoon, I danced hand in hand with several hundred costumed children in a circle round the square. We stamped our feet lightly to the rhythm of the drums and raised and dropped our hands in time. Officials in straw boaters made sure no gaps appeared, for Binche's civic rhetoric declares the unbroken circle "a ring of friendship, which shows that, amidst the joy of Carnival, all barriers of ideological and political difference collapse."[4] Afterwards, the children marched out of the square in their separate groups, armed with blood oranges in little wicker baskets. Diminutive musketeers from Dumas and whiskered pantomime cats tossed oranges at the crowd. Spectators caught the fruit and gave it back to have it thrown again. After dark, to the music of a brass band, we watched fireworks explode in the square outside the railway station. It was all over by 8:30 P.M. Children's Carnival ended by bedtime. Undressing, I dropped layers of confetti on my bathroom floor.

On Tuesday morning, Binche's pride and joy, the Gilles, came out. Dressed in padded suits in Belgium's national colors of black, yellow, and orange, with belts of bells around the waist, some nine hundred Gilles in their several *sociétés* marched the streets to pounding drums. On their feet, to supplement the rhythm of the bells and drums, the Gilles wore wooden clogs. They hid their faces behind pale masks with painted green lunettes and sideburns, mustache, and a daub of a goatee in the style of Napoleon III (1848–1871).[5] The masks were made of waxed cloth. A white skullcap, extending downwards over the ears and tied in a white bow beneath the chin, completed the disguise. Each man clutched in his right hand a broom twelve to eighteen inches long. (In earlier years, like those of the *txatxos* in Lantz, the brooms had been full-length weapons.) For now, the marching was informal, interrupted by long intervals spent standing in the street, drinking, outside bars. While they drank, they doffed their masks. They had not yet donned their feather headdresses.

I asked the meaning of their costumes. The masks, I was told, erased social distinctions and gave everyone the same identity. The lunettes ("a mask on a mask") reinforced this uniformity. The brooms were for driving out winter, the oranges a sign of spring. The white ruffs around their necks recalled the fashion at the court of Mary of Hungary. Younger sister of the emperor (and king of Spain) Charles V, Mary had built a sumptuous Renaissance palace in town in 1545 only to see it destroyed by the forces of Henry II of France in 1554. The feathers that the Gilles would wear that afternoon derived, they said, from Incas represented at a masque at Mary's court in 1549. I knew the sources of these theories. In Binche, as in Loíza, scholarly theory has become the material of folk informants.

There was also a company of Peasants, in dark blue coats, white trousers, and long-ribboned hats, who wore pale, bespectacled masks akin to those of the Gilles but clean-shaven. A group of Harlequins, mostly children, wore white ruffs, green hats, and dark and furry masks. A children's society of Pierrots wore black half-masks and loose tunics in pastel colors. Harlequins and Pierrots were borrowed from the world of the Comédie Italienne. This

11.2   Masked Gilles. Binche, 1999.

popular French version of the commedia dell'arte, successfully exploiting stock characters, masks, and plots, flourished in France from the sixteenth century until the end of the eighteenth century, when it lost its hold on the professional stage. It now survives in Carnivals and folk traditions.[6]

The Peasants, too, have their origin not in the rural landscape around Binche but in the commedia dell'arte. Many of the *zanni*, or valet-buffoons, of the commedia—such as Harlequin and Pierrot—were of peasant stock. When Pierrot first appeared on the French stage, in Molière's *Don Juan ou Le Festin de Pierre* (first performed on Carnival Sunday, 15 February 1665), he was listed as a *paysan* (peasant).[7] Writing of Binche's Carnival in 1900, Léo Claretie remarked that the Peasant's costume "recalls the Italian farce."[8] Other traces of the commedia dell'arte in Binche include the olive-tinted half-mask with a furred mustache worn by the town's Harlequins, which properly belongs to another commedia character, Brighella,[9] and, as we shall see, the Gilles themselves.

As the morning progressed in Binche, the several companies arrived in turn outside the old town hall, where each danced in a circle, every Gilles holding with his left hand his neighbor's broom (Fig. 11.2). Then, one by one, the *sociétés* crowded, dancing, into the main chamber of the town hall, where they faced the municipal authorities. For several minutes, drums beat, feet stamped, bells rang, and masked men brandished their symbolic weap-

11.3   Gilles in feathered headdresses. Binche, 1999.

ons in a faint memory of invasive challenge to authority. When the drums stopped, the clogs stilled, the Gilles unmasked, and the mayor greeted them with a brief and genial speech of welcome. Standing beside the mayor, in ceremonial costume, was the Prince of the Carnival of Alost, a town thirty-five miles to the north. He brought collegial greetings.

Over lunch, my neighbor at table told me that the Gilles' padded backs and chests were intended as a sign of wealth but that their clogs were the common footwear of an earlier century. I asked if commoners in clogs had once made fun of wealthy merchants. He didn't know, but he agreed that mockery was now lacking in Binche's Carnival. After lunch, I joined the formal cortege marching slowly down the broad Avenue Charles Deliège towards the Grande Place. In front were children's groups of Little Gilles and Pierrots. Harlequins and Peasants followed. Behind them walked the several companies of adult Gilles, each man now sporting a mushroom cloud of more than three hundred white ostrich feathers (Fig. 11.3).[10] All the masqueraders carried wicker baskets—or in the case of the Peasants, leather pouches—packed with blood oranges, which they tossed amiably into the crowd. (Some three hundred thousand oranges are thrown during Binche's

Carnival. Trucks meet a special train from Spain at Mons, load up, and drive the oranges to Binche, where merchants announce the fruit's arrival and its price.)[11] None but those in costume were supposed to enter the square, but a policeman kindly let me pass.

As we invaded the square, the Gilles hurled a barrage of oranges at Albert II and Paola, the king and queen of Belgium, who were visiting the Carnival this year. They waved politely from a balcony behind a screen. For all their lingering memory of insurgent threat, the Gilles were now a dignified and strangely tame embodiment of Carnival. Forming a massive circle round the margins of the square, they danced a *rondeau* (ring dance).

I ate supper at a common table in a crowded bar: a bowl of onion soup, soused herring, bread, and beer. An older couple told me Carnival had been much wilder in their youth: the Gilles had thrown so many oranges that the grandmother of the present king had seemed quite blood-bespattered.[12] Students from Brussels, armed with inflated pig's bladders, had attacked spectators, especially those in bowler hats, and, when the bladders burst, beaten passersby with remnant sticks. (Blaming Carnival excess on outsiders is a characteristic ploy of residents of Binche, but history records that "before 1914" it was "the young Binchois" males who wielded the bladders.[13] Claretie wrote in 1900 that any visitor not wearing a mask was in danger of attack by locals armed with bladders and oranges. Blows with remnant sticks sometimes drew blood.)[14] Binche's Carnival, the older couple told me, had also boasted higher aspirations. The wealthy bourgeoisie had dressed as aristocracy and danced at masked balls. Few balls survive these days; the expenses are prohibitive. Even to dress as a Gilles is costly: to rent a feathered headdress for the day costs ten thousand Belgian francs (U.S.$300).

After dark, wearing neither masks nor feathers, the Gilles stormed the square. A dense crowd stood around the edges, watching. Drums pounded, bands played loudly, and Bengal lights flared. The red lights cast monstrous shadows on the surrounding walls, creating the effect of fire without the danger. Then, after a final display of pyrotechnics, the Gilles danced a communal *rondeau* around the square. The show was over by 10:00 P.M., but I'm told informal drumming and dancing continued until daybreak. At dawn the police start confiscating drumsticks.[15]

It is tempting to find the origins of Binche's Carnival in the famous Fêtes de Binche of August 1549, when Mary of Hungary entertained her imperial brother Charles V and her nephew Philip II of Spain at her fortified palace just up the street from the Grande Place. After dinner one night, an elaborate sword dance was staged in the great hall of the palace. According to several eyewitness accounts, four plumed dancers in masks with long white beards escorted four ladies of the court onto the dance floor. When their "chaste" dance was interrupted by four "younger" dancers, also in feathers, the old men drew swords and fought their younger rivals. Taking advantage of this distraction, eight "savages" in feathers and "rustic" dress entered the hall and seized the watching women. Urban age and youth at once united against the wild invaders and a "terrible battle" ensued. This is the moment captured in a famous colored drawing of the sword dance. Then the wild men's attendants escorted the apparently willing women to a waiting chariot, the "savages" followed, and the courtiers were left bereft.[16]

There is something carnivalesque about this: wild men invade the urban safety of the court, seize its women, and disappear into the darkness. The women, abandoning both decorum and their men, go willingly. There also seems to be, in the drawing, a cousin of the cross-dressed Carnival *mam'zelle,* his role unnoticed and unexplained in any of the narrative accounts: one of the costumed ladies' maids, standing in the center foreground, is clearly bearded. But it was not the evening's social reversals that caught the eye of subsequent local historians; it was the feathers. For the Gilles, too, wear feathers.

In 1872 a journalist in Tournai published an article on Binche's Carnival in which he claimed that the Gilles were descendants of the feathered dancers who performed in Mary of Hungary's court in 1549 and that those dancers represented Incas conquered by the Spanish.[17] Despite the lack of any mention of Incas in the eyewitness accounts or of any documentary link between the summer games at Mary's palace and Binche's Carnival, the idea that the Gilles represented Incas gradually took hold. Eventually, according to Samuël Glotz, it became "a local carnivalesque article of faith to which it would have been sacrilegious for a good Binchois not to have adhered."[18]

Beginning in 1949, with the first edition of his *Carnaval de Binche,* Glotz attacked the theory of Spanish origins and advanced an alternative theory of his own. Criticizing the "amateurs of exoticism and romanticism" who had propagated the earlier "fantasy," Glotz suggested that the roots of Binche's Carnival were much older and owed nothing to Spanish ceremonial. Instead, he found in Binche's Carnival a spring fertility rite rooted in ancient local practice. According to Glotz, the short brooms carried by the Gilles are for driving out winter and the scattered oranges—imported ironically from Spain—represent the imminent arrival of spring. The exclusively male identity of the Gilles, their uniform masks, their belts of bells, their shuffling march, and the rhythmic pounding of their drums confirm Glotz's impression that the Gilles are descended from a prehistoric seasonal rite.[19]

Unfortunately, Glotz's theory, too, lacks documentary evidence. Moreover, it fails to account for all the data. Sensing this, the Gilles move to and fro between the theories. Asked about the brooms and oranges, they speak of winter and spring. Asked about the feathers, they talk of Mary of Hungary and the Incas. One Gilles told me that Glotz's book was "like a Bible" to him.[20] Others admit that the older theory "still has considerable credibility in the minds of the local populace."[21]

The historical record suggests a more disreputable origin for the Gilles, one that successive theories of courtly parentage and local antiquity concealed even as the Carnival itself was transformed from belligerent misrule to bourgeois respectability. The earliest extant references to Carnival in Binche are from the late fourteenth century. In 1394 six wooden candlesticks were purchased to illuminate the town hall at night during Carnival. Two years later, on Carnival Sunday, the town magistrate sent a servant to Beaumont, a town to the south of Binche, to buy "three or four vats" of wine.[22] Scattered references to Carnival follow, including, in 1708, mention of a schoolboy production of a *comédie* "under the aegis of the schoolmaster" and, later in the century, several measures prohibiting disguise.[23]

The first mention of the town's distinctive masked Gilles comes from 1795, less than a year after Napoleon's armies had overrun that part of the Hapsburg Empire that is now Belgium. When the newly installed Republican authorities banned all Carnival masquerades, one François Gaillard was arrested for appearing in the streets "masked, dressed in the costume known locally as the Gille [*sic*], and armed with a large stick."[24] Although this passing mention in a contemporary letter suggests that Gilles was no innovation in Binche in 1795, it does not tell us how much earlier Gilles had been known locally. Nor does it tell us what his costume was.

The name provides a clue. Gilles, like Harlequin and Pierrot, was a popular character in the Comédie Italienne. Just as the French Arlequin derived from the Italian Arlecchino and Pierrot from Pedrolino or Piero, so Gilles may owe his name to an Italian ancestor in the commedia dell'arte. Giglio is first recorded in Italy in 1531. Like Pedrolino, Pierrot, and Gilles, he "dressed in white flannel, and wore white shoes and a head-band of the same color."[25] Ironically, given Glotz's resistance to the idea of Spanish influence, Giglio's character may have been that of a Spanish servant who spoke a comic jargon of mixed Spanish and Italian.[26]

By the 1640s the role of Gilles the foolish servant was common enough on the French stage for more than one typecast comedian to adopt the stage name Gilles le Niais (Gilles the Simpleton). A writer and performer of popular songs by the name of de Tourniquet appeared under the pseudonym Gilles le Niais in 1646.[27] If we can trust a reference in Antoine Baudeau de Somaize's play, *Les véritables précieuses* (1660), the leader of a troupe of comic actors by the name of de La Force took an identical pseudonym. Victor Fournel believed this to be the same Gilles le Niais who left a "very rare" volume of plays.[28]

The titles of three of the many satirical pamphlets known collectively as Mazarinades—after Cardinal Mazarin, chief minister of France between 1642 and 1661—refer to Gilles le Niais. Although most of the Mazarinades were published during the civil war of the Fronde (1649–1652), one of those that mentions Gilles is undated and may have been directed against Mazarin's predecessor, Cardinal Richelieu, in power from 1624 to 1642. If so, it would be the earliest reference to Gilles in France. Another, printed in 1649, refers to Flanders and may be the first written record to place Gilles in territory that is now a part of Belgium.[29] By the end of the century, Gilles le Niais had found his way into learned French dictionaries. Antoine Furetière's *Dictionnaire universel* (1690), noting that *s'enfariner* (to sprinkle oneself with flour) is often used of "fools and comedians who daub their faces with flour to make people laugh," cites the example of Gilles le Niais.[30] (In the Comédie Italienne, instead of wearing a mask, Gilles traditionally powdered his face.) Gilles Ménage, in his *Dictionnaire étymologique* (1694), notes, under his entry for Gilles, "In my youth, there was a juggler [*bateleur*] in Paris who was called Gilles le Niais."[31]

In 1697 the commedia dell'arte troupes were banished from their home theater in Paris. For the next nineteen years, they performed without license at the city's outdoor fairs. Several actors played the part of Gilles—dropping the nickname but not the character of the Simpleton—during this period.[32] One was known as Gilles the Lame. His injury, sustained in a traffic accident, didn't prevent him from singing songs while "dancing on the tightrope with grace and lightness."[33] Another "was the first to dance on the rope wearing wooden clogs."[34] Clogs, then as now, may have been a distinctive part of Gilles's costume. Adelson Garin cites an unattributed description of Gilles as an "actor of farces, shod in clogs," and a seventeenth-century engraving of Gilles le Niais shows him wearing clogs very similar to those now worn by the Gilles of Binche.[35]

The personality of the fairground Gilles was not one that would please the bourgeoisie of Binche, for he was "a character of more simplicity than sense and of less decency than either."[36] He appeared most often in short *parades,* burlesque farces mounted on trestle stages outside the fairground theaters. The *parades* were designed to entice paying spectators inside for the full show. In Thomas-Simon Gueullette's *Le marchand de merdre* (*The Shit Merchant*), Harlequin persuades Gilles that there is money to be made in selling excrement. Gilles touts a barrel round the fairground, crying, in a fine parody of mercantile advertising, "Who wants my shit? Money for my shit! It's fresh."[37]

The roles of Gilles and Pierrot seem to have merged in the eighteenth century, with the former name becoming the more popular. Antoine Watteau's famous painting, known variously as *Le Grand Gilles* or *Pierrot* (ca. 1716–1719), depicts an actor in the common costume of Gilles and Pierrot: white shoes, baggy white trousers and tunic, white ruff, white skullcap, and straw-colored hat.[38] Gilles/Pierrot's white ruff is a more likely source of the one worn by the Gilles of Binche than is the fashionable dress of Mary of Hungary's court. The same is true of Gilles/Pierrot's skullcap. A seventeenth-century engraving of the comic Gilles, or Gilotin, shows a skullcap extended over the ears and tied in a bow beneath the chin in exactly the manner of the modern Gilles of Binche.[39]

Gilles/Pierrot's name appears in the police files more often than any other commedia character during the two decades of his banishment to the fairs. Pierrot "took an especial delight in confusing the police spies, who were never quite certain about the real meaning of his mime, although they knew, almost instinctively, that its nature was basically subversive, and that Pierrot's performance was designed to provoke his audience to jeer at the authorities."[40] He frequently appeared in the police files under the name Gilles.

Gilles/Pierrot's persistently subversive nature adds poignancy to Watteau's portrayal of him in a pose that has reminded many of paintings of Christ. In *Le Grand Gilles,* the character's hat, tilted backwards so that only the wide brim is visible, reminds the viewer of a halo. In Watteau's *Comédiens italiens* (ca. 1719–1720), the halo-hat is extended upwards by an effusion of light in the painted scenery immediately behind Pierrot's head and a gilt-edged oval in the architecture immediately above the light. The arrangement of the players, with Scaramouche to one side gesturing towards Pierrot at center stage, is reminiscent of the relationship between Pilate and Christ in Rembrandt's etching, *Ecce Homo.*[41] Whether Watteau's painting has so specific an artistic reference is impossible to prove, but the traces of a halo are indisputable and lend an aura of sanctity to Pierrot the innocent rogue.[42] The good burghers of Binche took a different approach. Rather than consecrate a comic simpleton, they ennobled Gilles, rendering his costume patriotic and his character respectable. This was not how he had arrived in town. Gilles's first recorded appearance in Binche, in 1795, was almost certainly as a commedia clown in the traditional white costume "known locally" and elsewhere "as the Gille." "Masked" and "armed with a large stick," in defiance of a Republican ban on Carnival masking, François Gaillard was making use of a long tradition of subversive Gilles to challenge local authority. Glotz doesn't like this idea. Well aware of Gilles's long commedia heritage, he denies its influence on the Gilles of Binche in anything but name.[43]

The transformation of Gilles was part of the gradual taming of Binche's Carnival over the course of the nineteenth century. The Republican authorities repeatedly banned all masks or confined them to the daylight hours of the "three last days of Carnival." The Dutch, who ruled the area briefly after 1815, and the burgomasters, who governed the town after Belgian independence in 1831, were no more favorable to Carnival masking. Permitting inoffensive masks a little later at night but still only on the three days of Carnival, a police decree of 1832 specifically prohibited "all disguises contrary to decency [or that imitate] the uniforms of clergy, military personnel, or civil servants." The same decree forbade revelers to carry any weapon or instrument "that might [be used to] wound the masqueraders or the spectators," to strike one another "with bladders [or] bags of powder," "to throw water, powder, or bran at people," or to make personal allusions under cover of a mask. Three years later, they insisted that there be "no tumult or anything else that could trouble the tranquility or the safety of [Binche's] citizens during Carnival."[44]

Oranges replaced the older custom of throwing bread or apples. The more exotic and expensive fruit "better corresponded" to the growing local "prestige of the character" of the Gilles[45] and, since it could neither be baked nor grown at home, meant more profit for the merchants. Trade during Carnival was assiduously protected by police decrees. When, on 16 February 1836, the movable date of Carnival Tuesday coincided with the fixed date of Binche's monthly horse fair, which had by then become "an event of considerable economic importance," masks were only permitted after 2:00 P.M. By then most of the trading was over. In the same year, the police banned the Carnival custom of "forcing oneself into a house or store" to demand free food and drink.[46]

Amid a prolonged litany of such prohibitions, which would not have been repeated had they been obeyed, one exempted the Gilles. In 1857 full-length brooms, which had been used as weapons by the Carnival masqueraders, were banned, but the ban specified, "This prohibition does not apply to the Gilles." Glotz believes that this exemption "shows the importance of the Gilles . . . even among the bourgeoisie. . . . Of all the masks, only [the Gilles] found grace in the eyes of the leading citizens."[47] On the other hand, the decree may have been nothing more than an attempt to limit the damage inflicted by the brooms by confining them to one character.

The Gilles were still something of a threat to good order in the 1860s. They appear by then to have exchanged their traditional commedia costume for something closer to that of a Carnival wild man, animal, or demon. A newspaper account from 1862 describes the Gilles as wearing "grey cloth decorated with figures of animals in all colors . . . , two formidable humps, an immense hooded cape, loaded with lace and ribbons, . . . [and] enormous clogs covered in sheepskin." Each Gilles carried "a broom without a handle," with which he struck the back of "unmasked companions." Another account from the same year mentions a "tapered hat, . . . covered with a profusion of lace, ribbons, and feathers."[48] Something of this wildness survives even in Claretie's account of the Carnival written, in the fictional context of a novel, as the century drew to a close.[49]

Gradually, however, the Gilles were domesticated. A full mask in the dignified style of Napoleon III was added sometime after 1850, perhaps replacing a more traditional commedia mask or a face whitened by flour.[50] (A reference to "gilles enfarinés [Gilles sprinkled with flour]" survives from Tournai in 1855.)[51] After the theory that the Gilles originated in a court masque of Incas was advanced in 1872, the feathered headdresses began to grow more splendid and coincidentally more restrictive of threatening carnivalesque movement. Royal lions ousted all the other animals from the costume by 1875, the same year that the national colors red, yellow, and black first dominated the Gilles' suits.[52] The Gilles lost any oppositional force they once enjoyed. As they became respectable, they allowed the bourgeois merchants and their sons to take part in a Carnival that, as Glotz insists, now "has nothing orgiastic about it" and has "limited" its "excesses."[53]

Other aspects of Binche's Carnival fell into place. The earlier "flirtation" of mam'zelles gave way to elegant "extravagance."[54] The masqueraders replaced brooms with toy swords or pretty parasols and now beat time in the air rather than on spectators' heads. Flour and bran have been replaced by confetti. Pig's bladders finally disappeared in 1970.[55] (By contrast, the Blancs Moussis [those dressed in white] of the Carnival in Stavelot, near the German border, are armed with brooms, four or five pig bladders apiece, and—clean kin to Laza's flour machine—"a blower-float which is able to hurl five kilos of confetti per second." Thus, the Walloon Department of Tourism happily reports, the Blancs Moussis "spread a cheerful panic among the spectators.")[56]

Against this background of growing respectability, the divergent theories of Carnival's origin in Binche make more sense, for they mask the Gilles' disreputable heredity while preserving a distant hint of danger. Even the bourgeoisie do not really want a Carnival that lacks all hint of the exotic or the oppositional. To suggest that the Gilles represented Incas and that they were brought to Binche by the imperial court of Charles V gave them an exotic aura and an aristocratic pedigree. As talk of empire and the imposition of foreign customs became unfashionable, it was better to find the ancestors of the Gilles in a pre-Christian seasonal rite. The temporally distant pagans of northern Europe replaced the geographically distant heathen of Peru. Both were far enough removed from modern Binche that they offered no real threat. Talk of Incas, Mary of Hungary, and pagan rites of spring add a safe little frisson of Carnival spirit to an annual celebration that, for all its value as entertainment and as an exercise in communal bonding, has made the world of Carnival safe for the bourgeoisie.

Perhaps, however, the old oppositional courage of the Gilles of Binche is not entirely lost but only stored away until needed. The German occupation of Belgium between 1940 and 1945 meant the deportation of many of Binche's citizens and the suspension of its Carnival. In a concentration camp in Wroclaw (Poland), six Binchois prisoners refused to yield. As Carnival approached, they made six Gilles costumes from packing cloth, applying lions, suns, coats of arms, and national flags in red, yellow, and black. They constructed two "feathered" headdresses and "lace" ruffs by cutting white packing paper into thin strips. They made wicker baskets. One of the men wrote later, "When [we] descended into the courtyard [in our costumes], there was an indescribable ovation and the whole camp (maybe three hundred prisoners) followed [us]."[57] Carnival at its best protests injustice.

I 2.
Devils and Decorum
(TRINIDAD)

ON MY FIRST DAY on the island of Trinidad, I was attacked by robbers, mesmerized by devils, and accused by an unwed mother of fathering her child. I had arrived in Port of Spain on Carnival Friday 1996, just in time for the old mas parade. While Binche summons the Romantic theory of rural pre-Christian ritual to dignify its Carnival, Trinidad invokes the classical precedent of Bacchanal to license Carnival excess. But like Binche's more restrained revels, Port of Spain's Carnival has a respectable purpose: it feeds the local economy, builds community, and diverts attention from a violent past. In both Binche and Trinidad, a pretty face obscures an older body of protest.

At least, that's the way it's supposed to work. But controlling the Carnival script is not as easy in a major Caribbean port as it is in a small Belgian market town. For more than a century, Port of Spain's drive towards commercialization and middle-class decorum has clashed with its refusal to relinquish violent memories of slavery. Caribbean notions of decorum are, of course, very different from those that prevail in Belgium. Carnival crowds in Port of Spain stretch for miles. The music is deafening and the costumes gaudy. The tropical heat allows the human body to be celebrated with greater freedom than in wintry Binche. But the excesses of fancy mas, as the commercially sponsored layer of Trinidad's Carnival is known, are, like Binche's orderly parades, affirmative rather than confrontational. It is old mas, with its traditional masqueraders and its eruption of misrule in the darkness of Jouvay (Carnival Monday) morning, that recalls the more aggressive early days of postemancipation Carnival. I began with the old mas parade.

The traditional masqueraders gathered in a downtown schoolyard.[1] Dame Lorraine, padded breasts and backside stretching her floral print dress, chatted with two of her "daughters." Fanning themselves in the oppressive heat, they mocked the pretensions of foreign plantation wives and their well-to-do descendants. Baby Dolls, played by black girls in whiteface, clutched infant dolls and baby bottles. The younger ones were too shy to demand support from "fathers" in the crowd, but an older Baby Doll accosted me. I bought my freedom from public scandal with a Trinidad dollar (worth about U.S.$0.15). Two foam rubber burrokeets (hobbyhorses) were even more sexually aggressive. Ridden by young men, the animals were visibly gendered: large male genitalia hung down between the back legs of one, while the other displayed a bright red vulva. The stallion frequently mounted the mare, shuddering in mock orgasm as it completed its pleasure.

Two Pierrots Grenades, dressed from head to toe in multicolored strips of fabric, displayed their eccentric spelling skills ("chicken in the car and the car can't go dats de way to spell Chicago"). In the old days, they used to fight with whips.[2] Midnight Robbers, wearing sequined capes and monstrous hats, blew whistles and brandished toy guns and daggers. Confronting one another, they dueled not with weapons but with bombastic tales of their own villainy.[3] One robber, who went by the name Admiral Benbow, later sat with me on a park bench. In his tirades, he said, he would accuse another robber of being "demonic, even Lucifer himself, who was incarnate as Goliath, Nebuchadnezzar, Herod, and Napoleon," and would announce that his own character knelt in submission to "none but the Master." Also making reference to biblical themes were a skeletal Grim Reaper and a masked demonic Bookman, inscribing our sins in a large book. The Bookman wore a white papier-mâché mask. "Is it a coincidence," I was asked by one of the masqueraders, "that Satan always look like this? He look very European to me."

A tambour-bamboo band beat hollow lengths of bamboo rhythmically against the ground. Tambour-bamboo developed in the late nineteenth century as an alternative to the traditional African drums banned by the British. Now the band accompanied a group of schoolboy stick fighters. Elsewhere in the yard, softer music came from a trio of Minstrel Boys, two black men and a woman in whiteface who sang plantation songs from the southern USA, simultaneously reversing the burlesque of white minstrels in blackface and honoring the memory of black slaves (Fig. 12.1).[4]

The most popular costumes in the yard were those of the Indians. Fancy Indians were modeled on the Plains Indians of North America. Black Indians imitated African and indigenous Caribbean modes of dress. A few Guarahoons, in bright red clothing, recalled the indigenous Warao people of the Orinoco delta who, until the 1930s, rowed their pirogues to Trinidad for trade. Older Trinidadians remember that the Warao painted themselves for festive occasions with a red berry dye. For blacks to dress as Indians is both

12.1   Theresa Morilla Montano leads the Minstrel Boys. Port of Spain, 1996.

to exploit the Carnival impulse to dress as those less "civilized" than ourselves and to identify with those who have resisted and sometimes defeated
white colonists.[5]

The most impressive figures were the blue devils. Daubed from head to
toe—skin and clothes—in blue mud and dressed in as little as shorts or as
much as coveralls and gum boots, they emerged at the last moment into the
schoolyard. They blew whistles and emitted high-pitched, rhythmic cries.
Their eyes had the glazed look of zombies or of men in trances. They chewed
a fruit whose juice and pulp mixed with saliva to produce an ample supply of
red drool that flowed over their chins and chests in graphic imitation of their
victims' blood. Those known as "beasts" were restrained at the end of long
chains or ropes by "imps." The beasts pulled forward or fell into contortions
and writhed on the ground while the imps goaded them. Some of the devils
wore masks or goggles, sprouted dark wings from their backs (see Fig. 12.3
below), carried pitchforks, or blew flames from bottled paraffin torches. At
times, the devils lunged fiercely at the crowd, a single finger jabbing the air
to denote the dollar demanded. Unlike many of the other masqueraders, the
devils stayed in character throughout, never breaking the illusion of posses-

sion to remove a mask or to pause for casual conversation. I saw them relax only once. When a traffic policeman stopped the parade at a downtown intersection, the blue devils rested. Waved on, they returned to full ferocity.[6]

The blue devils have deep roots, like much of Trinidad's Carnival, in the experience of slavery and emancipation. When the British captured Trinidad from Spain in 1797, they found an island largely populated by French colonists and their slaves. The French plantation owners had fled from other islands disturbed by ripples of the French Revolution. The colonial French Carnival was for the most part "a high-society affair of elaborate balls, masking and costuming, street parading in carriages, and house-to-house visiting[7] lasting from Christmas to Shrove Tuesday. But high society masking was also an opportunity to "dress down." According to one nineteenth-century account, "the favorite costume of the ladies was the graceful and costly 'mulatress' of the period, while gentlemen adopted that of the garden Negro, in Creole, *negue jadin,* or black field slave."[8] Such cross-racial masking indulged two "convenient white fantasies," drawn from the men's belief that their slaves were "sensuous" and "hedonistic" and the women's dreams of being desired by their husbands as were the men's "mulatto mistresses."[9] Slaves also imitated their white masters. The wife of a British plantation owner noted how on Christmas morning the slaves used to "flour each other's black faces and curly hair, and call out, 'look at he white face! and he white wig!' "[10] No doubt, more pointed mockery took place in private.

With the emancipation of Trinidad's slaves in 1834, the power of Carnival shifted from white to black. Mockery of upper-class social and military pretensions, the open election of black kings and queens (previously carried out in secret and understood by the authorities to threaten slave revolt),[11] and widespread *jamette* (underworld) participation in the Carnival prevailed. The French Creoles complained bitterly to the newspapers of the degradation of their Carnival and "withdrew from the festival, hoping it would die."[12] When it did not, the authorities took more active but eventually ineffective steps legally to prohibit or forcibly to suppress it.

One mas band that appeared soon after emancipation was a precursor of today's blue devil bands. During the 1848 Carnival, "gangs" of "negroes, as nearly naked as might be, bedaubed with a black varnish," took to the streets. One in each gang "had a long chain and padlock attached to his leg, which chain the others pulled." An English visitor, Charles Day, observed, "What this typified, I was unable to learn; but, as the chained one was occasionally thrown down on the ground, and treated with a mock bastinadoing it probably represented slavery."[13] Day's interpretation was almost certainly correct. In 1856 a writer to the *Port-of-Spain Gazette* grumbled that "devils filled the streets" overnight during Carnival. Two years later, another complained of "the hooting of a parcel of semi-savages . . . exhibiting hellish scenes and the most demoniacal representations of the days of slavery as they were forty years ago."[14]

Yet another report suggests that these scenes may have been related to the preemancipation practice of Canboulay (from *cannes brûlées* [burned canes]). "In the days of slavery," according to a government report in 1881, "whenever fire broke out upon an estate, the slaves on the surrounding properties were immediately mustered and marched to the spot, horns and shells were blown to collect them and the gangs were followed by the drivers cracking their whips and urging with cries and blows to their work." White men found it amusing during Carnival to dress as black slaves and march through the streets carrying torches in imitation of such a nighttime summons. After emancipation, the freed slaves co-opted this mimetic practice for very different ends, representing this scene instead "as a kind of commemoration of the change in their condition."[15] Carnival Canboulay, in other words, changed from a lighthearted (and grossly insensitive) elite depiction of slavery to an enacted remembrance by former slaves of their past humiliation and a celebration of its passing.

Suggesting that "the black varnish applied to an already dark skin" may have been a direct imitation of the white planters' makeup, Errol Hill wonders if "the freed slaves were imitating the white planters who had, in their turn, previously been imitating the bonded slaves."[16] This proposal is rendered even more likely by Day's observation that "every negro, male and female," who took part in the Carnival masquerade in 1848 "wore a white-coloured flesh mask, their wooly hair carefully concealed by handkerchiefs."[17] Wearing a white mask over the face and black varnish over the body recalled the offensive Carnival fantasy of white planters playing black field hands. Freed slaves thus imitated, in a single Carnival character, devils, white planters, and black slaves. To play both planters and devils suggested a kinship between the two. To play both devils and slaves recalled and protested the white demonization of blacks that had sustained slavery. Devils and slaves were, in traditional iconography or brute fact, chained and black.

During the second half of the nineteenth century, Carnival was increasingly dominated by Canboulay, by ritual stick fighting, and by *pissenlit* (piss in bed) bands, in which men dressed in white masks and women's nightgowns (or even soiled menstrual cloths) and indulged in sexual horseplay. Hill sees a great deal more than "frivolous enjoyment" in this, arguing that "it had a ritualistic significance, rooted in the experience of slavery and in celebration of freedom from slavery."[18] Whites had dressed as blacks. Now blacks dressed as whites, rendering the white men morally darker and the white women more vulgar than they had in jest pretended to be. The black performance was thus both a reminder of the hell the slaves had endured and a celebration of their new freedom to retort.

The authorities, however, perceived this freedom as a "threat to public order," and their fear culminated in the famous Canboulay Riots of 1881, a pitched battle between police and masqueraders armed with fighting sticks.[19] In 1884 Canboulay was banned. But serious Carnival mockery survived. The foreground of a contemporary engraving, "Carnival on Frederick Street, Port-of-Spain, 1888,"[20] is occupied by two scantily clad devils, one of whom is wearing a white mask or white face paint. Alongside and behind the devils are several "women," presumably played by men, in frilly dresses, bonnets, and whiteface. The devils are followed by two "sailors" in straw boaters and whiteface; a man in a top hat, with spectacles perched on a long, beaked nose that protrudes from a whitened face; and two bearded Minstrels, playing banjos. Among the crowd of masqueraders in the background is an Indian in whiteface with a feathered headdress. While the sailors wore whiteface to mock whites directly, others—such as the devils and the women—mocked whites playing blacks. Public opinion is portrayed on the faces of two sidewalk spectators at the far right margin of the engraving: a white clergyman looks on with distaste and a black woman grins with delight.

Having failed to suppress Carnival, aristocracy, government, and business instead joined forces to appropriate, tame, and prettify it. Commercial and government sponsors found that they could direct the development of Carnival more effectively by offering financial support and prizes for those aspects of Carnival they wished to encourage and by neglecting those they wished to discourage. Under such sponsorship, a growing middle class began to take to the streets in "fancy bands," depicting exotic or historical themes drawn from popular literature or the movies rather than from the painful memory of slavery. "Instead of playing tough, mean, dirty, evil, drunken, or fiendish,"[21] the middle-class masqueraders played rich and exotic. Today's fancy mas, which long ago superseded old mas in numbers, prestige, and economic impact, is the fruit—good or bad depending on your perspective—of a century of such prettification and commercialization. Although it is now undergoing something of a minor revival, old mas has lost much of its aggressive power.

Even the most aggressive of old mas characters can be tamed. When, on Carnival Saturday morning, I visited the home of D'Arcy (Johnnie) and Carole Lee in the fashionable residential district of St. Clair, I found several hundred sets of cardboard pitchforks, horns, and tails hanging in the backyard. Tins of blue "mud," made from Vaseline and colored pigment or from bentonite and water, were stacked nearby. Lee is a fourth-generation Chinese-Trinidadian dentist who for several years organized a Jouvay (from *jour ouvert* [opening day]) band of charitable devils, who would daub themselves with blue mud and beat biscuit tins in the streets in the early hours of Jouvay morning. In 1996 it cost TT$95 (about U.S.$15) to join Johnnie's band. All the proceeds were given to charity. A framed 1984 newspaper article on the wall of the Lee home reported that members of Johnnie's band had "cast off their fiendish attire and donned angelic robes" to make a substantial donation to a dialysis center. The Lees' group, which has since disbanded, was for middle-class residents of Port of Spain who wanted to "dress down" for charity and party in a safe neighborhood. While the Lees' charitable concerns were admirable, their "pretty" devils effectively obscured the role's traditional protest against slavery and other forms of economic exploitation.[22]

The matter of prettification is not a simple one. Consider the history of another Carnival genre, the steelpan bands. Made initially from large biscuit tins and finally from abandoned oil and chemical storage drums, steelpans replaced tambour-bamboo after World War II. They were war drums. Throughout the 1950s, working-class band members and their supporters fought each other in the streets of Port of Spain "with sticks, stones, broken bottles, razors, and the cutlasses that every Trinidadian has in his yard to keep down the grass." The introduction of the government-sponsored Panorama steelpan competition in 1963 reduced the violence. Middle-class Trinidadians began to join the bands, some "for the vicarious pleasure of associating with the roughness of steelband culture." When, in 1971, Amoco became the first oil company to sponsor a steelband, "the move into respectability was almost complete."[23]

With the shift from street fighting to sponsored competition, steelpan bands became more complex and less mobile. Today's pans come in every size, from the shallow tenor instruments, about six inches deep with a range of up to thirty-two notes, to the huge bass pans made from full-size forty-four-gallon oil drums.[24] Since each bass pan has a range of only four notes, the musician plays five or six bass drums at a time, whirling and leaping to strike the surrounding instruments. Each Panorama band consists of more than one hundred musicians. Once a battleground for street gangs, steelpan now enjoys an honored place in the competitive world of fancy mas.

The Panorama finals took place on Carnival Saturday evening, on an enormous permanent open stage (two hundred yards long and fifty yards wide) at the southern edge of the Queen's Park Savannah—one hundred acres of grassland just north of Port of Spain's downtown business district. A paying audience watched from the stands on either side. Blessed with a press pass, I roamed the stage. The density of drums, stacked one above another in several layers of hastily erected scaffolding, amplified the intensity. The bass players, concentrated each to his or her own cube of space at the four corners of the edifice, whirled like percussive dervishes. The tenor panmen, lined up front and center stage, traded places with one another in midphrase, each jumping into his neighbor's space without losing a beat. The driving rhythm and rapid melody of nearly two hundred steel drums was breathtaking. The Amoco Renegades won the competition for the second year in a row and the eighth time overall. They were to win again in 1997.

One might think that few would mourn the pacification of steelpan. But the Trinidadian novelist Earl Lovelace has argued that it was not only the rhythm but also the violence of the early steel bands that linked them to their roots in the African drums and stick fighting of postemancipation Canboulay. It was "all we had," Lovelace writes, "to express the breadth of violence" into which "the poorest had been emancipated." Lovelace doesn't advocate a return to street fighting, but he does worry that steelpan now "remains frozen in the mode of the European classics, the melodic line emphasized at the expense of the rhythmic," and that it is increasingly incapable of "moving people to dance."[25] Something vital is lost in the prettification that makes the streets safe for Carnival.

The same tension between fancy mas, with its aspirations to lavish display, and old mas, with its memories of slavery and emancipation, crackled on Sunday night. I watched the King and Queen finals at the Savannah stage. The elaborate costumes of the fancy kings and queens, "explod[ing] like a bursting star"[26] from the central face of the wearer, weighed so much they had to be supported on wheels. The winning king costume, *Rainforest*, measured 22 feet high, 22 feet wide, and 24 feet long, weighed 200 pounds, and cost between TT $60,000 and $70,000 (U.S.$10,000–$11,600). It unleashed its own pyrotechnic display as it crossed the stage.[27] Its designer, Geraldo Vieria, claimed a kind of religious inspiration for his work, telling an interviewer that the idea for *Rainforest* came as he watched the beauty of rain falling across the mountains behind the Savannah. "I clasped my hands together," he recalled, "and said, 'Thank you, Lord, that will be my 1996 design, falling rain.'"[28]

The Calypso Monarch Finals followed. Like so much else in Trinidad's Carnival, calypso has its sights set in two directions at once. On the one hand, it remembers its roots in a plantation economy, where slaves found the transplanted African tradition of extemporaneous song, with its possibilities for oblique patois criticism of the masters, a way to "conjure power out of [their] situation of powerlessness."[29] On the other hand, it drifts inexorably towards the kind of "party music" likely to achieve success on the world music stage. Most of those competing for the Calypso crown manage to straddle the gap, setting political commentary to a lively beat. The winner in 1996 was Cro Cro, one of whose songs—considered racist by some—berated the Afro-Caribbean community for an electoral apathy that had given victory in the recent national elections to the first prime minister of East Indian heritage. The runner-up, Brother Marvin, was more inclined to harmony. He sang "Jahaji Bhai" (Brotherhood of the Boat), challenging the myth of pure African descent and wagering with Afro-Caribbeans that, somewhere in their genealogy, they'd find "a man in a dhoti."[30]

I left the Savannah stands before the last calypso was sung, making my way on foot to Darceuils (pronounced "dark eyes") Lane in the working-class district of Belmont. There, around 1:00 A.M., I joined the Merry Darceuils mas band for Jouvay morning. Band members shared rum and "dirtied up" by daubing themselves with white or yellow mud. One youngster stood before a shard of mirror, carefully turning his close-cropped hair into a helmet of yellow mud. A cardboard float, designated the slave ship *Middle Passage,* waited for us to haul it through the city streets.

The theme of this year's band was "I'm a slave to . . . ." Playing off the human tendency to exchange one form of slavery for another, band members wore cardboard headpieces depicting such items as beer bottles, televisions, and window frames decorated with lace curtains. Thus they portrayed addiction to alcohol, passive entertainment, and gossip. Loose cardboard handcuffs dangled from their wrists. The band "captain" complained of the "commercialization" of fancy mas. His own Carnival vision had its roots in intelligible protest: "You see, we free, but if you notice the pictures, the chains has been broken, but are still on our hands because we still slaves to this, slaves to that, so this is the whole t'ing. Mas is really a form of protest, showin' the masters of this time, or the Establishment, that you was not pleased with certain things that they was doin'. . . . Mas is a portrayal. You are saying somethin'."[31]

Some of the teenagers, slaves to sexual temptation, wore earrings made of condom packages. There was a strong smell of marijuana. The band's "king," his face painted in black and white quadrants, his arms in black, and his legs in yellow, wore a crown that resembled television screens and a satellite dish. Mocking the ornate wheeled body masks pushed across the Savannah stage by the "fancy" kings and queens, he pushed a ramshackle baby buggy bearing an increasingly dilapidated cardboard television. Where fancy mas privileges "transcendent glitter," the Jouvay bands value "transgressive dirt."[32]

We were led by African-style drummers in the back of a pickup truck. In our disorderly march towards the downtown harbor, we were joined and intersected by other bands and random individuals. I saw men and women covered, like ghoulish spirits, in white paint. Some had grinning skulls painted on the backs of their heads, which made them seem to be walking backwards, their bodies strangely twisted at the neck. Others were smeared from head to toe in thick, black motor oil, heirs to the Jab Molassies (from *diables* [devils] covered in molasses) who had once owned the streets during Canboulay.

When we reached the judging stand near Independence Square—for even Jouvay has succumbed to the restraint of competition—we had a run-in with the police. Our truck driver lacked the necessary permit from the Traffic Office. Grudgingly, the drummers unloaded their instruments and slung them round their necks. While the rest of us pushed and pulled our dilapidated slave ship past the reviewing stands, the drummers led on foot. I don't think we won a prize that year, but in 1997 the Merry Darceuils rebounded with "One Mornin' in a Coal Mine," representing South African and Appalachian miners as examples of an exploited workforce. They won third place in the Jouvay Small Band competition.[33]

Afterwards, I walked slowly back to the Savannah. As the sun came up, I met some of Johnnie Lee's devils. They had played in the streets of St. Clair, staying clear of downtown and crossing the upscale Savannah stage for their competitive review. Now they were heading home. As for me, I managed three hours of sleep before catching a ride to Arima, some twenty-five miles east of Port of Spain.

In the heat of the afternoon, I joined what my notes describe as "the world's longest, densest, most intimate throng of dirty dancers" as it marched, ahead of a sixteen-wheel truck piled high with the speakers of a deafening sound system, into the center of Arima. One black youth had streams of red mud flowing from a head caked with white mud, as if he—or the white role he'd adopted—had been severely beaten. An older man, clothed in the motley dress of a medieval European fool, played the traditional Jab Jab (Devil Devil), threatening us with his whip. ("Jab Jab . . . put

12.2　Winin'. Port of Spain, 1996.

on a costume, a happy clown costume, but inside that costume is a fierce warrior. They fight back.")[34] Most were simply dirtied up with colored mud.

We performed repeatedly an exuberant jump-and-wave to the amplified music. Spread across the road in rough formation, we moved left and right to the year's most popular Road March: "We must all unite an' stop de fuss an' fight,/Movin' to de right. . . ."[35] And almost everybody wined. Any definition of wining sounds pedantic, but here goes: wining (from winding your hips or "winin' yo' behin'") is an overtly sexual movement of the pelvis, usually performed in full physical contact with a partner or in an erotic row of masqueraders one behind the other (Fig. 12.2). It pervades Trinidadian Carnival. I refrained, more from a sense that I'd look silly than from any misplaced sense of virtue. But one young woman, painted blue from head to toe, writhed against my thigh anyway, leaving a blue stain that later required explanation to my understanding wife.

Then, as dusk settled over the island, I made my way north to Paramin Mountain, one of the island's more traditional communities.[36] Patois is still the first language of many of its older residents; I had attended a joyous patois mass in the tin-roofed village church on Sunday morning. Now, the village

12.3   Blue devil. Paramin Mountain, 1996.

square was crowded with spectators. Against the walls, vendors were selling soft drinks, beer, and shark-and-bake (Trinidad's equivalent of fishburger). There were no streetlights.

Paramin Mountain is the home to the most accomplished of Trinidad's blue devils, some of whom had joined Friday's old mas parade. Two blue devil bands were already roaming the village streets. Others soon joined them. The larger bands, numbering seven or eight members apiece, were accompanied by musicians beating biscuit tins and blowing plastic whistles. I saw just one young woman taking part; otherwise, the devils were all men. They were variously clothed in shorts or jeans; some of the men were bare-chested, others wore loose-fitting shirts. Some wore dark glasses, false fangs, face paint, or masks. As in Port of Spain, the beasts were roped and goaded by imps. One beast wore a store-bought werewolf mask, with pointed ears, red pupils, sharp fangs, and shaggy hair. From his back grew wings, made of blue netting fitted to bamboo frames, that stretched three feet above his head (Fig. 12.3). Most of the devils were daubed with blue mud, but some were covered instead with white powder (Fig. 12.4), and at least one was smeared with black grease. The devils moved through the crowd, creating their own playing spaces and then demanding money from villager and visitor alike.

Their performance consisted of various acts of transgression, ranging from the comparatively innocent—climbing telephone poles and trying unsuccessfully to enter the school against the objections of the principal—to the scatological and obscene. Scatological mimesis included ripping open another devil's trousers while he rolled on the ground and pretending to wipe his backside with leaves. The obscene seemed to focus on pretended acts of homoeroticism or homosexual rape: fellatio, anal intercourse, and anal penetration with a baseball bat. Most of the aggressors in the mimed assaults wore powdered whiteface. I supposed this, too, was a comment both on plantation life and on power relationships in general: those with unrestrained power (white plantation owners and their kin) humiliate subordinates. Women and children were present, and no one seemed to take the least offense at this depiction of obscene political reality.

The devils were not entranced; they were consummate actors. When a white woman broached the subject of "devil worship" with one of the blue

12.4   Devil in white powder. Paramin Mountain, 1996.

devils, he was offended. Displaying a bundle of one hundred TT$1.00 bills, he asked straightforwardly, "Why do you think we do it?"[37] There was an unexpected sense of decorum about the whole performance. Although the devils came face-to-face with us, they never touched us. Once I saw a devil down half a bottle of beer in a single swig, pour the rest over his head, and then, without breaking stride, bend and roll the empty bottle gently into the gutter out of harm's way. In 1998, when I returned to Paramin Mountain, I saw a band of blue devils gently but firmly remove an intrusive drunk from their space. His inebriation, being real, spoiled their play.

By 9:00 A.M. on Carnival Tuesday, I was back at the Savannah for the all-day parade of fancy mas bands across the stage. Fancy mas resembles the aristocratic Carnival of slaveholding days, providing an opportunity for the expanding professional and middle classes to "dress up" in ornate and showy costumes or to "dress down" in skimpy costumes and indulge in fantasies of sensuality. Some bands made reference to unifying narratives or themes, such as "People of Ancient Kingdoms" or "Tribes of the Shifting Sands." The most inventive was Peter Minshall's Callaloo, whose "Song of the Earth" incorporated orderly mud men, silver-winged stilt-walkers (*moko jumbies* of African heritage) (Fig. 12.5),[38] delicate burrokeets in the form of fantastic horses, elephants, mice, and griffins, and several other truly pretty versions of traditional Carnival characters. "Song of the Earth" won the 1996 Band of the Year competition. Others bands, such as Poison, offered little more than color-coordinated sequined bikinis (Fig. 12.6). I spent hours atop the television scaffold just a few feet from the stage watching scantily clad young women plead with the camera crew to capture their wining on live broadcast. According to the official logbooks for 1996, it took Poison sixty-three minutes to cross the Savannah stage.[39] Among its six thousand members, most of them women, was the wife of the prime minister.

Some of the smaller fancy bands preserved an element of protest. Brian "Tico" Skinner and Associates adapted Canboulay's "slavery is hell" theme to current politics. By way of reference to the recent hastily called general election, they dressed as devils with briefcases and marched under a banner proclaiming "Snap Election Is Hell" (Fig. 12.7). In previous years they had staged "Recession Is Hell" and "I.M.F. Is Hell." A few traditional characters braved the competition. A trio of Minstrel Boys were the first to cross the stage, delivering a sweetly audible rendition of "Way Down Upon the Swanee River." The arrival of the fancy bands, with their deafening sound systems, overpowered any subsequent old mas characters.

Fancy mas bands now provide the most popular means of participation

12.5   Moko jumbies (Song of the Earth). Port of Spain, 1996.

in Trinidad's Carnival, providing an opportunity for the release of sexual energy, the display of showy costumes (both ornate and skimpy), the celebration of the body, and the exuberance of an all-day mobile street party. For some, it is a form of easy self-indulgence. For those who painstakingly design or fabricate the costumes, it requires skill, self-discipline, and time. It also feeds the economy. Trinidad's Carnival generates an estimated U.S.$60 million each year in increased commercial activity. Foreign tourists spend a further U.S.$200 million. Fancy mas, which at its worst requires only a taste for alcohol, scantily clad women, and dancing in the sun, attracts 98 percent of these visitors.[40] Commercial and government sponsorship naturally inclines towards the promotion of fancy mas.

Fancy mas promotes what derisive Carnival resists. Embraced by government and commerce, it exalts the power of the economy, encouraging the middle class to indulge in extravagant sensual or exotic fantasy. Fancy mas

12.6 Members of Poison pose for the television cameras. Port of Spain, 1996.

democratizes opulence, allowing participants the temporary illusion of an extravagance that is still in reality the permanent privilege of the wealthy, and it replaces the deflating mockery of the mighty that is arguably the most enduring impulse of Carnival. It invites its participants to aspire to grandeur rather than to laugh at pretension. In doing so, it conceals rather than reveals injustice.

Old mas, on the other hand, preserves the memory of pain. Brian Honoré, the leader of a younger generation of Midnight Robbers, told me that the celebration of emancipation requires the depiction of the horrors that preceded it. "We keep playing old mas," he said, "for the same reason as that guy made *Schindler's List*. We don't want it to happen again." Blue devils, Dames Lorraines, and Baby Dolls recall the injustices of the patriarchal white plantations. Stick fighters, Midnight Robbers, and Jab Jabs boast of strong resistance.

Even so, the extravagant fantasies of fancy mas and the commemorative protests of old mas leave an intervening space where Carnival once thrived. For Carnival at its best not only indulges dreams of opulence and memorializes past offenses; it also deflates present pretensions. Just as the Feast of Fools deposed the present bishop from his seat, exalting the least of the choirboys, so the Carnivals of Laza and Lantz mock the ascetic and hierarchical impulses of a church that still exerts considerable power in parts of Spain. Similarly, Carnival in Trinidad once took to the streets to mock the white colonists who laid claim to uninterrupted power after emancipation.

Mockery of the powerful is considerably easier in a hierarchical society, for its targets are more readily identified. But the larger the aspiring middle class, the more ethnically blended the culture, and the more impersonal the channels of power in a global economy, the harder it is to identify an opponent that is not us. An economy that creates a relatively prosperous middle class, in a way that slavery never even dreamed of doing, is difficult for a whole community to parody. There are those in Port of Spain, such as the Merry Darceuils or Tico Skinner and Associates, who bring the sharp edge of Carnival laughter to bear on the injustices of the global economy, but they are a minority. The modern urban Carnival, in Trinidad and elsewhere, will have to address the moral problems of its patrons more directly if it is not to subside into a commercially sponsored street party that substitutes spectacle and economic stimulus for critical and theological potency.

12.7 Snap Election Is Hell (Brian "Tico" Skinner and Associates). Port of Spain, 1996.

13.
The Sins of the Carnival Virgin
(BOLIVIA)

ORURO'S CARNIVAL faces some of the same problems as that of Port of Spain but in a very different climate and with stronger religious roots. Oruro squats high in the Bolivian altiplano, striking many travelers as "a mean, forbidding town, hugging the bare hillside," where "all is grey monotony even in the noon sunlight of a bright winter day."[1] At 12,144 feet above sea level, Oruro can be bitterly cold at night even in the summer months. Lacking the encircling snowcapped mountain peaks of La Paz or the rich artistic heritage of colonial Potosí, it has little to offer the visitor by way of compensation.

Since Inca times, Oruro has been a mining town. Unlike its wealthier sister, Potosí, it failed to transform its temporary prosperity into permanent architectural glories and so has the air of a boomtown that never quite made the grade. Depleted of its silver by the end of the Spanish colonial period, in the late nineteenth century Oruro became the hub of Bolivia's tin-mining industry. By 1947 the metal content of the ore had declined too far to support commercial interests and the government took over the mines. In 1985 the nationalized mines were closed. Some have reopened under private management, but falling prices have limited profitability. Unemployment hovers over the town like a persistent cloud.[2]

Enclosing the entrance to an ancient mineshaft, in the side of the hill that steeply elevates the western edge of town, is the Santuario del Socavón (Sanctuary of the Mineshaft), a large, partially whitewashed stone church. On the wall behind the main altar is a gilt-framed fresco of the Virgen del Socavón. Once a year, on Carnival Saturday, the sanctuary is packed with tens of thousands of costumed devils, savages, and blacks, who throughout the day remove their ornate and terrifying masks and kneel to pay her homage.

Oruro's Carnival is the feast day of Oruro's Virgin. Originally the Virgin of Candlemas, traditionally honored on 2 February, she is now known locally as the Virgin of the Mineshaft. Legend has it that on the Saturday of Car-

nival in 1789 a bandit known as Nina-Nina or Chiru-Chiru was mortally
wounded in a street fight, perhaps by the father of the girl with whom he was
eloping. In his dying, the amorous bandit was comforted by the Virgen de la
Candelaría. Some accounts say that a life-size image of the Virgin, painted
on the wall of a deserted house, had been the object of his weekly devotion;
others report that the painting miraculously appeared on the wall of the bandit's own abode after his death.[3] The story adds that a troupe of masked devils
first danced in honor of the Virgin in the next year's Carnival.[4] The present
sanctuary, built to house her image, was completed in 1891.[5]

Behind this legend of the Carnival bandit lurks another historical reality.
During the Great Rebellion of Túpac Amaru II, which spread south along
the Andean highlands from its starting point in Cusco, Oruro survived its
own brief but bloody revolution. Exacerbated by fears of imminent Indian
attack, tensions in Oruro between the majority Creole population and the
minority ruling class of peninsular-born Spaniards (chapetones) erupted into
a full-scale uprising.[6] On the night of Saturday, 10 February 1781, a mob of
several thousand Creoles set fire to the house of a Spanish shopkeeper, killing eleven Spaniards and five black slaves. A hastily organized Sunday morning procession of the Holy Sacrament failed to calm the situation, which
further deteriorated when some four thousand Indians, armed with conch
trumpets, slingshots, and nooses, arrived "to defend the Creoles." The Creoles welcomed their temporary allies but must have watched with mixed
feelings as the Indians danced around the charred Spanish corpses, inflicting
further wounds with stones and knives. A procession of the Holy Christ of
Burgos was no more pacifying than its predecessor.[7]

For several days, the Indians roamed the town, firing their slings, sacking
houses and churches, and killing any Spaniards they could find. One terrified
Spanish man, disguised in women's clothes, hid among a group of praying
women but was betrayed by his shoes. He was stripped and killed. More Indians arrived, swelling the occupying army to as many as fifteen thousand.[8]
On 14 February, an order was given by the leading Creoles that everyone in
the town had to dress like Indians and chew coca leaves. Only the clergy was
exempt. The members of the governing Creole council chose to dress as Inca
royalty. During a parade celebrating the new mode of dress, the participants
shouted "Viva Túpac Amaru!"[9]

On 15 February, a messenger arrived in Oruro, claiming to be from Túpac
Amaru himself. He instructed the Indians to respect churches and clergy, to
do no harm to Creoles, and to persecute none but chapetones. Moreover, he
assured the Indians of imminent victory: Túpac Amaru would enter La Paz

"by Carnival [*por Carnestolendas*]."[10] Enticed by individual payments from the Oruro treasury and by orders of their own *caciques* (chiefs), the Indians began to return to their villages. By 16 February, Oruro was comparatively calm. Of a population of some five thousand people, twenty-seven Spaniards, thirteen black slaves, one Creole, and one Frenchman had been killed.[11] The Indians launched further attacks during March and April, but the Creoles and remaining Spaniards united to repel them.

The messenger's promise that Túpac Amaru would enter La Paz "by Carnival" is striking. In 1781 Carnival Saturday fell on 24 February, placing Oruro's uprising almost exactly halfway between Candlemas and Carnival. Much of what happened in Oruro during the six days of Indian occupation was, if one disregards the terror and the loss of life, remarkably carnivalesque. Religious processions dueled ineffectually with secular parades. Europeans and Creoles disguised themselves as Indians. A Spaniard resorted to cross-dressing in a vain attempt to save his life. Thousands of armed Indians (paradigmatic wild men from beyond the boundaries of urban society) roamed the colonial city streets, overturning existing hierarchies of power.

Carnival itself followed closely on the uprising. Astonishingly, by 19 February most Orureños were "thinking only of games and drunken revelry." Few details of the festivities survive beyond a seasonally appropriate redistribution of wealth. "Throughout Carnival," one witness grumbles, the city markets were full of "robbers" selling looted gold and silver back to its owners or to "*cholos* and mestizos," who made the most of the opportunity to "inherit" precious metal at a steep discount.[12] By 1784 it was "customary" to "rejoice, dance, play, and form *comparsas* [companies of masqueraders]" for the city's Carnival. That year, one large *comparsa* of three hundred members mocked ruling class fears that there would be a fresh uprising "during Carnival" by singing mischievously:

Courageous Orureños
Are noble-hearted folk
Who never have intended
To fashion new revolts.

The Spanish *corregidor*, reinstated after the rebellion, walked behind the *comparsa*, watching carefully and refusing it entry to the main square.[13]

Arrests of those implicated in the uprising began in 1784 and continued through 1791. Judicial proceedings lasted until 1801, when a general amnesty was granted to surviving fugitives and prisoners.[14] Mining production, already in decline by 1781, came to a complete halt after the uprising. It was against this background of judicial retribution and economic decline that, on Carnival Saturday 1789, the Virgin of the Mineshaft is said to have appeared to the dying bandit. Unlike the Virgin of the Rosary, whose image in the Church of Santo Domingo was so venerated by the *chapetones* that the rebels of 1781 had wanted to behead it,[15] the Virgen del Socavón favored Creoles, Indians, miners, and bandits. She also appears to have tolerated indigenous deities or "devils." By 1790, if the legend is correct, Oruro's miners had moved Candlemas to Carnival and added indigenous gods, masked as Christian devils, to the week's festivities.[16]

A generation later, in the midst of armed struggle for independence from the Spanish crown, an archangelic warrior was summoned to defeat the devils. The first stage of the Andean wars of independence (1809–1816) left the royalists in control; the second stage (1823–1825) left Bolivia an independent nation. In 1818, according to credible oral history, Oruro's parish priest, Ladislao Montealegre, composed the *Narrative of the Seven Deadly Sins*, a dramatized "moral tale depicting the struggle between Saint Michael and the Seven Deadly Sins."[17] Although he may have wanted to redirect both the remembrance and the present threat of rebellion into more virtuous channels, Montealegre seems instead to have furnished an enduring public transcript for the devils. Despite alternating periods of "decline and prosperity"[18] in the nineteenth century, the devils and their morality play are now flourishing. Several thousand devils dance through the streets of Oruro each year before the narrative is staged on Carnival Monday.

A Carnival that honors a Virgin and dramatizes an ambiguous defeat of demonic sins by the saintly archangel brings us full circle to our starting point in days of saints and virgins, emphasizing once again the close kinship between supposedly pagan Carnivals and overtly Christian festivals. We end, as we began, with devils going to church. Julia Fortún believes that Oruro's supernatural street fighters are kin to the combative Michael and "twenty-three devils" who led the fifteenth-century Barcelona Corpus Christi procession and whose Catalan descendants still dance in such towns as Berga and Vilafranca del Penedès.[19] Like Oruro's *relato* (dramatic narrative), the Catalan dances often feature a *diablesa* (female devil); and, in a related Catalan dance, the Devil leads the Seven Deadly Sins into battle against the opposing Virtues and an angel.[20] Although Fortún has found no documentary evidence of historical influence, her thesis is inherently plausible.

But if the iconography of the morality play derives from Catalan sources, the durability of Oruro's Carnival is rooted in its recollection of the 1781 uprising. Not only does the *entrada* of the Carnival masqueraders visually recall the "*entrada* of the Indians"[21]—as an eyewitness described the indigenous invasion of Oruro—but the names of some *comparsas* and of the streets and squares through which the Carnival entry passes make explicit the remembrance of rebellion. Two of the *comparsas*, "in homage to the Revolution of 10 February 1781," are named after Sebastian Pagador, one of the Creole heroes of the uprising.[22] So is the street where the *entrada* starts and which it crosses a second time on its way to the central Plaza 10 de Febrero.

As a fixed historical referent, the uprising allows for a shifting series of contemporary connotations. Initially, Oruro's Carnival played on Spanish fears of a renewed insurgency. After 1825 Carnival celebrated Oruro's uprising as a precursor of national independence while simultaneously creating an alternative world in which the indigenous miners and their gods again ruled the streets before succumbing to the pale-faced Spanish Michael. By the early part of the twentieth century, Oruro's elite was denouncing Carnival as a "mixture of paganism and superstition" that furnished only an "absurd repetition of past epochs."[23] Today, the professional classes dominate Oruro's Carnival and the national government markets the *entrada*, with its festive representations of multiple ethnicities, as "a metaphor for the national unity of Bolivia."[24]

The *Narrative of the Seven Deadly Sins* is no longer staged by miners but by the Gran Tradicional Auténtica Diablada Oruro, formed for the purpose in 1904 by a guild of butchers.[25] When I saw the play in 2000, it was performed early in the afternoon of Carnival Monday at one end of the Avenida Cívica, a broad parade ground permanently lined with bleachers just below the Santuario del Socavón. Montealegre's text, substantially modernized in 1945 by Rafael Ulises Peláez, had been further streamlined to intensify the action.[26] An audience of several thousand watched from the bleachers and the slopes of the hills beyond; hundreds crowded onto the paved parade ground for a closer look. Devils marked out a playing area. A trumpet heralded the action. Saint Michael and an unnamed companion angel entered the circle. Each wore a silver-colored mask with pink eyes and a winged helmet, a white tunic with a pink cross sewn across the chest, white gauze wings, and pale blue or white cape, trousers, and shoes. Each clutched a plastic shield and a sword, from whose handle dangled three handkerchiefs in the Bolivian national colors, red, yellow, and green (Fig. 13.1).

Lucifer approached. Seated astride the shoulders of an assistant and wearing a huge, black, fanged and horned mask, he towered over the angels. A thick black wig flowed over his shoulders. Dressed in a heavy sequined cape

13.1   Saint Michael. Oruro, 2000.

and trousers and flourishing a demonic trident in his gauntleted hand, he roared out his challenge to Michael. Lest the audience forget, Lucifer summarized his origins in proud rebellion against God and his enduring intent to destroy all Christians. His words, otherwise inaudible beneath his mask, were broadcast over loudspeakers.

Slipping from his assistant's shoulders, Lucifer accosted Michael, who scraped the ground with his foot like a bull and boasted of his own power. Another actor, in a beaked mask and real condor's wings, danced between them, flapping his wings and grounding the action in the Andean world. After an exchange of vaunting speeches and ineffective angelic sword thrusts, Lucifer was joined by Satan (Fig. 13.2), who assured the watching "demonic hordes" of certain victory in the battle for "unwary human hearts." Michael threatened both devils with judgment, which, he said, would have to take place outside "the temple of the Virgin of the Mineshaft, the patroness of the miners of Oruro" because "devils cannot enter the temple. They cannot profane that holy place with their infamous presence." Michael's boast was of course qualified by the audience's awareness that thousands of devils had already gone inside the temple to visit the Virgin on Saturday. Lucifer and Satan knelt in token submission to the archangel before running off to join the circle of watching devils (Fig. 13.3).

Lucifer and Satan were followed, one by one, by the Seven Deadly Sins: Pride, Avarice, Lechery, Anger, Gluttony, Envy, and Sloth. Masked and costumed as ferocious devils, the Sins took turns challenging Michael and boasting of their transgressions. Stagehands planted flares that filled the playing area with variously colored smoke, so thick that at times the actors briefly disappeared from view. Condors wafted through the colored clouds. Avarice admitted that in his eagerness to accumulate wealth, he had engaged in "unjust oppression." Anger removed his mask and flung it to the ground, where Michael crushed it with his feet. Gluttony asked the archangel for food and wine. Sloth, clutching a beer bottle, could barely make it into the arena. Supported by two white bears, he slipped and slurred his challenge to Michael.

The text implied that the sins were being "humiliated," forced to confess their iniquities before retiring to the depths of hell, "conquered" by Michael's "power," but the performance suggested otherwise. The Sins remained loud and defiant throughout, all but Sloth (who had to be helped) running out of the playing area undeterred. After the Sins had retired, Michael invited the crowd to name the opposing Virtues. The loudspeakers roared out the answer: Humility, Generosity, Chastity, Patience, Temperance, Charity, and

13.2 Satan in smoke. Oruro, 2000.

13.3   Satan kneels before Saint Michael. Oruro, 2000.

Diligence. As each Virtue was named, the contesting Sin, still very much alive, ran across the playing area.

One Sin remained: China Supay. Once played by a cross-dressed man, China Supay is now acted by a young woman in a short skirt and a pale-faced mask with horns and big blue eyes. Supay was one of the more mischievous pre-Hispanic deities of the region, demonized by the Spaniards.[27] China Supay is his wife. She entered the circle laughing. "I am the temptation of the flesh," she announced, "symbol of human perdition." Michael retreated before this object of lust. China Supay offered not the least pretense of submission. Instead, she confidently assured Michael, "Pure angel, I can tempt you and carry you to hell." Once she had left, still laughing, Michael shouted after her, "You'll never tempt me." The band struck up. The play was over.

In an influential essay on Oruro's Carnival, Thomas Abercrombie has argued that the morality play embodies an ethnically charged message of renunciation. For its mestizo performers and audience, he believes, the Sins represent "the savage condition of the Indian who lives in each of us." Sensuality in particular is located, for the mestizo male, "in the bodies of indigenous women." The play invites its audience to renounce these temptations, "for the sake of God and country," by "attending to the example of the Virgin's renunciation of sexuality."[28] This strikes me as too simple a reading of the performance. Abercrombie neglects the possibility of a hidden transcript more suited to the play's historical origins and Carnival context, and he trusts the clerically scripted word more than its good-natured performance.

Certainly the morality play enacts a virtuous Catholic public transcript of victory over sin, but this is challenged by a number of contrary factors, both in the performance itself and in its larger Carnival context. In two other plays that followed the *relato,* characters died dramatically and at length, as do the devils in some Catalan devil dances. But, in Oruro, the devils visibly survived their confrontation with Saint Michael. As for China Supay—the "temptation of the flesh," whose defeat is required by Abercrombie's reading of the play—she didn't even kneel to Saint Michael. She left still laughing.

Several observers have commented that Saint Michael seems "pallid and emasculated" compared to the fearsome devils that oppose him.[29] During the dancing that filled the parade ground immediately before and after the play's performance, Michael was visually outshone and vastly outnumbered. While a few archangels danced up and down in pink and white, hundreds of devils cavorted in a wild array of colors splashed liberally across their high boots, skintight trousers, beaded capes and tunics, long wigs, and monstrous masks (Fig. 13.4). Their masks are among the most complex headpieces in the festive world: "Bulging, billiard-ball eyes studded with bright artificial stones and huge grinning silver teeth, hideously pointed, leer grotesquely out of an exuberant tangle of horns and ears and tusks, painted in a wild cacophony of colours, and crowned by a three-headed viper or other misshapen reptile."[30] Some masks are crowned with whole stuffed condors. No two masks are alike.[31] Dancing alongside the devils, a number of China Supays provocatively swung their hips and twirled their skirts (Fig. 13.5). The odds were stacked against the virtuous archangel. The audience's eyes were on the devils' masks and the China Supays' thighs. Winning the aesthetic war in performance is a common folk means of challenging an officially scripted defeat.

It was not only in the massed dancing immediately before the play that the conventional forces of virtue were outnumbered and outclassed. "Saint Michael wins the *relato* up at the church," a street vendor told me on Friday evening, "but here, in the streets, it's like hell itself, there are so many devils." The Carnival's Grand Entry of Pilgrimage, a parade of all the costumed masqueraders, began at 6:00 A.M. on Saturday in the northern suburbs—"near the old Indian settlement"[32]—and ended five miles later at the Sanctuary of the Mineshaft at about 5:00 A.M. on Sunday, only to begin all over again an hour later. While any single company of "pilgrims" took only about five hours to cover the parade route, masqueraders filled the streets

13.4   Devil. Oruro, 2000.

13.5   China Supays. Oruro, 2000.

for almost two whole days. Of the fifty *comparsas* that took part in the parade, five of the largest were *diabladas* (companies of devils). Music for the *diabladas*, as for many of the other *comparsas*, was provided by a series of brass bands marching between the *comparsa*'s different squadrons. The "pilgrimage" was loud, boisterous, colorful, and sensual.

Insofar as the male devils represented the mortal sins of Christian tradition and their female counterparts enacted an invitation to lust, a carnivalesque inversion of conventional religious morality clearly ruled the streets during the two days of the *entrada*. It is another common strategy of Catholic folk performers to concede the virtuous triumph of the church at the close of a fiesta in exchange for a prolonged expression during the fiesta of those sensual aspects of human nature ordinarily condemned by the church. Devotion to the Virgin sanctifies the transgression. It was for just this reason that the street vendor preferred Oruro's Carnival to its more famous counterpart in Rio de Janeiro. "Rio's Carnival has no religious dimension," he told me. "It's just a pagan festival, full of half-clothed women."

But Oruro's devils represent more than the Deadly Sins of Christian theology. They also recall the indigenous gods of the region. Scholars have identified the devils with the local god Supay or Huari, who resisted and survived colonization by both the Incas and the Spaniards.[33] Now known as Tío (literally, "Uncle," but possibly an ambiguous corruption of the Spanish *díos* [god] or *diablo* [devil]), Supay's underground power is still acknowledged by Oruro's miners. On Carnival Friday, in the mines, *ch'allas* (offering rituals) are made before an image of the Tío. The squat, caped statue resembles that of a conventional Christian devil, with red mask, thick gloves, and three-pronged pitchfork. Indigenous miners acquiesced in the early Catholic identification of Supay with the Christian devil, drawing comfort from the power of "the enemy of their enemy."[34] Tío still rules the underground realm of the mines, insisting that the offensive name Jesus not be uttered there.[35]

The devils were not the only "pilgrims" to represent the indigenous world. Nearly half of the *comparsas* performed folkloric versions of rural Indian dances. Some imitated the llama herders of the high altiplano. A group called Suri Sicuri bore enormous circular feathered headdresses, worn horizontally, that touched the ground when the dancers bent at the waist. Other dancers, whirling slings in mock combat, recalled the indigenous martial art of the *tinku*. From time to time the driving rhythm of drums and *tarkas* (wooden flutes) or *zampoñas* (Andean reed pipes) offered an alternative to the brass bands. The largest of the "Indian" *comparsas* were those representing Tobas. Generally regarded as the least civilized of Bolivia's Indians, the Tobas live along the low-lying border between Bolivia and neighboring Argentina and Paraguay. Each of the three Toba *comparsas* boasted several hundred male and female dancers. The men wore tall feathered headdresses, long colored skirts, and masks locked in fierce grimaces and decorated with warpaint and nose plugs (Fig. 13.6). Many brandished spears. The women wore briefer costumes. The dance steps, characterized by great bounding leaps and massed forward surges, recalled "hunting and war dances."[36]

The unimpeded passage of so many exuberant Indians through the streets of Oruro during the two-day *entrada* recalls the indigenous invasion of the city in 1781, insinuating a barely hidden transcript of resistance into the public transcript of penitential submission. Many Orureños, as a waiter in my hotel put it, feel "betrayed by a national government that has shut down the mines and now pours all its money into promoting agriculture around Cochabamba." Frustrated, they readily identify with the celebrated attempt of local Indians to recapture Oruro from the powerful outside forces that impoverished and marginalized them.

Consider, too, the juxtaposition on Carnival Monday afternoon of the *Narrative of the Seven Deadly Sins* and *The Death of Atahualpa*. Performed

13.6   Tobas. Oruro, 2000.

shortly after the morality play, *The Death of Atahualpa* challenged, even in its written text, the former's clerical interpretation of human sin and demonic temptation.[37] In this Andean adaptation of the theme of Moors and Christians, the Spanish contingent consisted of three bearded Spanish soldiers in colonial armor, two carrying swords and one an arquebus, and a Spanish friar in a black cassock bearing a Bible and a cross. The soldiers represented Francisco Pizarro, Diego de Almagro, and an anonymous king of Spain, while the friar was named Hernando de Luque.[38] The "heathen" contingent consisted of forty Inca lords and princesses in ornate cloaks and feathered headpieces. They were led by Atahualpa, the Inca ruler executed by Pizarro in July 1533.

Throughout the play, the Indians spoke Quechua and the conquistadors spoke Spanish. The text, its original composed perhaps as early as the sixteenth century by a native Quechua speaker, embodied "a beautiful and painful indigenous interpretation of the conquest."[39] Atahualpa and the Incas were noble, generous, and dignified, peacefully welcoming Pizarro and placing themselves and their wealth at his service. Pizarro and the Spaniards were aggressive, impatient, proud, and greedy for precious metal, repeatedly denouncing the Indians to their faces as "barbarians." For their part, the Incas privately described the strange-looking Spaniards as a great red crowd of thick-necked, "bearded enemies . . . ; on their heads three-pointed horns like those of a stag tossing tossing; faces pressed together like white flour; knotted red beards divided at the jawbone like those of billy goats."[40] Within the world of the play, this was nothing more than an effort to describe the foreign in terms of the familiar, but in the immediate context of its performance it recalled the masked, horned, and sometimes bearded Sins.[41]

The malevolence of the Spaniards was especially evident in their manipulation of mutual incomprehensibility. Almagro presented Atahualpa with a written order in Spanish, commanding the Inca to submit to Spanish rule on penalty of death. Understanding neither Spanish nor the concept of a written language, the Inca consulted his advisers, who puzzled over inscriptions that seemed to them like "spread rooster claws" and "a mass of black ants." Almagro reported to Pizarro, "These barbarians do not want to obey." When Pizarro's own querulous attempts to communicate with the Indians also failed, he deemed Atahualpa's execution justified.[42] Luque obstinately offered Atahualpa a Bible, which the Inca ruler examined briefly and returned. "To me," he responded, "it says absolutely nothing."[43]

The princesses mourned Atahualpa's death, tearfully pleading for his revival.[44] Then three members of the ruler's family took turns predicting the future of the Spaniards in language deliberately reminiscent of God's biblical curse on Adam (Genesis 3:17–19): the Spaniards would gain their livelihoods "by the sweat of their brows," and whatever small amounts of silver and gold they might "take from the ground" would "return to dust."[45] Spanish colonization was thus identified with the original human capitulation to demonic temptation and sin. The play closed with the king of Spain rebuking Pizarro for having taken the life of "a great king, perhaps even stronger than I."[46] As the play's editors remark, it was a conclusion that by tactfully exonerating the Spanish crown, "avoided conflict with the colonial authorities."[47]

The Death of Atahualpa unequivocally sympathized with the Incas, portraying the Spaniards as prime examples of the sins of pride, avarice, anger, envy, and sloth. The play's "depiction of the Spaniards," Manuel Vargas insists, "is diabolical."[48] The Inca play thus directly challenged the public transcript of the preceding morality play, offering an alternative, retrospective reading of its moral. If the public transcript of the first play identified the demonic Sins with the Indians, the second performance openly reversed that judgment, identifying the Sins with the Spaniards. In Mario Unzueta's 1945 account of a fiesta in Toco (Cochabamba), the *comedia* of "Saint Michael" and "a legion of devils" immediately followed *The Death of Atahualpa*, allowing the diabolic sins of the *comedia* to be identified even more clearly with the Europeans.[49]

13.7 *Morenos* with armadillo noisemakers. Oruro, 2000.

Folk plays, however, are rarely about the past alone. In earlier years, some of the Spanish soldiers in the Oruro play wore "present-day army uniforms."[50] The national colors still hang from Saint Michael's sword. In terms of the present Bolivian situation, the retrospective reading of the morality play called to repentance the successors of Pizarro, protected by government policies, who still exploit miners and indigenous campesinos for personal power and profit.

The Death of Atahualpa was not the only Carnival presentation to point the finger of sin at white colonial mine owners and their heirs. The most crowded of the *comparsas* during the Entry of Pilgrimage were the five *morenadas* (companies of blacks). Rank upon rank of *morenos* (blacks), even more numerous than the devils, danced noisily through the Carnival streets of Oruro on Saturday and Sunday (Fig. 13.7). Many reappeared during the march past of *comparsas* that framed the dramatic presentations on Monday. Most observers agree that the *morenos* represent African slaves imported to work in colonial silver mines or vineyards.

"Many of the older miners" in Oruro, June Nash reported in 1979, "speak of stories they heard from their parents, who saw the brutality of the *caporals* [overseers] exercised to an even greater degree against the slaves than against the Indians." One seventy-year-old miner told her "that Indians of his parents' generation would bury the dead bodies of slaves thrown out of the mines when they died."[51] Because of their inability to endure the Andean climate, African slaves proved more profitable to their owners in the vineyards of the tropical lowlands.

Early *moreno* masks, with their black skin, flattened noses, and thick, red lips, were simple caricatures of African features.[52] More recent ornamentation sometimes obscures the African referent. The dancers carry rotating ratchet noisemakers, sometimes made of armadillos, whose abrasive rhythm recalls "the steps of their chained feet" or "the sounds of the cranks turning the wine presses."[53] The *morenos'* tiered costumes of hooped and beaded cloth represent casks of wine or the heavy burden of mined silver. In either case, "the rich and heavy costume is not wealth for themselves, it is for their master."[54]

The Carnival critique of colonial slave masters is unintentionally directed back at Oruro's elite (many of whom are themselves dressed as *morenos*) by the lavish display of gold and silver that precedes each *comparsa*. A vehicle richly decorated with brightly colored cloths and hung with an abundance of gold and silver cups, plates, and other utensils drives ahead of the dancers. For the duration of the parade, these ostentatious displays of wealth are designated "offerings to the Virgin."[55] They are, of course, the inherited fruit of colonial mining and, perhaps, a distant memory of the Carnival redistribution of wealth in 1781.

Originally an Indian representation of the cruelty inflicted on blacks by a privileged elite in the name of commercial profit, the *morenada* is now danced primarily by "doctors, engineers, auditors, lawyers, . . . dentists,"[56] and their families, who alone can afford the expensive costumes. The young women of the *morenadas* wear short skirts and low-cut tops. Indicative of the degree to which the *morenada* may be losing its social conscience is the outgrowth, since the 1970s, of several independent squadrons of *caporales*, young men and women who crack their whips and strut their stuff in sequined pants and the most revealing skirts of all, transforming brutal overseers into photogenic dancers. Nevertheless, amid the glitter and the gold, the message of the *morenada* is still legible in performance. It is neither the Incas of the past nor the rural Indians of the present nor the impoverished miners placating the Tío who are guilty of the mortal sins of Christian theology. It is those who have exploited them.

When they reached the end of the parade route on Saturday, the dancers climbed the steps of the sanctuary, removed their masks, and made their way (mostly on their knees) up the nave to the altar rail. From about noon on Saturday until the early hours of Sunday morning, the sanctuary was filled with waves of black slaves, ornate devils, highland Indians, lowland "savages," and scantily clad young women. Men who had borne heavy masks and hot costumes the full length of the parade route sweated profusely. Women in high-heeled boots hobbled painfully and dropped to their knees with relief. Tobas, armed with all the regalia of paganism, knelt before the altar. Panoplies of feathers, cornucopias of masks, and a wild profusion of colors brightened the church. Brass bands and indigenous *tarkas* and *zamponas* filled it with music.

At the altar rail, each group of pilgrims was blessed by a friar. Then, the group's band struck up a folk hymn to the Virgin and the pilgrims made their way to the right of the altar, past a statue of Saint Michael set in a niche of the sanctuary wall. None that I saw paid it the least attention. For all that he might win Monday's staged battle against the devils of the *relato*, the archangel was of no importance at this culminating moment of the *entrada*. The Sins, the devils, the blacks, and the Indians belonged to the Virgin.

Passing counterclockwise around the enclosed altar area, the pilgrims knelt again as they arrived at the narrow walkway separating the back of the altar from the sacred fresco of the Virgen del Socavón. Tightly packed, the kneeling pilgrims shuffled by, faces raised to gaze in adoration at the Virgin. This was no distant and generic Virgin. This was the Virgin of the Mineshaft, who had comforted a romantic bandit in his dying, who took no offense at the miners' placation of the underground Tío, and who now blessed the slaves, the savages, the peasants, the demonized, and even the flawed middle class who, sanctioned by Carnival, had displayed their own excess. Each *comparsa* had paraded its own image of the Virgen del Socavón, but the fresco on the wall was the original from which all the reproductions drew their power. As they stood, the pilgrims turned to face the Virgin, backing out through a door near the altar with their eyes still on her image.

I saw no evidence of renunciation. Tobas, llama herders, warriors, and devils had danced freely in the circle outside the church. As they climbed the steps to the sanctuary, the female *caporales* had swung their hips and revealingly twirled their short skirts. Although the dancers had unmasked inside the church, they had done so not in renunciation of their role but to gaze freely on the Virgin and to receive a more personal blessing from her.

Their passage through the sanctuary was no forced surrender to a moralistic church but a voluntary act of gratitude to a Virgin who over the centuries has shown mercy to the sinful and the demonized.

Sunday's reiteration of the *entrada* offered further proof that the blessing of the Virgen del Socavón requires neither renunciation of the flesh nor repentance for rebellion against repressive authority. Sunday's parade was noticeably more relaxed than Saturday's had been. Devils, slaves, and Incas tied colored balloons to their masks. Carnivalesque figures absent on Saturday, such as a caricature of the president of Bolivia and a man in a tight skirt dancing a comic rumba, appeared on Sunday. The sanctuary was closed. The Virgin had blessed the celebrations and the masqueraders needed no further license.

Augusto Beltrán, commenting in 1962 on the exuberance and satire of Sunday's *entrada*, acknowledged that by Sunday "the occasional tourist might suspect" that Oruro's Carnival had lost its religious moorings. But Beltrán denied any impropriety, arguing that the increase of "joy, beauty, and wit" was firmly grounded in "the religious foundation" of Oruro's Carnival. Remembering that Oruro's Virgin of the Mineshaft was also the mother of Christ, he reminded the skeptical tourist that "Christ, the son of Mary," had said, "I have come that they may have life, and may have it abundantly" (John 10:10).[57] This is a startling gloss of the dominical saying but one that is full of insight into both Carnival and Christianity. The joyous celebration of embodied humanity and the strong critique of oppressive social hierarchy, characteristic of Carnival in Oruro as elsewhere, is grounded not in pagan resistance to Christianity but in the very heart of the Christian story. The child born to Mary affirmed humanity in all its comic fleshliness and, according to his mother's song, embodied a God who "puts down the mighty from their seat and exalts the humble."

IN PART ONE I proposed six heuristic principles for the study of religious festivals. By way of drawing our journey to a close, we can reflect on the assistance afforded by these principles not only in the study of patronal saints' days festivals but also now in the exploration of the ostensibly triumphalist feast of Corpus Christi and the avowedly "pagan" festival of Carnival.

First, Scott's distinction between public and hidden transcripts has helped me to read the mask of such diverse festivities as Corpus Christi in Camuñas and Cusco and Carnivals in Laza and Lantz. Into public transcripts that invoke an allegorical triumph of virtue over sin, the European iconography of martyrdom, the burial of Carnival by Lent, and the parade of a captured bandit, folk performers have insinuated hidden transcripts that protest the mistreatment of Jews by the Inquisition, imagine the end of indigenous subordination to the economic interests of mestizos, bawdily assert a millenarian vision of freedom and plenty for the poor, and enact the triumph of Christian Carnival over pagan Lent. Scott's distinction has not so much given me eyes to see as language to describe what is masked (and so displayed) in popular religious festivals.

Second, I have trusted folk performances to reveal their meanings without recourse to corroborative verbal testimony. In some cases, the embodied signs of a hidden transcript have been so obviously at odds with the festival's public transcript as to demand an alternative explanation. Camuñas's pilloried pope and mock inquisition are a case in point. So are San Sebastián's parrots, bare-breasted women, and Chuncho warriors. In other cases, the signs of the hidden transcript have been seamlessly woven into the whole, signaling their dissent less obtrusively but more pervasively. Lantz's Carnival mimicry of a Corpus Christi procession and the frightening but ultimately harmless fire of Berga's Patum are good examples. In a few cases, such as Armando Espinosa's acknowledgment in San Luis Huexotla that "Santiago is the sun" or Brian Honoré's observation in Trinidad that "we keep playing old mas for the same reason as that guy made *Schindler's List*," I have been fortunate enough to garner some verbal confirmation of what the performance was already telling me in a rich profusion of embodied signs. Even in these cases, however, I have learned more from the performance itself than I have from any other source. To privilege the speech of the "informant" or the writing of the scholar over articulate folk performance is to close one's ears to the chosen medium of the performers themselves.

Third, I have found that both Corpus Christi and Carnival—for all the difference in their official postures of Catholic triumphalism and pagan riot—can display a creative folk theology in dialogue with the official dogma of the church. Whether in their rejection of the threat of hell in Berga, their Carnival embrace of the Magnificat in Laza, their portrayal of Christ as a cheerful scapegoat for communal sins in Lantz, their devotion to a Virgin who prefers local demons, savages, and bandits to strangers armed with swords and sacred texts in Oruro, or their protests against injustice perpetrated in the name of Christianity in Camuñas, Cusco, and Port of Spain, folk performers enact an alternative theology. The festive God of folk theology is one who "puts down the mighty from their seat and exalts the humble," who "fills the hungry with good things," who prefers fireworks and dancing to pomp and ceremony, who chooses muddy flesh over homiletic word, and who excludes none from his embrace but those who would exclude others.

Fourth, I have been confirmed in my suspicion of official explanations of fiestas, especially those backed by uncontested scholarship. Glotz's account of the local roots of Binche's Carnival in dignified pre-Christian seasonal ritual collapses under close historical scrutiny, revealing the Gilles's disreputable but much more interesting origins in an imported and very ribald commedia dell'arte clown. Yugo Santacruz's repackaging of Corpus Christi in Camuñas as a pious *auto sacramental* is equally misleading, but at least it had the virtue of protecting the fiesta from ecclesiastical suppression. Now that the danger has passed, his theory is treated with some suspicion even in Camuñas.

Fifth, large-scale urban fiestas have been heavily contested, often along class lines. In Cusco, middle-class mestizos dress as Incas to lay claim to a romanticized indigenous past and to promote tourism, while suburban Indians mask themselves as mestizos to protest economic exploitation and to dream of a messianic reversal of fortunes. In Trinidad, the rhetoric of pagan Bacchanal licenses middle-class indulgence and promotes tourism, while old mas counters by insisting on the memories of slavery. Oruro's Carnival, lacking a substantial tourist infrastructure and sharing a common devotion to a single Virgin, is less contested. It has, however, been the site of upper-class withdrawal in the past and is now, in its proliferation of "Indian" dances, beginning to slip towards the middle-class romantic *indigenismo* of Cusco's Inti Raymi parades.

Sixth, windows onto the hidden transcript of a fiesta have been more likely to open in its deliberately hybrid elements than in those that aim at purity and fail. While the romanticized "indigenous" dancers of Cusco and Oruro were more interesting than their counterparts outside the basilica of Guadalupe, none bore the same wealth of hidden transcripts as the genuinely Indian dancers of San Sebastián who masked themselves as blue-eyed blacks, Chunchos, Qollas, and Majeños. Similarly, in La Mancha, it was not the purified Corpus Christi of Toledo that embodied a hidden transcript of folk theology but the hybrid dancers of Camuñas, who enacted and accepted their own heritage (or, at least, that of their neighbors) as Christian Jews.

The apostle Paul wrote that in Christ "there is neither Jew nor Greek, slave nor free, male nor female" (Galatians 3:28). He later added "barbarian" (Colossians 3:11) to the list of prohibited hierarchical rankings. One of the great failings of the church, according to the masked theology of folk fiestas, is to have substituted for these classical categories of difference not only the racial construct of black and white and the ethnic distinction of European and Indian but also an eternal division of Christian and non-Christian. In Spain, Sariñena's *coloquio* of Moors and Christians, Camuñas's defense of persecuted Jews, Vilafranca's incorporation of demons, bandits, giants, dwarfs, and saints into a single worshiping body, and Berga's inclusive vision of those unharmed by fire, all reject the division between Catholic and infidel in whose conservative defense Franco launched the Spanish Civil War. A similar denial of hierarchical limits to God's favor is found in the Americas: in Loíza's joyous exodus, alongside Santiago de los Niños, of the poor, the women, the dead, the little devils, the cross-dressed, and the crazy; in Mexico's proliferation of maternal images of the Virgin of Guadalupe and her namesake Maringuilla (Malinche), extending divine blessing far beyond the single clerically controlled image in the basilica; in San Luis Huexotla's refusal of forced conversion and celebration of indigenous Christianity in its *danza de los santiagos;* and in Oruro's Carnival devotion of demons, savages, blacks, and Indians to the all-embracing Virgen del Socavón.

Most patronal saints' day celebrations and the hidden transcripts of some Corpus Christi festivities give physical form to this inclusive folk theology. But of all the Christian festivals, Carnival is most faithful to the vision that God is with us not in the dizzying distinctions of constructed hierarchy but in the muddiness of our common humanity. One could argue that such a carnivalesque folk theology is nothing more than the radical good news of the gospel narratives rephrased in festive form. It is a sad commentary on the church's entanglement with power that such good news so often has to be insinuated into the public square in the form of hidden transcripts.

Notes

CHAPTER 1. *Demons and Dragons*

1. For Torras's own account of Manresa's *festa major* and *correfoc*, see Torras i Serra, *Manresa*, pp. 47–52, 56–62; for a historical overview of Manresa's various festivals, see Torras i Serra, "Festes."

2. Sarret i Arbós, *Historia*, pp. 127–128; Sarret i Arbós, *Historia religiosa*, p. 60.

3. Gasol, *Manresa*, pp. 85–86, 103; see also Torras i Serra, *Manresa*, p. 27.

4. For Zaragoza in 1399, see Milá y Fontanals, *Obras*, 6:237; and, in 1414, Shergold, *History*, pp. 115–120; Aubrun, "Débuts," pp. 301–302. For Barcelona in 1424, see Milá y Fontanals, *Obras*, 6:376–379; Very, *Spanish*, pp. 37–39. For Manresa, see Torras i Serra, "Festes," p. 479.

5. Torras i Serra, "Festes," pp. 478–483; Torras i Serra, *Manresa*, pp. 19–33.

6. Amades, *Costumari*, 3:78–80; Milá y Fontanals, *Obras*, 6:247, 250.

7. Torras i Serra, "Festes," pp. 485–486; Torras i Serra, *Manresa*, pp. 25, 33, 49; Sarret i Arbós, *Historia religiosa*, pp. 298–300.

8. For a description of the crypt, see Sarret i Arbós, *Historia religiosa*, pp. 91–92.

9. For the general turmoil of these years in Spain, see Thomas, *Spanish*. For Manresa in particular, see Sardans i Farràs, "República." For the anarchist takeover of Manresa's town hall, see Bookchin, *Spanish*, p. 244. For the attacks on churches in Manresa, see Sardans i Farràs, "República," p. 426; Junyent i Maydeu, *Manresa*, p. 140; Gasol, *Manresa*, p. 46. Such attacks were widespread in Republican-controlled Spain after Franco and other generals launched the Nationalist rebellion in July 1936.

10. Caro Baroja, *Carnaval*, p. 144.

11. Lovelace, *Salt*, pp. 90–91.

12. Burke, *Popular*, p. 199.

13. Montes Camacho, *Proceso*, p. 15. For Oruro's Carnival, see below, chap. 13.

14. Ibañez, personal communication, 5 October 1998. A description of the ceremony at Montserrat can be found in Amades, *Costumari*, 5:853–856.

15. Burke, *Popular*, p. 192.

16. Ibid., p. 193.

17. Ibid., pp. 207–243.

18. Scott, *Domination*, p. 136; Harris, *Aztecs*, pp. 23–27. Both Scott and I intend "public" and "hidden transcripts" in a figurative sense, including a much wider range of speech and nonspeech acts than can be reduced to mere writing.

19. Harris, *Aztecs*, pp. 20–27, 243–250; Harris, *Dialogical*, pp. 108–119.

20. Harris, *Aztecs*, p. 23.

21. Milá y Fontanals, *Obras*, 6: 376.

22. Bové, *Penedès*, p. 81; Milá y Fontanals, "Algunas," p. 30.

23. These dates are given in *Balls de la festa major*.

24. Amades, *Costumari*, 1:514–524; Milá y Fontanals, *Obras*, 6:286–291; Bové, *Penedès*, pp. 105–111; Bertran, *Ball*.

25. Fribourg, *Fêtes*, p. 65, reports that stick dancers in Aragon use old cart wheel spokes because they are a good source of dry holm oak, which makes a particularly good sound when struck and is otherwise hard to find.

26. "The name derives from the expression '*fer figa*,' which means to make faces (*fer ganyotes*), and refers to the constant exchange of jibes between the dancers. (Marta Ibañez, personal communication, 25 April 2000).

27. For the *ball pla* and other dances mentioned in this paragraph, see the relevant entries in Pujol and Amades, *Diccionari*.

28. *Balls*; Bové, *Penedès*, pp. 67–69.

29. Farmer, *Oxford*, pp. 181–182.

30. See Forrest, *History*, for a summary of the various theories (including those of Cecil Sharp) of the rural, pre-Christian origins of morris dancing and for careful documentation of the historical origins of the morris in various forms of aristocratic and courtly dance gradually diffused into rural England.

31. Noyes, "Mule," pp. 1–2.

32. Steinberg, *Sexuality*, p. 106.

33. Ibid., p. 251.

CHAPTER 2. *Flowers for Saint Tony*

1. Fahissa, *Falla*, pp. 101–104. For the traditional Aragonese *jota*, see Arco y Garay, *Notas*, pp. 474–478.

2. Fribourg, who worked in Sariñena between 1975 and 1985, includes the serenading tour of the *joteros* among "those ancient ritual elements that have disappeared" (*Fêtes*, pp. 23, 112). It has since been reintroduced.

3. Fribourg, *Fêtes*, pp. 73–74, 84, reports that the majorettes and *mairalesas* arrived in Sariñena from urban festivals in the 1970s. *Mairalesa* is the feminine form of *mayoral* (community representative) and is considered more Aragonese than *reina de la fiesta*.

4. For a detailed discussion of the *danzantes'* costumes, see Fribourg, *Fêtes*, pp. 60–67.

5. Beltrán Martínez, *Dance*, p. 174; see also Fribourg, *Fêtes*, p. 60.

6. The Aragonese bagpipe differs from those used in other parts of Spain. Fribourg, *Fêtes*, p. 71, reports that "Sariñena takes pride in having been the last [village] in Aragon to preserve the true Aragonese bagpipe (until 1974) and the first to revive its use (in 1980), at which time there were only three surviving examples, two of which were in Sariñena."

7. Fribourg, *Fêtes*, pp. 69, 74.

8. Epton, *Spanish*, p. 179, writes that basil is "supposed to be an antidote against the powers of evil." See also Alford, *Singing*, p. 50. In Sariñena, I was told that it was a symbol of nature (*la naturaleza*). Fribourg, *Fêtes*, pp. 77–78, regards it as a visible sign of "integration" into the fiesta.

9. Fribourg, *Fêtes*, pp. 55–56, 113.

10. Although the honor guard of dancers is an ancient tradition, the offering of fruit and flowers at Sariñena's fiesta mass may be a recent innovation (Fribourg, *Fêtes*, pp. 90–91, 113).

11. Bosch's triptych lends itself to varied interpretations, of which this is the most widely accepted. See Gibson, *Bosch*, pp. 77–99; Orienti and de Solier, *Bosch*, pp. 82–100; Beagle, *Garden*.

12. For a full treatment of the remarkable artwork of Albi's cathedral, which includes a number of much happier scenes, see the two volumes of Biget and Escourbiac, *Sainte-Cécile*.

13. Adams, *Mont*, p. 78.

14. Thomas, *Spanish*, p. 54.

15. Brown, *Cult*, p. 50.

16. The foundational text of liberation theology is Gutiérrez, *Theology*. For an introduction to base communities, see Cleary, *Crisis*, pp. 104–124; and, for the study of the Bible in these communities, see Mesters, *Defenseless*.

17. Fribourg, *Fêtes*, p. 103.

18. One onlooker told me the boys were called *volantes* because "their twirling skirts make them look as if they're flying." But Jaime Martín Coto said, "They are called *volantes* not because they fly but because they are initiates. The word *volantes* means initiates. They are apprentices, invited by their fathers, uncles, or brothers to learn the dance. As they grow they become *danzantes*." He also provided me with a copy of the script of Sariñena's *coloquio de moros y cristianos*, a variant of which is printed in Arco y Garay, *Notas*, pp. 198–223.

19. Fribourg, *Fêtes*, p. 68. The Mayoral and Rabadán are leaders who speak on behalf of their community, a role often adopted by the chief shepherds in a pastoral economy.

20. Charlemagne passed through Aragon in 778, the rear guard of his retreating army being wiped out by Basques—or, in the epic *Chanson de Roland*, by Moors—at Roncesvalles.

21. This conciliatory ending, which is not included in the Sariñena text published by Arco y Garay, *Notas*, pp. 198–223, may be found instead in the Sena text of Arco y Garay, pp. 172–174.

22. Fribourg, *Fêtes*, p. 110, mistakenly suggests that the penultimate *mudanza*, in which a knot of swords is placed around the first shepherd's neck, represents the beheading of the Turkish general. The episode is known as the *degollau* (beheading), but it is the Christian Mayoral rather than the Turkish General whose head is placed in the knot (Larrea Palacín, *Dance*, p. 15). The variously named knot, nut, or rose is a common figure in European sword dances. When placed over the head of one of the dancers (usually the leader), it visually suggests a beheading, but it does so without any necessary narrative connotation.

23. Morera, *Extro-historia*, pp. 24–56, 131–133.

24. Ibid., p. 48.

25. Ibid., p. 120. For the Aragonese offensive of March 1938, see Thomas, *Spanish*, pp. 787–793. Thomas estimates that "at least 75,000 or so Moroccan 'volunteers' . . . fought for Franco" (p. 908).

26. Morera, *Extro-historia*, p. 145.

27. Harris, *Aztecs*. For a close reading of two modern *fiestas de moros y cristianos* that embody the desire for *convivencia*, see Harris, "Muhammed." See also Albert-Llorca, "Maures," pp. 6–8.

28. Spanish humor can seem a little strange to outsiders. According to Fribourg, *Fêtes*, p. 98, in 1978 Sariñena staged a comic bullfight (*charlotada*) during its patronal saint's day festival. The picadors and toreros, who somehow succeeded in killing the bulls, were all dwarfs.

CHAPTER 3. El Mas Chiquito de To' Los Santos

1. Zaragoza, *St. James*; Ungerleider Kepler, *Fiestas*; Rodríguez, *African*, pp. 16–17, 47–52; Vissepo, *Herencia*; Martínez Sosa, *Fiestas*; Malavé, *Tercera*.

2. Alegría, "Fiesta," pp. 126, 130.

3. Alegría, *Fiesta*, pp. 2–3; Zaragoza, *St. James*, pp. 46–47.

4. Álvarez Nazario, *Elemento*, pp. 81–83.

5. Alegría, *Fiesta*, pp. 22–25; Zaragoza, *St. James*, pp. 47, 58–59, 92–93.

6. Alegría, *Fiesta*, p. 23.

7. Alegría, "Fiesta," p. 126.

8. Sued Badillo and López Cantos, *Puerto Rico*, pp. 167–168; Álvarez Nazario, *Elemento*, pp. 44–49, 55–60. For a comprehensive history of the transatlantic slave trade, see Thomas, *Slave*.

9. Álvarez Nazario, *Elemento*, pp. 25–26; Curtin, *Rise*, p. 120.

10. Álvarez Nazario, *Elemento*, pp. 366–367.

11. Ibid., p. 51. Dorsey, "Puerto Rico," pp. 266, 273, is equally emphatic. In a detailed study of Puerto Rico's participation in the slave trade during the nineteenth century, he writes of the "near absence" of a "Yorùbá factor."

12. I am grateful to Judith Bettelheim for drawing my attention to these influences.

13. Herskovits, *Myth*.

14. Raboteau, *Slave*, p. 52.

15. Herskovits, "African," p. 640; Alegría, "Fiesta," p. 133n2; Bascom, *Shango.*

16. Bettelheim, personal communication, 12 March 1999; Drewal, personal communication, 7 September 2000.

17. I was told that all three images used to be allowed entrance to the church, "but the priests objected" to the masked *vejigantes* and *locas* that accompanied the other two. Alegría's film includes footage of Santiago de las Mujeres leaving the church in Loíza.

18. In the Roman Catholic Church, red is the obligatory liturgical color for days of apostles and martyrs. A red stole over a white cassock is the simplest form of priestly observance. The traditional Yorùbá association of red and white with Shangó is coincidental.

19. Alegría, *Fiesta,* pp. 58–59.

20. Alegría, "Fiesta," p. 130.

21. Bascom, *Yoruba,* p. 111.

22. Drewal, personal communication, 7 September 2000.

23. Alegría, "Fiesta," p. 130; Alegría, *Fiesta,* p. 56n2.

24. For Puerto Rico, see López Cantos, *Fiestas,* pp. 168–174. For modern Mexico, see Harris, *Aztecs,* pp. 3–17, 243–250.

25. For the medieval fool, see Southworth, *Fools,* pp. 4–7, pls. 4(b), 8(b); Chambers, *Medieval,* 1:385–387. For modern Carnival, see Cocho, *Carnaval,* pp. 138, 150–151; Harris, "Carnival," pp. 158–159; Giroux, *Carnavals,* p. 36.

26. "Relación verídica," p. 178. Scarano, "Jíbaro," p. 1416, glosses *vejigante* in this instance as "a monster who teased festival-goers with the contents of a cow's bladder, often urine or feces." Even in the context of Carnival, I have not seen inflated bladders filled with anything but air. Bonafoux, "Carnaval," pp. 108–109, claims to have seen "Carnival coconuts" filled with urine and "fecal matter," but his claim is disputed by his editor.

27. López Cantos, *Fiestas,* pp. 195, 204.

28. Bonafoux, "Carnaval," p. 111.

29. Pertinent excerpts from *Nenen de la ruta mora* are included in Martínez Sosa, *Fiestas.* See also Palma, *Muestras,* pp. 166–167.

30. The song was Nigel and Marvin's "Movin'." See Mason, *Bacchanal,* p. 179, for a list of Road March winners.

31. Although photographs (Alegría, *Fiesta,* pp. 54–55) and film footage (Alegría, *Fiesta;* Martínez Sosa, *Fiestas*) from the 1940s and 1950s show *caballeros* on horseback, all were on foot in 1997.

32. Zaragoza, *St. James,* p. 108.

33. Alegría, *Fiesta,* p. 54. See also Ungerleider Kepler, *Fiestas,* p. 66.

34. Until his recent death, Castor Ayala was the premier mask maker in the region. His son Raul Ayala now makes masks according to his father's designs.

35. See Harris, *Aztecs,* pp. 10–11, 240–242, for Mexican and New Mexican *viejos* and *abuelos* (grandfathers) with similar roles and masks.

36. Zaragoza, *St. James,* p. 116.

37. So, in nineteenth-century San Juan, did the images of Nuestra Señora de la Soledad (Our Lady of Solitude) and the resurrected Christ greet one another in the street before dawn on Easter Sunday? See López Cantos, *Fiestas*, p. 69, and Scott, "Walker's," p. 43.

38. Vissepo, *Herencia*; Bilby, "Caribbean," p. 191.

39. Alegría, "Fiesta," p. 131.

40. Scott, "Walker's," p. 43; Álvarez Nazario, *Elemento*, p. 304.

41. Álvarez Nazario, *Elemento*, pp. 303–320; see also Mauleón Benítez, *Español*, pp. 91–99.

42. For an extended study of Loiceño Spanish, see Mauleón Benítez, *Español*.

43. The *viejo* identified his mount, made from plastic tubing, burlap sacks, and straw, as a "mula" (mule). Given the high level of Catalan immigration to Puerto Rico in the nineteenth century, it probably had its roots in the traditional hobbyhorses and ill-tempered mules of Catalan festivals. For Catalan immigration, see Cifre de Loubriel, *Formación*; and Sonesson, *Catalanes*. For an identical Puerto Rican *mula* in New York, see Sciorra, "'We're not here,'" pp. 37–38.

CHAPTER 4. *The Cross-Dressed Virgin on a Tightrope*

1. *El Heraldo de México*, 13 December 1998, estimated the number of visitors "since 8 December" at "more than six million people." *Excelsior*, 13 December 1998, cited the Office of Public Security as its source for the figure of "almost seven million in the last 72 hours." These figures may be exaggerated.

2. Mexica is now believed to be a more precise designation of the inhabitants of Tenochtitlan-Tlatelolco. The broader term Aztec covers many Yuto-Aztecan groups in Mesoamerica.

3. Sahagún, *Historia*, pp. 704–705 (bk. 11, chap. 12, app.). Until very recently, most scholars accepted Sahagún's assertion without question (see, for example, Harrington, "Mother," pp. 32–35; Taylor, *Magistrates*, p. 279). Burkhart, "Cult," pp. 207–209, 221, was the first to issue a serious challenge. Poole, *Lady*, pp. 78–80, 215, endorsed and disseminated Burkhart's suspicions.

4. For an excellent study of the origins of the Guadalupe cult, see Poole, *Lady*. For a history of its shifting theological underpinnings, see Brading, *Mexico*.

5. For the construction of the two basilicas, see Brading, *Mexican*, pp. 119, 336; Mullen, *Architecture*, p. 121.

6. Burkhart, "Cult," p. 206.

7. Laso de la Vega, *Story*, pp. 78–79.

8. See ibid., pp. 60–61, for the text, and pp. 37–39, for editorial comment on the meaning of *macehualtzintzli*. The *Nican mopohua*—so named after its opening words ("Here is recounted")—is the longest of several parts of

Laso de la Vega's *Huei tlamahuicoltica* ("By a great miracle . . ."), which also includes opening and closing prayers, an account of subsequent miracles connected with the image of Guadalupe, and an epilogue.

9. Laso de la Vega, *Story*, pp. 68–69.

10. Ibid., pp. 64–67.

11. Ibid., pp. 76–79.

12. Ibid., pp. 64–65.

13. Poole, *Lady*, pp. 99–100.

14. Taylor, *Magistrates*, p. 282.

15. Ibid., pp. 285–286.

16. Harris, "Moctezuma's."

17. Lockhart, *Nahuas*, p. 374.

18. Rostas, "Production," p. 211.

19. Stone, *Sign.* González, "Concheros," offers a more recent study of the dance.

20. Rostas, "Production," p. 220; Stone, *Sign*, p. 7; González, "Concheros," p. 216.

21. Rostas, "Production," pp. 210–211.

22. Rope walking was known in Europe at least by the twelfth century, and some of the early accounts include dancing in the funambulist's repertoire. In July 1590, for example, "an Hungarian and other of the Queen's Majesty's players and tumblers" entertained a crowd in the English city of Shrewsbury. A rope being "tight[en]ed and drawn straight upon poles erected" in the Corn Market, the Hungarian "went to and fro" on the rope, "dancing and turning" while holding "a long pole in his hands" (Somerset, *Shropshire*, 1:247). Other early records survive from countries as far apart as Ireland (Fletcher, *Drama*, p. 231), Switzerland (Chambers, *Medieval*, 1:70–71), and Spain (Esses, *Dance*, 1:677–678).

23. Burkhart, "Cult," pp. 207–208; see also Burkhart, *Before*, p. 11.

24. Burkhart, "Cult," p. 209.

25. See, for example, Paz, *Labyrinth*, pp. 65–88; and Cypess, *Malinche*. Recent feminist efforts to reclaim the historical Malinche as a strong, independent woman who deployed official male power to her own advantage have not yet changed the popular perception.

26. Harris, "Moctezuma's."

27. Ibid., pp. 171–172.

28. Laso de la Vega, *Story*, pp. 112–113.

29. Lutterman-Aguilar, "Virgin," p. 1.

30. Cisneros, "Guadalupe."

CHAPTER 5. *A Polka for the Sun and Santiago*

1. For the church, convent, and Mendieta's residence, see Urquiza Vázquez, *Convento*. For the Aztec ruins, see Batres, *Exploraciones*; García García, *Huexotla*, pp. 77–98; Kelly, *Complete*, pp. 66–67.

2. Sahagún, *Florentine*, 9:13–14 (bk. 8, chap. 4); Sahagún, *Historia*, 2:286.

3. For a summary of Huexotla's early history, population estimates, and archaeology, see Brumfiel, "Specialization," pp. 30–45.

4. For a map of Lake Texcoco and its precontact cities, including Huexotla, see Thomas, *Conquest*, p. 4. For Cortés's visit, see Vetancurt, *Teatro*, 2:138–139.

5. Vetancurt, *Teatro*, 3:199; Montoya Castro, *Huexotla*, p. 22.

6. Latrobe, *Rambler*, p. 138.

7. The patron saint of Huexotla is San Luis Obispo, known outside the Spanish-speaking world as Saint Louis (1274–1297), Franciscan bishop of Toulouse.

8. Urquiza Vázquez, *Convento*, p. 120, wrote in 1993 that the *danza de los santiaguitos* was "introduced [to Huexotla] from neighboring villages 75 years ago." If she is correct and if Armando's date for the introduction of the brass band is also accurate, then the change in instrumentation took place shortly after the dance arrived in Huexotla.

9. Jáuregui, "Santiago," p. 203.

10. For street maps of Huexotla, see García García, *Huexotla*, p. 18; Montoya Castro, *Huexotla*, p. 20. For a brief discussion and photograph of the bridge, see Romero de Terreros, "Huexotla."

11. Jáuregui, "Santiago," p. 168.

12. Schwartz, *Curse*, pp. 1–4, 34–37, 79–83, 118–119.

13. For a diagram of the initial lineup at San Pablo Ixáyotl, see Jáuregui, "Santiago," pp. 172–173. For a detailed choreography of the dance at San Pablo, see Ramírez and Valle, "Coreografías," pp. 372–385.

14. For the influence of European dance bands on Mexican folk music, see Thomson, "Ceremonial."

15. Jáuregui, "Santiago," p. 183.

16. Ibid., p. 198.

17. Ibid., p. 203.

18. Urquiza Vázquez, *Convento*, pp. 67–68.

19. Jáuregui, "Santiago," p. 192.

20. Latrobe, *Rambler*, pp. 139–140.

21. Dominguez Assiayn, "Filosofía," p. 214. Ricard, *Spiritual*, p. 277, gives credence to this account, but his source is hard to track down because his endnotes are numbered incorrectly.

22. Scott, *Domination*, p. 136.

CHAPTER 6. *Dancing under Friendly Fire*

1. For the accounts entry, see Ingram, *Coventry*, p. 230; for a discussion of the staging, see King and Davidson, *Coventry*, p. 48; for the biblical reference to a final conflagration, see 2 Peter 3:10.

2. Brown, *Cult*; Abou-El-Haj, *Medieval*, pp. 7–32.

3. Brown, *Cult*, pp. 67–68.

4. Rubin, *Corpus*, pp. 14–82; Zika, "Hosts."

5. For text and analysis of the bull, see Franceschini, "Origine." For the birth and early development of the feast, see Rubin, *Corpus*, pp. 164–212.

6. For the list of representations, see Milá y Fontanals, *Obras*, 6:376–379. For summaries in English, see Very, *Spanish*, pp. 37–39; Shergold, *History*, pp. 56–57.

7. For the English Corpus Christi plays in general, see Kolve, *Play*; for the York plays in particular, see Beadle, *York Plays*; Beadle, "York Cycle."

8. Motolinía, *Historia*, pp. 67–74 (trat. 1, cap. 15); Harris, *Aztecs*, pp. 134–147.

9. Korotaj, Szwedkowska, and Szymanska, *Programy*, p. 433; Dabrówka, "Anything," pp. 7–9.

10. Turner, *History*, pp. 115–122. For the staging of devils and hell in European medieval drama, see Massip, "Infierno"; and, in the English Corpus Christi plays, Cox, *Devil*, pp. 19–38.

11. Very, *Spanish*, pp. 106–107, 114–117.

12. Ibid., pp. 107–108.

13. Ortiz, "Uses"; Noyes, "Mule," pp. 409–425.

14. The procession was abolished by Berga's clergy, for whom the participation of the Spanish army in the procession was "a serious grievance," the small number of participants walking near the host an embarrassment, and the vibrancy of the preceding *entremesos* a reminder that "the procession was out of their hands in more ways than one." To their credit, the clergy encouraged the secular growth of the *entremesos* as an expression of Berguedan identity. See Noyes, "Mule," pp. 427–429.

15. Although the first record of a Corpus Christi procession in Berga dates from 1527, the *tabal* and the first of the *entremesos* are not documented until 1623 (Armengou, *Patum*, p. 22; Noyes, "Mule," pp. 234, 297). For the claim that the Patum was instituted in 1394, see Armengou, pp. 40–46; Noyes, pp. 221–227.

16. Armengou, *Patum*, pp. 28–32; Noguera i Canal, *Visió*, pp. 22–30; Noyes, "Mule," pp. 221–225, 367–370.

17. Huch i Guixer, *Patum*, p. 29. For a recent history of the giants, see Rumbo i Soler, *Història*.

18. Farràs, *Patum*, p. 12.

19. Noyes, "Mule," p. 427.

20. For the music of the various dances, see Huch, *Patum*, pp. 114–123; Armengou, *Patum*, pp. 129–152.

21. The escape of the fourth Turk is clearly visible both on my video footage from 1996 and on the film of the 1994 Patum that I bought from Berga's Foto Luigi.

22. Noyes, "Mule," p. 374, calls this "a tremor of pleasure fulfilled." See also Farràs, *Patum*, p. 12.

23. Noyes, "Mule," p. 174.

24. Ibid., pp. 384–385.

25. Farràs, *Patum*, p. 20.

26. Bernstein, *Formation*, p. 262.

27. Noyes, "Mule," pp. 459–460.

28. Farràs, *Patum*, p. 62. Noyes, "Mule," pp. 452–455, disputes Farràs's reading.

29. Neumann, *Geistliches*, 1:306–308. For the probable text of the play, see Schneider, *Eisenacher*. For a scholarly discussion of the incident, see Gras, "*Ludus.*"

30. Barth, *Humanity*, pp. 61–62.

CHAPTER 7. *A Confraternity of Jews*

1. Fita, "Inquisición," pp. 294–296; English translation from Kamen, *Spanish*, pp. 207–208.

2. Kamen, *Spanish*, pp. 60, 329.

3. Ibid., pp. 48, 302. For a brief and disturbingly laudatory history of the Inquisition in Toledo, see Moreno Nieto, *Diccionario*, pp. 203–208.

4. Molinié, "Rite," p. 133.

5. The morality play reading is most fully developed by Yugo Santacruz, *Danzantes*. See also González Casarrubios, *Fiestas*, pp. 97–103. Caballero Santacruz, "Danza," p. 31, calls this the "official interpretation."

6. Molinié, "Rite," p. 133. See also the photographs and captions in Romero Aranda, *Imagenes*, pp. 20–22.

7. Jiménez, "Panoramica," pp. 154–157. For a history of the various military orders, see Seward, *Monks*. For the Knights of Malta in particular, see Sire, *Knights* (for Consuegra, see pp. 140–143, pl. xiv.)

8. Held, *Inquisition*, pp. 150, 153.

9. Molinié, "Rite," pp. 134, 144.

10. Kamen, *Spanish*, p. 202.

11. Ibid., p. 13.

12. González Casarrubios, *Fiestas*, p. 102.

13. Molinié, "Rite," p. 134.

14. Caballero Santacruz, "Danza," p. 27.

15. Forrest, *History*, p. 168.

16. For the late courtly origins of the European sword dance, the English morris dance, and the Spanish *danza de moros y cristianos*, see, respectively, Corrsin, *Sword*; Forrest, *History*; Harris, *Aztecs*.

17. Yugo Santacruz, *Danzantes*; Molinié, "Rite," p. 137.

18. Yugo Santacruz, *Danzantes*, p. 13.

19. Fernandez Calvo, "Manifestaciones," p. 195.

20. Brugarola, "Fiestas"; Moreno Nieto, *Provincia*, pp. 106–107; Epton, *Spanish*, p. 104; Moreno Nieto, *Diccionario*, p. 70.

21. Brugarola, "Fiestas," p. 76.

22. Cf. Romero Aranda, *Imágenes*, p. 119, and Held, *Inquisition*, pp. 86 (fig. 68), 131 (fig. 115).

23. Molinié, "Horca," p. 117.

24. Cf. Romero Aranda, *Imágenes*, pp. 128-129, and Held, *Inquisition*, p. 130 (figs. 112-113).

25. Held, *Inquisition*, p. 57; Kamen, *Spanish*, p. 190.

26. Molinié, "Rite," p. 138.

27. Julian Navarro, reprinted in *Programa*, p. 39.

28. Molinié, "Rite," pp. 140, 144-146.

29. Ibid., p. 138.

30. For the order of the procession in 1997, see *Programa*, pp. 8-9. For a lavishly illustrated description of the procession and its participants, see López Gómez, *Procesión*.

31. *Programa*, p. 9. See also López Gómez, *Procesión*, pp. 73-75.

32. *Programa*, p. 9. See also López Gómez, *Procesión*, pp. 81-93.

33. Kamen, *Spanish*, p. 207.

CHAPTER 8. *Saint Sebastian and the Blue-eyed Blacks*

1. As the father of Christian monasticism, Anthony of Egypt (251-355) is also known as Anthony the Abbot. The Order of Hospitallers of Saint Anthony, founded ca. 1100, kept pigs that were allowed by special privilege to run free in medieval streets.

2. Santisteban Ochoa, "Documentos," p. 31, prints a document, written in 1732, in which the episcopal donation of the silver "carro" (cart) is recorded. Fiedler, "Corpus," p. 285, reports that the gold and silver monstrance was added in 1745. The weight and other measurements are printed in several descriptive brochures readily available in Cusco during Corpus Christi.

3. For a detailed account of the conquest, see Hemming, *Conquest*.

4. Ibid., pp. 425-450.

5. Toledo, *Fundación*, pp. 87-90. For the date of the declaration, see Mariátegui Oliva, *Pintura* (1951), p. 12.

6. Dean, *Inka*, pp. 31-38.

7. Cieza de León, *Incas*, pp. 190-193 (pt. 2, chap. 29), Sallnow, *Pilgrims*, pp. 39-40; Fiedler, "Corpus," pp. 245-278; Dean, *Inka*, pp. 32-38.

8. Garcilaso, *Royal*, 1:244-245 (pt. 1, bk. 5, chap. 2); Dean, *Inka*, p. 38.

9. Garcilaso, *Royal*, 2:1415-1416 (pt. 2, bk. 8, chap. 1). Cf. Garcilaso's similar description of Inti Raymi at 1:356-358 (pt. 1, bk. 6, chap. 20). Dean, *Inka*, pp. 200-201, contends that Garcilaso's descriptions of the two festivals are "intentionally analogous," reflecting his desire "to demonstrate how the Inkas had prepared the way for Christianity in the Andes."

10. Esquivel y Navia, *Noticias*, 2:41.

11. Dean, *Inka*, pp. 15, 32.

12. Garcilaso, *Royal*, 2:1417-1419 (pt. 2, bk. 8, chap. 1). See also Esquivel y Navia, *Noticias*, 1:178.

13. For the 1615 reference, see Dean, *Inka*, p. 255. For the dance's pre-Hispanic origins, see Guaman Poma, *Nueva*, 1:230-234 [fols. 322-323]; Randall, "Qoyllur," pp. 45-47; Sallnow, *Pilgrims*, p. 221.

14. Blanco, *Cuzco*, p. 106.

15. Esquivel y Navia, *Noticias*, 2:183n. The text is not clear. Perhaps, as Mariátegui Oliva, *Pintura* (1951), p. 14, believes, the "masked Indian dancers, dressed as Spaniards," replaced an unidentified banned dance.

16. Fiedler, "Corpus," p. 285. Cahill, "Popular," p. 93n, disputes Fiedler's interpretation.

17. Cahill, "Popular," pp. 71–72.

18. Esquivel y Navia, *Noticias*, 2:175–176n; Dean, *Inka*, pp. 82–83.

19. Cahill, "Popular," p. 79.

20. The series originally boasted eighteen paintings, of which twelve now belong to the Museo Arzobispal del Arte Religioso in Cusco, four are in private collections in Santiago, Chile, and two are unidentified (Dean, *Inka*, p. 64, 232–233). In 1835 Blanco, *Cuzco*, p. 63, admired the "delicate brushwork" of the paintings, which were "nailed to the walls" of the church of Santa Ana "in expensive gilded frames," and reported that the parish had refused their sale to "several foreigners." The four paintings now in Santiago appear to have been sold between 1895 and 1907 (Dean, *Inka*, p. 233). They were in good condition when located by Mariátegui in 1952 and 1983. In 1951 Mariátegui Oliva, *Pintura*, p. 7, lamented the "deplorable state" of the twelve paintings that still hung unidentified and unguarded "on the adobe walls of this modest temple" of Santa Ana. These were moved to the Museo Arzobispal in 1968. Fifteen of the paintings are reproduced in black-and-white in Mariátegui Oliva, *Pintura* (1951) and *Pintura* (1954). Fourteen, including the one that Mariátegui had not yet found, are reproduced (some in color) in Dean, *Inka*, figs. 8–21, pls. I–V. The twelve paintings still in Cusco are reprinted in color in Flores Ochoa, "Historia," figs. 14–24, 29, and, in the subsequent "catalogue," figs. 33–44. See also Mesa and Gisbert, *Historia*, I:pls. XXV–XXVII, II:pls. 229–242.

21. Jaye and Mitchell, "Iconography," p. 98.

22. Mesa and Gisbert, *Historia*, 1:179; Dean, *Inka*, pl. IV. For the mischievous behavior of children in the paintings, see Dean, "Naughty."

23. Dean, *Inka*, pp. 84–87, 93–95.

24. Ibid., pp. 88–89.

25. Ibid., p. 97

26. Ibid., pp. 182–199. Mariátegui Oliva, *Pintura* (1951), p. 32, believes the military corps to be a group of Indian dancers.

27. Castro, *Relación*, p. 57.

28. Dean, *Inka*, p. 23.

29. For the use of wood paste in processional statues, see Webster, *Art*, pp. 105–107.

30. Ibid., pp. 4–5, 112.

31. Mendoza, *Shaping*, pp. 97–99. For a detailed account of San Jerónimo's role in Cusco's Corpus Christi, see Roca Huallparimachi, "Jerónimo."

32. Cánepa Koch, *Máscara*, pp. 110–11, 243; Mendoza, *Shaping*, pp. 77–79; Villasante Ortiz, *Paucartambo*, pp. 114–116; Verger, *Fiestas*, figs. 62–63.

33. Gow, "Gods," pp. 232–233; Randall, "Qoyllur," pp. 54–55, 78. See also Mendoza, *Shaping*, pp. 164–206; Cánepa Koch, *Máscara*, pp. 105–106, 240–

241; Villasante Ortiz, *Paucartambo*, pp. 77–78; Pilco Loaiza, *Danzas*, pp. 75–82; Verger, *Fiestas*, figs. 90–92.

34. Fiedler, "Corpus," pp. 217, 248–250. See also Blanco, *Cuzco*, p. 66.

35. The two "kings" told me they represented "Spanish Catholics." Neither Cánepa Koch, *Máscara*, pp. 102–105, nor Pilco Loaiza, *Danzas*, pp. 27–31, mention such "kings," describing the dance instead as being led by a single Chuncho chief, but Sallnow, *Pilgrims*, p. 222, notes a crowned king at the head of the Chunchos.

36. Randall, "Qoyllur," pp. 45–46; Gow, "Gods," pp. 226–228. For the Ñaupa Machu, see also Allen, *Hold*, pp. 54–57.

37. Randall, "Gods," pp. 77–78; Silverman-Proust, "Representación"; Cánepa Koch, "Ch'unchu."

38. Randall, "Qoyllur," p. 55. See also Ramirez, "Novena," pp. 80–81; Gow, "Gods," pp. 232–233; Sallnow, *Pilgrims*, pp. 233–234. Allen, *Hold*, p. 250, notes that neither she nor other "more recent observers" have seen the battle at Qoyllur Rit'i. Both Ramirez, "Novena," p. 84, and Cánapa Koch, *Máscara*, p. 103, call the unmasked dancers Q'ara Chunchos (poor Chunchos). Gow and Randall call them Wayri Chunchos, but Gow, p. 45n, confesses that he has "come across no good explanation for the name *wayri*."

39. Cánepa Koch, *Mascara*, pp. 226–234.

40. Mendoza, *Shaping*, p. 194.

41. Allen, "Bear-Men," p. 43.

42. For the pilgrimage to Qoyllur Rit'i (and the *ukukus'* role therein), see Ramirez, "Novena"; Gow, "Gods," pp. 1–6, 214–239; Randall, "Qoyllur"; Sallnow, *Pilgrims*, pp. 177–242; Allen, *Hold*, pp. 190–200; Poole, "Accommodation."

43. Allen, "Bear-Men."

44. Fiedler, "Corpus," p. 131, reported four parrots in 1980.

45. Cusihuamán, *Diccionario*, p. 46. See also Silverman-Proust, "Representación," pp. 68–69; Guaman Poma, *Nueva*, 1:234 (fol. 323).

46. Flores Ochoa and Flores Nájar, "'Mamacha,'" p. 284.

47. Cánepa Koch, *Máscara*, pp. 106–10, 241; Villasante Ortiz, *Paucartambo*, pp. 90–98; Mendoza, *Shaping*, p. 77, figs. 7–8.

48. Cánepa Koch, *Máscara*, pp. 216–219, 226–227; Mendoza, *Shaping*, pp. 188–191; Gow, "Gods," pp. 232–233.

49. Mendoza, *Shaping*, p. 169. For the pile of bodies, see pp. 193–194.

50. The traditional order of the procession was reversed in 1969 to save the church the embarrassment of the crowd dispersing after the passage of the saints and dances but before the arrival of the archbishop and the host (Fiedler, "Corpus," p. 189). See Roca Hallparimachi, "Jerónimo," p. 25, for a description of the procession in 1961.

51. Villasante Ortiz, *Paucartambo*, pp. 116–117; Cánepa Koch, *Máscara*, pp. 112–114; Verger, *Fiestas*, figs. 60–61. In some versions of the Qoyacha, the women also wear masks.

52. *Machukuna* is the plural form of *machu*. For the role of the *machu* in the *contradanza*, see Cánepa Koch, *Máscara*, p. 110, 242–243, 321–322. For

the malevolence (and generative powers) of the *machukuna*, see Allen, *Hold*, pp. 54–57, 63; Gow, "Gods," pp. 234–236.

53. Fiedler, "Corpus," pp. 172–173, 186; Milne, *Fiesta*, p. 108.

54. Mendoza, *Shaping*, p. 59. For unvarnished accounts of rural Carnival, its dances, and its ritual battles, see Sallnow, *Pilgrims*, pp. 136–139, 154–157; Allen, *Hold*, pp. 182–189.

55. Mendoza, *Shaping*, pp. 48–83.

56. Valcárcel, in Verger, *Indians*, p. 3. See also Fiedler, "Corpus," pp. 177, 245; Gisbert, *Paraíso*, p. 250.

57. Cánepa Koch, *Máscara*, pp. 108–110, 241–242; Villasante Ortiz, *Paucartambo*, pp. 102–105.

58. Fiedler, "Corpus," p. 48.

59. Compare the *maqt'a* mask in Mendoza, *Shaping*, fig. 18, with the Indian face in Verger, *Indians*, fig. 20. For the role of the *maqt'a*, see Cánepa Koch, *Máscara*, pp. 119–121; Villasante Ortiz, *Paucartambo*, pp. 121–122.

60. Mendoza, *Shaping*, p. 113.

61. Mendoza, *Shaping*, pp. 109–163; Cánepa Koch, *Máscara*, pp. 111–112, 243; Villasante Ortiz, *Paucartambo*, pp. 109–111; Pilco Loaiza, *Danzas*, pp. 83–88.

62. Fiedler, "Corpus," pp. 138–164.

63. Dean, *Inka*, p. 211. For a history and critique of the modern Inti Raymi, see Fiedler, "Corpus," pp. 338–366; Dean, *Inka*, pp. 200–218.

CHAPTER 9. *A Scattering of Ants*

1. Chambers, *Medieval*, 1:294.

2. Golby and Purdue, *Making*, p. 26.

3. Ladurie, *Carnival*, pp. 307–308.

4. Kinser, *Carnival*, pp. 3–6.

5. Chambers, *Medieval*, 1:327–328; Tilliot, *Memoires*, pp. 19–20.

6. Chambers, *Medieval*, 1:317–318.

7. Ibid., 1:287, 2:279–282.

8. Wasson, *Devon*, p. 325; Hutton, *Stations*, p. 100.

9. Tilliot, *Memoires*, p. 6; see also Lever, *Sceptre*, p. 12. Muchembled, *Popular*, p. 73, notes that in early modern France, "feces were not the object of profound disgust that they are in our own day."

10. For England, see Chambers, *Medieval*, 1:321–323, 352–368; Hutton, *Stations*, pp. 99–104; and such scattered references in the Records of Early English Drama series as Wasson, *Devon*, pp. 319, 325–326; and Klausner, *Herefordshire*, pp. 221–225, 277–278, 539. For Bohemia, where even the young John Huss took part, see Chambers, *Medieval*, 1:320–321. For Spain, see Alonso Ponga, *Religiosidad*, pp. 14–17, and Amades, *Costumari*, 1:217–229. For Portugal, see Vilhena, "Origem," pp. 237–238.

11. Chambers, *Medieval*, 1:325.

12. Southworth, *Fools*, pp. 52–53.

13. Knight, "Bishop," p. 157.

14. Chambers, *Medieval*, 1:277; see also 1:309, 340, 345–346.

15. Amades, *Costumari*, 1:219, 226.

16. Duffy, *Stripping*, pp. 13–14.

17. Chambers, *Medieval*, 1:293.

18. Cochis, "Bishop," p. 100.

19. Chambers, *Medieval*, 1:296.

20. Muchembled, *Popular*, p. 141.

21. Grinberg and Kinser, "Combats," pp. 69–71. See also Kinser, *Rabelais's*, p. 51.

22. Humphrey, *Politics*, pp. 64–65. For an earlier transcription of the same document, see Hudson and Tingey, *Records*, 1:345–346. For the political context of the Norwich masquerade, see Humphrey, pp. 63–82.

23. Kinser, *Rabelais's*, p. 50.

24. Tilliot, *Memoires*, gives an extensive eighteenth-century account of the Mère Folle. See also Petit de Julleville, *Comédiens*, pp. 193–232.

25. Petit de Julleville, *Comédiens*, pp. 193–199; cf. Muchembled, *Popular*, p. 140.

26. Petit de Julleville, *Comédiens*, pp. 199–214; Davis, *Society*, p. 99.

27. Davis, *Society*, pp. 97–123.

28. Ibid., p. 109.

29. Pettit, "Protesting."

30. Muchembled, *Popular*, p. 142.

31. Petit de Julleville, *Comédiens*, pp. 231–232.

32. For a more complete account of my visit to Galicia, including brief reports on Carnivals in Verín, Viano do Bolo, Manzaneda, and Xinzo de Limia, see Harris, "Carnival."

33. For the meaning of *peliqueiro*, see below. *Cigarrón* may be a variant of *zaharrón*, meaning a masked fool, wild man, or demon (Caro Baroja, *Carnaval*, pp. 217–224). Despite their distinct names, the two figures dress and act almost identically.

34. Risco, "Notas," p. 164.

35. Ibid., p. 165.

36. Tenorio, *Aldea*, p. 126.

37. The troupes of costumed maskers and musicians in Manzaneda's Carnival are also called *foliôns* (merry companies). The Galician *foliôns*, like the synonymous Portuguese *foliões*, may be derived from the French *folie* (folly), providing an etymological link between Galician Carnival and the French Feast of Fools (see Vilhena, "Origem").

38. Risco, "Notas," pp. 186–187; Risco, "Etnografía," pp. 622–623. The *peliqueiro*'s outfit is expensive. Cocho, *Carnaval*, p. 116, reports that it cost about 100,000 pesetas ($700) in 1990. In 1998 a mask and headpiece alone sold for 45,000 pesetas ($300).

39. *Laza*, p. 3.

40. Lozano, *Entroido*.

41. Gonzalez Reboredo and Mariño Ferro, *Entroido*, p. 50. See also Caro Baroja, *Carnaval*, p. 361.

242 + NOTES TO PAGES 150–160

42. Risco, "Notas," p. 186; Risco, "Etnografía," p. 618.

43. Muñoz, personal communication, 4 June 1999.

44. Mariana Regalado, personal communication, 23 May 1999.

45. Regalado, "*Ounhas.*"

46. Risco, "Notas," p. 195. For other examples of *vaquillos* (little cows), see Caro Baroja, *Carnaval*, pp. 243–251.

47. *Laza*, p. 5.

48. Regalado, personal communication, 14 June 1999.

49. Risco, "Notas," p. 181.

50. For a study of Laza's *testamento*, see Regalado, "*Ounhas.*" For the text of the 1969 Laza *testamento*, see Dasairas, *Entroido*, pp. 97–103. For discussion of *testamentos* elsewhere, see Risco, "Notas," pp. 354–359.

51. Lozano, *Entroido*.

52. Regalado, "*Ounhas.*"

53. Bouza-Brey, "Máscaras"; Taboada Chivite, *Etnografía*, pp. 56–61; Manuel Mandanes Castro, cited in Amado Rolán and Barreal Novo, *Laza*, p. 4; *Laza*, p. 3.

54. Gonzalez Reboredo and Mariño Ferro, *Entroido*, pp. 53–4. See also Cocho, *Carnaval*, pp. 190–191.

55. Lynch, *Christ*, pp. 107–109.

56. Dasairas, *Entroido*, pp. 47–48.

57. Cocho, *Carnaval*, pp. 47–48.

58. Dasairas, *Entroido*, pp. 45–46.

59. Oman, *History*, 2:179–95, 223–6.

60. Barreiro Fernández, *Historia*, 1:115–16.

61. Risco, "Etnografía," p. 622.

62. Martin, *Military*; Chartrand, *Napoleonic*. Caro Baroja, *Carnaval*, p. 361, recognizes the Napoleonic style of the *peliqueiros'* bicorn hats but regards the maskers themselves as "archaic."

63. Cocho, *Carnaval*, pp. 135–42; Harris, "Carnival," pp. 158–159.

64. Gonzalez Reboredo and Mariño Ferro, *Entroido*, pp. 27, 129, 179–181.

CHAPTER 10. *The Bandit and the Fat Man*

1. For a study of the Aragonese dialect of the Valley of Bielsa, including a glossary that extends to the names of Bielsa's Carnival figures, see Badía Margarit, *Habla*.

2. For a similar figure, known as the *vieja* (old woman), in the Carnival of Zaldundo (Alava), see García Rodero and Caballero Bonald, *Festivals*, pp. 74, 275.

3. The original is owned by the judge's grandson, also named Rafael Pañart, whose family has been in Bielsa for several centuries. A Remon de Penyar is recorded in the 1495 census of Bielsa (Bielza de Ory, *Estudio*, p. 48).

4. Badía Margarit, *Habla*, pp. 46–50; Bielza de Ory, *Estudio*, p. 120.

5. Roma Riu, *Aragón*, pp. 81–83.

6. Frazer, *Golden*, 4:220–233.

7. Caro Baroja, *Folklore*, pp. 5–6.

8. Caro Baroja, *Folklore*, p. 11, suggests that the Basque word *ziripot* is synonymous with the Castilian *cipote*, meaning chubby or obese.

9. Aranburu Urtasan, *Danzas*, p. 81.

10. Caro Baroja, *Folklore*, p. 14.

11. Iribarren, "Estampas," pp. 411–414; Caro Baroja, *Carnaval*, pp. 195–196 and illustrations following p. 208; Caro Baroja, *Folklore*, pp. 15–19; Garmendia Larrañaga, *Carnaval*, pp. 152–156.

12. For Basque folk instruments, including the *txistu*, see Aranburu Urtasan, *Danzas*, pp. 102–111.

13. Lanz's *zortzikoa*, a variety of *mutildantzak* (all-male circle dance), is well known even among the Basque diaspora. See Aranburu Urtasan, *Danzas*, pp. 53–82; Ysursa, *Basque*, p. 38.

14. Iribarren, "Estampas," pp. 415–416.

15. Alford, *Pyrenean*, p. 157.

16. Iribarren, "Estampas," p. 412. Caro Baroja, *Folklore*, p. 15, reports that some in Lantz believe Miel is synonymous with Mikel (Michael), while others connect it to the Castilian word *mil* (thousand). *Otxin* is said to be "the name of an ancient coin." Miel Otxin might be loosely translated as Mickey Megabucks.

17. News item, published 26 February 2001, on http://www.noticiasde navarra.com/ediciones/20010226/navarra/d26navo503.php/.

18. Harris, *Dialogical*, pp. 108–119.

19. Garmendia Larrañaga, *Iñauteria*, pp. 34–36, 94; Irigoien, *Ihauteriak*, p. 42.

20. Aubailly, *Deux*; Hérelle, *Théâtre*, pp. 77–94.

21. García Rodero and Caballero Bonald, *Festivals*, pp. 74, 275; Ysursa, *Basque*, p. 38.

22. See, for example, Grinberg and Kinser, "Combats," p. 65. Irigoien, Dueñas, and Larrinaga, *Ihauteriak*, p. 42, notes that the Basque hobbyhorse is "sometimes associated with death."

23. Hérelle, *Théâtre*, pp. 30–33, 59–60; Irigoien, Dueñas, and Larrinaga, *Ihauteriak*, p. 43.

24. Iribarren, "Estampas," pp. 419–420 and illustration following p. 416; García Rodero and Caballero Bonald, *Festivals*, p. 223.

25. Lleo Cañal, *Fiesta*, pp. 41 and illustration facing p. 16.

26. López Estrada, "Fiestas," p. 316.

27. Ysursa, *Basque*, p. 38.

CHAPTER 11. *Safe for the Bourgeoisie*

1. For color photographs of Binche's Carnival, see Evrard, *Binche.*

2. In Binche's Carnival, satire seems to be confined to the hours after dark on the Monday before Carnival weekend, known as *la nuit des Trouilles* (night of the coarse ones). See Glotz, *Carnival* (1983), p. 54.

3. Glotz, *Carnaval* (1983), p. 54.

4. Ibid., p. 60.

5. Glotz, *Carnaval* (1975), p. 20; Revelard, "Carnaval," p. 242.

6. For a history of the commedia dell'arte, see Duchartre, *Italian;* Richards and Richards, *Commedia.*

7. Dick, *Pierrot,* p. 53.

8. Claretie, *Carnaval,* p. 126.

9. Compare the Brighella mask in Rudlin, *Commedia,* p. 85, with the Harlequin mask in Glotz, *Carnival* (1983), p. 64.

10. Revelard, "Carnaval," p. 240. Until the beginning of the twentieth century, the Gilles wore tall headdresses of just eight feathers, some of which were colored (Garin, *Binche,* pp. 198–199).

11. Glotz, *Carnaval* (1975), p. 17; Glotz, *Carnaval* (1983), p. 56.

12. Queen Elisabeth, widow of Albert I (1909–1934) and grandmother of Albert II (1993–), visited Binche on Carnival Tuesday 1951 (Garin, *Binche,* p. 80). She was then seventy-four years old.

13. Glotz, *Carnival* (1975), p. 21.

14. Claretie, *Carnaval,* pp. 119, 130, 133.

15. Glotz, *Carnaval* (1983), p. 49.

16. For eyewitness accounts of the *Fêtes de Binche,* see Calvete, *Felicísimo,* 2:1–69; Alvarez, *Relation,* pp. 89–110; Heartz, "Divertissement," pp. 340–342. For commentary, see Glotz, *Marie,* pp. 7–148; Heartz, "Divertissement"; Devoto, "Folklore"; Wangermée, *Flemish,* pp. 155–160; Harris, *Aztecs,* pp. 198–202. For a color reproduction of the drawing, see the cover of Glotz, *Marie;* for a black-and-white reproduction, see Jacquot, *Fêtes,* 2:pls. xxvii–xxviii. There are several discrepancies among the accounts and between the accounts and the drawing.

17. Glotz, *Carnaval* (1975), pp. 31–35; Glotz, *Carnaval* (1983), p. 77.

18. Glotz, *Carnaval* (1983), p. 78.

19. Glotz, *Carnaval* (1975), pp. 37–40; Glotz, *Carnaval* (1983), pp. 25, 73, 78; Glotz, *Marie,* pp. 149–144. See also Garin, *Binche,* p. 19.

20. Hugues Deghorain, personal communication, 17 December 1998. See also Revelard, "Carnaval." Michel Revelard, Glotz's successor as curator of Binche's International Carnival and Mask Museum, has endorsed Glotz's theories in his own work.

21. Garin, *Binche,* p. 18.

22. Glotz, *Carnaval* (1983), p. 27.

23. Ibid., p. 26.

24. Letter, 11 February 1795, reprinted in Glotz, *Carnaval* (1983), pp. 30–31.

25. Duchartre, *Italian,* p. 254–255. Doutrepont, *Types,* 2:74, favors the Italian origin. Celler, *Types,* p. 119, and Panofsky, "Gilles," p. 324, do not.

26. Mic, *Commedia,* p. 33n.

27. Fournel, *Spectacles,* p. 266.

28. Somaize, *Véritables,* pp. 60–61; Fournel, *Spectacles,* pp. 265–266.

29. Moreau, *Bibliographe,* 1:313–314 (no. 1072), 1:366 (no. 1257), 2:242 (no. 3935).

30. Furetière, *Dictionnaire,* s.v. "Enfariner."

31. Cited in Panofsky, "Gilles," p. 325n.

32. Pougin, *Dictionnaire,* p. 404.

33. Campardon, *Spectacles,* 1:218.

34. Parfaict, *Dictionnaire,* 3:21.

35. Garin, *Binche,* p. 19; Storey, *Pierrot,* illus. 8.

36. Storey, *Pierrot,* p. 79.

37. Gueullette, *Théâtre,* 1:235.

38. For a color reproduction of Watteau's painting, which now hangs in the Louvre in Paris, see Posner, *Watteau,* pl. 57 (p. 233).

39. Duchartre, *Italian,* p. 254.

40. Dick, *Pierrot,* p. 148.

41. Panofsky, "Gilles," has made the case most strongly for the resemblance between Watteau's Gilles/Pierrot and Rembrandt's Christ. A fine old copy of the lost original of Watteau's *Comédiens italiens* hangs in the National Gallery, Washington, D.C. For a color reproduction, see Vidal, *Watteau,* illus. 144 (p. 147).

42. Posner, *Watteau,* p. 265, objects to such a conclusion on the grounds of impropriety.

43. Glotz, *Carnaval* (1975), p. 38; Glotz, *Carnaval* (1983), p. 73. In 1890, Claretie, "Gilles," p. 159, assumed that the Gilles of Binche "united" the *bouffon* of the "Italian farce" and the "Inca chieftain" of Mary of Hungary's masque. See also Claretie, *Carnaval,* pp. 135–137. In 1899, Ernest Matthieu rejected all theories of Indian or courtly origins, insisting that the foolish Gilles of the commedia was a feature of several popular expressions in the region long before the first evidence of his appearance in Binche's Carnival in 1795. For a summary of Claretie and Matthieu's views, see Glotz, *Marie,* pp. 168–170, 175–180.

44. Glotz, *Carnaval* (1983), pp. 28, 32.

45. Ibid., p. 75.

46. Ibid., pp. 32, 34–35. In 1905, Delattre, *Pays,* p. 154, wrote, "On the fifteenth day of each month, the streets [of Binche] fill with horses for a celebrated fair." Perhaps, in 1836, the monthly horse fair had extended to a second day.

47. Glotz, *Carnaval* (1983), p. 34.

48. Glotz, *Carnaval* (1975), p. 26; Glotz, *Carnaval* (1983), p. 75.

49. Claretie, *Carnaval,* pp. 118–144.

50. Glotz, *Carnaval* (1983), pp. 46, 75.

51. Glotz, "Carnaval," p. 6.

52. Glotz, *Carnaval* (1983), pp. 37, 74–75.

53. Ibid., p. 38.

54. Ibid., p. 68.

55. Ibid., p. 45.

56. *Folklore,* p. 7. See also Glotz, "Carnaval," p. 8; and, for a photograph of the Blancs Moussis, Giroux, *Carnavals,* p. 36.

57. Garin, *Binche,* p. 45.

CHAPTER 12. *Devils and Decorum*

1. For an overview of traditional Carnival characters, see Crowley, "Traditional"; Hill, *Trinidad*, pp. 87–93; Stegassy, "Cupid." For the recent revival of traditional characters, see Riggio, "Resistance," p. 19. For a helpful glossary of Trinidad Carnival terms, including the names of traditional characters, see Martin, "Trinidad."

2. Carr, "Pierrot." The 1956 version of Carr's article contains a lengthy transcript of "a typical dialogue in Creole between two seasoned Pierrot Grenade masqueraders" (pp. 286–314). The dialogue is omitted from the 1988 reprint. For the spelling of Chicago, see Stegassy, "Cupid," p. 99.

3. Crowley, "Midnight"; Honoré, "Midnight."

4. The Tennessee Jubilee Singers, the first U.S. "minstrels" to tour Trinidad (twice between 1888 and 1891) were not whites in burlesque blackface but black singers who "presented their music formally" (Cowley, *Carnival*, pp. 114–115). Theresa Morilla Montano (Fig. 12.1), who led the Minstrel Boys —the best-known minstrel group in Trinidad—until her death in 2001, at the age of eighty-four, told me, "We have to sing songs that the black slaves in America would have sung."

5. For a comparison of Carnival Indians in Trinidad and New Orleans, see Bellour and Kinser, "Amerindian." For Carnival Guarahoons, see Stegassy, "Cupid," pp. 98–99, 103.

6. For a history of the devil bands between 1906 and 1956, see Procope, "Dragon."

7. Hill, *Trinidad*, p. 11.

8. Ibid., p. 11; see also Pearse, "Carnival," pp. 17–18.

9. Johnson, "Introduction," p. xiii.

10. Carmichael, *Domestic*, 2:290.

11. Johnson, "Introduction," p. xiv.

12. Ibid., p. xiv. See also Hill, *Trinidad*, p. 17.

13. Day, *Five*, 1:313–314.

14. Quoted in Hill, *Trinidad*, p. 25. See also Pearse, "Carnival," p. 28.

15. Quoted in Hill, *Trinidad*, p. 22. See also Pearse, "Carnival," p. 18; Cowley, *Carnival*, p. 21.

16. Hill, *Trinidad*, p. 24.

17. Day, *Five*, 1:314.

18. Hill, *Trinidad*, p. 21.

19. Cowley, *Carnival*, pp. 84–90; Pearse, "Carnival," pp. 30–34; Hall, "Lennox."

20. The engraving by Melton Prior, originally published in the *Illustrated London News* (5 May 1888, pp. 496–497), is reproduced in Hill, *Trinidad*, following p. 52; Cowley, *Carnival*, p. 109; Bellour and Kinser, "Amerindian," p. 150.

21. Crowley, "Traditional," pp. 83–84.

22. Chang, "Chinese," pp. 216, 218–219.

23. Mason, *Bacchanal*, pp. 59–61.

24. Gay, "Brief."
25. Lovelace, "Emancipation," pp. 56–59.
26. La Fay, "Carnival," pp. 698–699.
27. Riggio, "Vieira," pp. 198–201.
28. Ibid., p. 199.
29. Lovelace, *Salt*, p. 171.
30. Rohlehr, " 'Getting,' " pp. 90–91.
31. Walsh, "Jouvay," p. 139.
32. Ibid., p. 145.
33. Ibid., pp. 145–146.
34. John Cupid, in Stegassy, "Cupid," p. 101.
35. Nigel and Marvin's "Movin'." See Mason, *Bacchanal*, p. 179.
36. Muller, "Paramin."
37. Milla Riggio, personal communication, 16 February 1996.
38. See, for example, Martin, "Trinidad," p. 230; Huet and Savary, *Dances*, pp. 122–123, 149.
39. Mason, *Bacchanal*, p. 105.
40. Ibid., pp. 122–125.

CHAPTER 13. *The Sins of the Carnival Virgin*

1. Anstee, *Bolivia*, p. 112.
2. For the early history of Oruro, see Crespo Rodas, "Fundación"; Cornblit, *Power*, pp. 5–10. For its mines in particular, see Nash, *Eat*, pp. xxiii, 22–24.
3. Villarroel, "Novena," first published the story of the amorous bandit Nina-Nina in 1908, having copied it from an undated manuscript. In 1925, Zaconeta, "Virgen," pp. 69–75, gave literary form to the "traditional" story of Chiru-Chiru, who robbed the rich to help the poor. Fortún, *Danza*, pp. 29–35, reprints Villarroel's account and summarizes two versions of the Chiru-Chiru legend. Other summaries of the stories can be found in Costas Arguedas, *Diccionario*, 1:261–262, 2:342–344; Vargas Luza, *Diablada*, pp. 13–15; Anstee, *Bolivia*, pp. 117–118.
4. Vargas, "Carnaval," p. 108; Zaconeta, "Virgen," pp. 76–77.
5. Beltrán Heredía, "Historia," p. 192. The sanctuary was dedicated on 8 February (Carnival Sunday) 1891, a year in which Carnival Tuesday coincided with the anniversary of the 1781 uprising.
6. Two eyewitness accounts of the Oruro uprising survive. Menéndez, "Relación," supports the Creoles, while Echeverría, "Diario," takes the side of the Spaniards. Intriguingly, the former is dated 27 February (Carnival Tuesday) 1781, while the latter is dated 13 April (Good Friday) 1781. On the question of authorship, see Siles Guevara, "Sucesos," p. 49, and Robins, *Mesianismo*, pp. 105–106. Siles Guevara's speculative identification of the second author as "a Mercederian . . . , Fray Echenique, to whom I have already alluded above" (p. 49), appears to contain a misprint. He has mentioned the Mercederian friar José de Echevarría (p. 48), who publicly condemned

the uprising, but no Fray Echenique. Cornblit, *Power*, pp. 137–209, gives a substantial modern account of the uprising.

7. Echeverría, "Diario," pp. 284–291; Menéndez, "Relación," pp. 313–318.

8. Robins, *Mesianismo*, p. 127.

9. Echeverría, "Diario," pp. 291–298; Menéndez, "Relación," pp. 318–321. For the specifics of the indigenous clothing, see Beltrán Avila, *Capítulos*, p. 175. For the Inca dress, see Robins, *Mesianismo*, pp. 129–130. For the parade, see Cajías, "Objetivos," p. 415; Cajías, *Cocinar*, p. 13. For a more informal parade involving drums, bugles, and flag waving, see Beltrán Avila, *Capítulos*, p. 304.

10. Echeverría, "Diario," p. 297.

11. Robins, *Mesianismo*, pp. 107, 121, 131. The number of dead given by Menéndez, "Relación," p. 324, varies only slightly.

12. Beltrán Avila, *Capítulos*, pp. 308–309.

13. Ibid., pp. 197–198.

14. Ibid., pp. 195–209; Robins, *Mesianismo*, pp. 138–141.

15. Cajías, "Objetivos," p. 418; Cornblit, *Power*, p. 179.

16. Zaconetas, "Virgen," pp. 76–88.

17. Vargas, "Carnaval," p. 108. For the identity of the play's author, see Fortún, *Danza*, p. 8.

18. Vargas, "Carnaval," p. 108.

19. Fortún, *Danza*, pp. 3–7. Intriguingly, the music to which Oruro's devils now dance closely resembles that of Berga's *salt de les maces*, which also pits masked devils against an outnumbered Michael. I have compared the music on my videotapes of Berga's 1996 Patum and Oruro's 2000 Carnival. Both have the same driving 6/8 rhythm and the same pattern of repeating measures, while the variant melodies are too close to be unrelated. The music for the *salt de les maces*, printed in Armengou, *Patum*, 131–132, and Huch i Guixer, *Patum*, p. 115, was written by the Berguedan composer Joan Trullàs i Vivó in 1963. Before then the *maces* danced, as they still do in their evening performances, to an unaccompanied drumbeat (see Armengou, *Patum*, p. 84). Various older melodies for the Oruro devil dance were published in 1961 by Fortún, *Danza*, pp. 75–82, but none resemble the tune to which Oruro's devils marched in 2000. Likewise, none of the several melodies described (but not transcribed) by Flores Barrientos, "Breve," pp. 134–136, and Montes Camacho, *Proceso*, p. 22, suggest recent Catalan influence. Unless Trullàs i Vivó drew from an earlier Bolivian tune, I can only suppose that Oruro's recent adoption and adaptation of the Berga tune was suggested by Fortún's proposed link between the two traditions.

20. Amades, *Costumari*, 5:235–236; Milá y Fontanals, *Obras*, 6:283; Noyes, "Mule," p. 307; Bertran, "Devils'," pp. 139–140.

21. Echeverría, "Diario," p. 291.

22. Montes Camacho, *Proceso*, p. 29–34. For Pagador's famous speech, calling the Creoles to rise up against "the tyranny of the *chapetones*," see Echeverría, "Diario," p. 277. For a summary of Pagador's historical identity

and his subsequent canonization as a precursor of Bolivian independence, see Robins, *Mesianismo*, pp. 141–143.

23. Newspaper article (1938), cited by Kuenzli, "Interstices," p. 28.

24. Kuenzli, "Interstices," p. 41.

25. Montes Camacho, *Proceso*, pp. 18–24.

26. Montealegre's text has not survived in its entirety. Fortún, *Danza*, 9–21, prints the first few speeches of Montealegre's text, as remembered in 1953 by Zenón Goitia, who had been performing the narrative since 1904, and the whole of Peláez's text. Montes Camacho, *Proceso*, pp. 143–155, also prints Peláez's text. For the date of Peláez's revision, see Beltrán Heredía, "Historia," p. 192. Comparison of Peláez's text with my videotape of the 2000 performance reveals judicious cutting by someone with a keen sense of dramatic action. The most substantial cuts are from the early debate between Michael, Lucifer, and Satan, allowing the action to proceed more quickly to the rapid and more varied confrontations between Michael and the Seven Deadly Sins.

27. Beltrán Heredía, *Carnaval*, pp. 13–17; Vargas, "Carnaval," pp. 99–106.

28. Abercrombie, "Fiesta," pp. 282, 304.

29. Anstee, *Bolivia*, p. 123.

30. Ibid., p. 122.

31. For the history of Oruro's devil masks, see Vargas Luza, *Diablada*, pp. 49–68; Noch, "Mascareros." For the manner in which the masks are made, see McFarren, "Mascarero"; Delgado-P. "Devil," pp. 142–146. The masks have a curiously oriental appearance, prompting some local mask makers in the 1980s to try to "purify the Oruro masks of alien 'Hindu' influences" (Noch, "Mascareros," p. 136). The original "oriental" influence may have been nothing more sinister than the Chinese dragon trade mark on imported Horniman's tea, which was popular in Oruro in the late 1930s (Vargas Luza, p. 53). By 1953 Antonio Viscarra—one of the more prominent mask makers of La Paz—was drawing inspiration for his devil masks from "a magazine in which a great number of Tibetan masks were reproduced" (Fortún, *Danza*, pp. 66–67).

32. Abercrombie, "Fiesta," p. 304.

33. Vargas, "Carnaval," pp. 101–102; Abercrombie, "Fiesta," p. 280.

34. Nash, *Eat*, p. 164. For photographs of the image of the Tío, see Vargas, "Carnaval," pp. 100, 103. Delgado-P. "Devil," pp. 133–134, suggests that Oruro's devil masks have their origin not so much in European images of the demonic as in indigenous representations of deified llamas.

35. Nash, *Eat*, pp. 138, 156–159; Vargas, "Carnaval," pp. 97–107.

36. Vargas, "Carnaval," p. 86. According to Nash, *Eat*, p. 132, the dance was introduced to Oruro by "miners who fought in the Chaco War [1932–1935] . . . and were impressed by [Toba] customs," but Montes Camacho, *Proceso*, p. 47, dates the formation of the Gran Conjunto Tradicional de Tobas to 1917.

37. A text of the Oruro play, as performed in 1942, was published by

Dargan and Hernando Balmori, *Conquista*. An almost identical text, furnished by the president of the Hijos del Sol but with its Quechua orthography "corrected," was published in 1986 by Montes Camacho, *Proceso*, pp. 156–195. Another variant of the play, from Chayanta (Potosí), has been published by Lara, *Tragedia*. Excerpts from the kindred Toco (Cochabamba) text can be found in Unzueta, *Valle*, pp. 133–143, and, in English translation, in Goins, "Death." The Oruro play differs in several respects from both the Chayanta and Toco versions. The Chayanta text, for example, is entirely in Quechua, the Spaniards only "moving their lips" before being translated into Quechua by an interpreter, while, in the Oruro play, the two groups speak mutually incomprehensible languages. (Dargan and Hernando Balmori, *Conquista*, include both the bilingual version and a fully Spanish translation.) The several texts may be variant adaptations of a common original, thought by Lara (pp. 12–13, 48) to be traceable to the known performance in Potosí in 1555 of a play in Quechua and Spanish about "the arrival of the Spaniards in Peru" and the "unjust imprisonment" and execution of Atahualpa. For the 1555 Potosí performance, see Arzáns, *Historia*, 1:98; and, for a 1641 Potosí play on the same theme, 2:86.

38. The historical Luque, a priest, stayed in Panama to look after the financial and political interests of Pizarro's preliminary expeditions to Peru in 1524–1528. Other versions of the play correctly name the friar Vicente de Valverde, a Dominican who traveled with Pizarro and Almagro during the successful conquest of Peru in 1530–1533.

39. Lara, *Tragedia*, p. 47. Lara is describing the Chayanta play, but his words apply equally well to the Oruro version.

40. Dargan and Hernando Balmori, *Conquista*, pp. 89–90; cf. Lara, *Tragedia*, pp. 70–71.

41. Vargas, "Carnaval," p. 95, cites the same passage as evidence that the "Indians (while respecting and worshipping their native devil, Supay), began to identify their [Spanish] enemies with the imported Devil."

42. Dargan and Hernando Balmori, *Conquista*, pp. 92–98.

43. This incident is not in the text published by Dargan and Hernando Balmori but does show on my videotape. Cf. Lara, *Tragedia*, p. 131, and Wachtel, *Vision*, p. 39.

44. In some versions of the play, their prayers are answered. A 1942 performance of the play in La Paz reportedly ended with "the resurrection and triumph of Atahualpa." See Dargan and Hernando Balmori, *Conquest*, pp. 47, 100; Wachtel, *Vision*, p. 38.

45. Dargan and Hernando Balmori, *Conquest*, pp. 99–100.

46. Ibid., p. 101.

47. Ibid., p. 48.

48. Vargas, "Carnaval," p. 95.

49. Unzueta, *Valle*, p. 143.

50. Wachtel, *Vision*, p. 35 and photographs following p. 40. See also Dargan and Hernando Balmori, *Conquest*, pl. 9.

51. Nash, *Eat*, p. 131.
52. Noch, "Mascareros," p. 134.
53. Vargas, "Carnaval," p. 88; Nash, *Eat*, p. 131.
54. Vargas, "Carnaval," p. 88.
55. Ibid., p. 85. See also Beltrán Heredía, *Carnaval*, p. 30.
56. Nash, *Eat*, p. 131.
57. Beltrán Heredía, *Carnaval*, p. 34.

Bibliography

Abercrombie, Thomas. "La fiesta del carnaval postcolonial en Oruro." *Revista Andina* 10 (1992): 279–352.

Abou-El-Haj, Barbara. *The Medieval Cult of Saints.* Cambridge: Cambridge University Press, 1994.

Adams, Henry. *Mont Saint Michel and Chartres.* [1904]. New York: Penguin, 1986.

Albert-Llorca, Marlène. "Maures et Chrétiens à Villajoyosa." *Archives de Sciences Sociales des Religions* 91 (1995): 5–19.

Alegría, Ricardo. *La Fiesta de Santiago Apóstol en Loíza Aldea.* San Juan, PR: Colección de Estudios Puertorriqueños, 1954.

———, director. *La Fiesta de Santiago Apóstol en Loíza Aldea, July 1949.* Film. San Juan, PR: Centro de Investigaciones Arqueológicos de la Universidad de Puerto Rico, 1949.

———. "The Fiesta of Santiago Apostol (St. James the Apostle) in Loíza, Puerto Rico." *Journal of American Folklore* 69 (1956): 123–134.

Alford, Violet. *Pyrenean Festivals.* London: Chatto and Windus, 1937.

———. *The Singing of the Travels.* London: Max Parrish, 1956.

Allen, Catherine J. *The Hold Life Has: Coca and Cultural Identity in an Andean Community.* Washington, D.C.: Smithsonian Institution Press, 1988.

———. "Of Bear-Men and He-Men." *Latin American Indian Literature* 7 (1983): 38–51.

Alonso Ponga, José Luis. *Religiosidad popular navideña en Castilla y León.* Salamanca: Junta de Castilla y León, 1986.

Alvarez, Vicente. *Relation du beau voyage que fit aux pays-bas, en 1548, le prince Philippe d'Espagne . . .* Trans. M.-T. Dovillée. Brussels: Presses Académiques Européennes, 1964.

Álvarez Nazario, Manuel. *El elemento afronegroide en el español de Puerto Rico.* San Juan, PR: Instituto de Cultura Puertorriqueña, 1974.

Amades, Joan. *Costumari català.* 5 vols. Barcelona: Salvat Editores, 1950–1956.

Amado Rolán, Nieves and Moncho Barreal Novo. *Laza Entroido.* Ourense: Excma. Deputación Prov. de Ourense, 1990.

Anstee, Margaret Joan. *Bolivia*. London: Longman, 1970.
Aranburu Urtasan, Mikel. *Danzas y bailes de Navarra*. Pamplona: Temas de Navarra, 2000.
Arco y Garay, Ricardo del. *Notas de folklore altoaragonés*. Madrid: Consejo Superior de Investigaciones Científicas, 1943.
Armengou, Josep. *La Patum de Berga*. [1968]. Barcelona: Columna, 1994.
Arzáns de Orsúa y Vela, Bartolomé. *Historia de la villa imperial de Potosí*. [1736]. 3 vols. Eds. Lewis Hanke and Gunnar Mendoza. Providence: Brown University Press, 1965.
Aubailly, Jean-Claude, ed. *Deux jeux de Carnaval de la fin du moyen âge*. Geneva: Droz, 1978.
Aubrun, Charles-V. "Sur les débuts du théâtre en Espagne." In *Hommage à Ernest Martineche*, ed. Mário Cardozo, pp. 293–314. Paris: Editions d'Artrey, 1939.
Badía Margarit, Antonio. *El habla del Valle de Bielsa*. Barcelona: Instituto de Estudios Pirenaicos, 1950.
Balls de la festa major. Brochure. Vilafranca del Penedès: Comissió Coordinadora de Balls de la Festa Major, 1991.
Barreiro Fernández, Xosé Ramón. *Historia contemporanea de Galicia*. 4 vols. La Coruña: Ediciones Gamma, 1982–1984.
Barth, Karl. *The Humanity of God*. Trans. John Newton Thomas and Thomas Weiser. Richmond, Va.: John Knox Press, 1960.
Bascom, William. *Shango in the New World*. Austin: African and Afro-American Research Institute of the University of Texas at Austin, 1972.
———. *The Yoruba of Southwestern Nigeria*. New York: Holt, Rinehart and Winston, 1969.
Batres, Leopoldo. *Exploraciones en Huexotla, Texcoco y "El Gavilan."* Mexico City: J. I. Guerrero, 1904.
Beadle, Richard. "The York Cycle." In *The Cambridge Companion to Medieval English Theatre*, ed. Richard Beadle, pp. 85–108. Cambridge: Cambridge University Press, 1994.
———, ed. *The York Plays*. London: Edward Arnold, 1982.
Beagle, Peter S. *The Garden of Earthly Delights*. New York: Viking, 1982.
Bellour, Helene and Samuel Kinser. "Amerindian Masking in Trinidad's Carnival." *Drama Review* 42, no. 3 (1998): 147–169.
Beltrán Avila, Marcos. *Capítulos de la historia colonial de Oruro*. La Paz: La República, 1925.
Beltrán Heredía, Augusto. *El Carnaval de Oruro*. Oruro: Comité Departmental de Folklore, 1962.
———. "Historia del 'diablo' del Carnaval de Oruro." In *Perfiles de Oruro*, ed. Elias Delgado Morales, pp. 183–193. Oruro: Alea, 1987.
Beltrán Martínez, Antonio. *El dance aragonés*. Zaragoza: Caja de Ahorros de la Inmaculada, 1982.
Bernstein, Alan E. *The Formation of Hell*. Ithaca, N.Y.: Cornell University Press, 1993.

Bertran, Jordi. *El ball de Serralonga.* Quaderns de la Festa Major 2. Tarragona: Ajuntament de Tarragona, 1987.

―――. "The Devils' Dance in Catalonia." In *European Medieval Drama,* eds. Sydney Higgins and Fiorella Paino, pp. 133–142. Camerino: Università degli Studi di Camerino, 1999.

Bielza de Ory, Vicente, et al. *Estudio historico-geografico del Valle de Bielsa (Huesca).* Huesca: Diputación Provincial, 1986.

Biget, Jean-Louis and Michel Escourbiac. *Saint-Cécile d'Albi: Peintures.* Toulouse: Odysée. 1994.

―――. *Saint-Cécile d'Albi: Sculptures.* Graulhet: Odysée. 1997.

Bilby, Kenneth M. "The Caribbean as a Musical Region." In *Caribbean Contours,* ed. Sidney W. Mintz and Sally Price, pp. 181–218. Baltimore: Johns Hopkins University Press, 1985.

Blanco, José María. *El Cuzco en 1835.* Cusco: Biblioteca del Instituto Americano de Arte, 1957.

Bonafoux, Louis. "El carnaval en las Antillas," *Boletín Histórico de Puerto Rico* 5 (1918): 107–111.

Bookchin, Murray. *The Spanish Anarchists.* Harper and Row, 1977.

Bouza-Brey, F. "Máscaras galegas de origen prehistórico." In *Homenagem à Martins Sarmento,* ed. Mário Cardozo et al, pp. 73–82. Guimarães: Sociedade Martins Sarmento, 1933.

Bové, Francesc de P. *El Penedès.* [1926]. Vilafranca del Penedès: Joan Solé i Bordes, 1990.

Brading, D. A. *Mexican Phoenix: Our Lady of Guadalupe—Image and Tradition across Five Centuries.* Cambridge: Cambridge University Press, 2001.

Brown, Peter. *The Cult of the Saints.* Chicago: University of Chicago Press, 1981.

Brugarola, Martín. "Las fiestas del Corpus en Camuñas." *Surco* 76 (1948): 29–31.

Brumfiel, Elizabeth Margarethe Stern. "Specialization and Exchange at the Late Postclassic (Aztec) Community of Huexotla, Mexico." Ph.D. dissertation, University of Michigan, 1976.

Burke, Peter. *Popular Culture in Early Modern Europe.* [1978]. Rev. ed. Aldershot, Hampshire: Ashgate, 1994.

Burkhart, Louise M. *Before Guadalupe: The Virgin Mary in Early Colonial Nahuatl Literature.* Austin: University of Texas Press, 2001.

―――. "The Cult of the Virgin of Guadalupe in Mexico." In *South and Meso-American Native Spirituality,* ed. Gary H. Gossen in collaboration with Miguel León-Portilla, pp. 198–227. New York: Crossroad, 1993.

Caballero Santacruz, Florentino. "La Danza." In *Imagenes de una danza,* ed. Gabriel Romero Aranda, pp. 27–31. Toledo: Diputación Provincial de Toledo, 1994.

Cahill, David. "Popular Religion and Appropriation: The Example of Corpus Christi in Eighteenth-Century Cuzco." *Latin American Research Review* 31, no. 2 (1996): 67–110.

Cajías, Fernando. *Cocinar y tirar piedras: Mujeres en la revolución del 10 de Febrero de 1871*. Oruro: Centro de Investigación y Servico Popular, 1997.

―――. "Los objetivos de la revolución indígena de 1781: El caso de Oruro." *Revista Andina* 1 (1983): 407–428.

Calvete de Estrella, Juan Cristóbal. *El felicísimo viaje del alto y muy poderoso príncipe don Felipe*. [1552]. 2 vols. Madrid: Sociedad de Bibliófilos Españoles, 1930.

Campardon, Émile. *Les spectacles de la foire*. Paris: Berger-Levrault, 1877.

Cánepa Koch, Gisela. "Los ch'unchu y las palla de Cajamarca en el ciclo de la representación de la muerte del Inca." In *Música, danzas y máscaras en los Andes*, ed. Raúl R. Romero, pp. 139–178. Lima: Pontificia Universidad Católica del Perú, 1993.

―――. *Máscara: Transformación e identidad en los Andes*. Lima: Fondo Editorial, 1998.

Carmichael, Mrs. (A. C.) *Domestic Manners and Social Conditions of the White, Coloured, and Negro Population of the West Indies*. [1833]. 2 vols. New York: Negro Universities Press, 1969.

Caro Baroja, Julio. *El Carnaval*. Madrid: Taurus, 1965.

―――. *Folklore experimental: El Carnaval de Lanz (1964)*. Pamplona: Diputación Foral de Navarra, 1965.

Carr, Andrew T. "Pierrot Grenade." *Caribbean Quarterly* 4 (1956): 281–314. Abbreviated version reprinted in *Trinidad Carnival*, ed. Gerard A. Besson, pp. 197–207. Port of Spain: Paria, 1988.

Castro, Ignacio de. *Relación del Cuzco*. [1795]. Lima: Universidad Nacional Mayor de San Marcos, 1978.

Catholic Encyclopedia, The. [15 vols. New York: Robert Appleton, 1907–12.] www.newadvent.org/cathen/.

Celler, Ludovic. *Les types populaires au théâtre*. Paris: Lepmannssohn et Dufour, 1870.

Chambers, E. K. *The Medieval Stage*. 2 vols. London: Oxford University Press, 1903.

Chang, Carlisle. "Chinese in Trinidad Carnival." *Drama Review* 42, no. 3 (1998): 213–219.

Chartrand, René. *Napoleonic War*. London: Brassey, 1996.

Cieza de León, Pedro. *The Incas*. Ed. Victor Wolfgang von Hagen. Trans. Harriet de Onis. Norman: University of Oklahoma Press, 1959.

Cifre de Loubriel, Estela. *La formación del pueblo puertorriqueño*. San Juan, PR: Instituto de Cultura Puertorriqueña, 1975.

Cisneros, Sandra. "Guadalupe the Sex Goddess." In *Goddess of the Americas*, ed. Ana Castillo, pp. 46–51. New York: Riverhead Books, 1996.

Claretie, Léo. "Les Gilles de Binche." *Illustration* no. 2713 (23 February 1895): 156, 159.

―――. *Le Carnaval de Binche*. Paris: Paul Ollendorf, 1900.

Cleary, Edmund L. *Crisis and Change*. Maryknoll, N.Y.: Orbis, 1985.

Cochis, Simonette. "The Bishop of Fools." In *Fools and Jesters in Literature,*

Art, and History, ed. Vicki K. Janik, pp. 96–105. Westport, Conn.: Greenwood Press, 1998.

Cocho, Federico. *O Carnaval en Galicia*. Vigo: Xerais de Galicia, 1990.

Cornblit, Oscar. *Power and Violence in the Colonial City*. Trans. Elizabeth Ladd Glick. Cambridge: Cambridge University Press, 1995.

Corrsin, Stephen D. *Sword Dancing in Europe*. London: Hisarlik Press, 1997.

Costas Arguedas, Jose Felipe. *Diccionario del folklore boliviano*. 2 vols. Sucre: Universidad Mayor de San Francisco Xavier de Chuquisaca, 1967.

Cowley, John. *Carnival, Canboulay and Calypso*. Cambridge: Cambridge University Press, 1996.

Cox, John D. *The Devil and the Sacred in English Drama, 1350–1642*. Cambridge: Cambridge University Press, 2000.

Crespo Rodas, Alberto. "La fundación de la Villa de San Felipe de Austria y Asiento de Minas de Oruro." *Revista Histórica* (Lima) 29 (1966): 304–326.

Crowley, Daniel J. "Midnight Robbers." *Caribbean Quarterly* 4 (1956): 263–274. Reprinted in *Trinidad Carnival*, ed. Gerard A. Besson, pp. 164–185. Port of Spain: Paria, 1988.

———. "The Traditional Masques of Carnival." *Caribbean Quarterly* 4 (1956): 194–223. Reprinted in *Trinidad Carnival*, ed. Gerard A. Besson, pp. 42–90. Port of Spain: Paria, 1988.

Curtin, Philip D. *The Rise and Fall of the Plantation Complex*. Cambridge: Cambridge University Press, 1990.

Cusihuamán G., Antonio. *Diccionario quechua: Cuzco-Collao*. Lima: Ministerio de Educación, 1976.

Cypess, Sandra Messinger, *La Malinche in Mexican Literature*. Austin: University of Texas Press, 1991.

Dabrówka, Andrzej. "Anything But a Game: Corpus Christi in Poland." Paper presented at the 35th International Congress on Medieval Studies, Western Michigan University, May 2000.

Dargan, Ena and Clemente Hernando Balmori. *La conquista de los españoles: Drama indígena bilingüe quechua-castellano*. Tucumán, Argentina: Universidad Nacional de Tucumán, 1955.

Dasairas, Xerardo. *O Entroido en Terras de Monterrei*. Vilaboa: Edicions do Cumio, 1990.

Davis, Natalie Zemon. *Society and Culture in Early Modern France*. Stanford: Stanford University Press, 1975.

Day, Charles W. *Five Years' Residence in the West Indies*. 2 vols. London: Colburn, 1852.

Dean, Carolyn. *Inka Bodies and the Body of Christ: Corpus Christi in Colonial Cuzco*. Durham: Duke University Press, 1999.

———. "Who's Naughty and Nice: Childish Behavior in the Paintings of Cuzco's Corpus Christi Procession." In *Native Artists and Patrons in Colonial Latin America*, ed. Emily Umberger and Tom Cummins. *Phoebus* 7: 107–126. Tempe: Arizona State University, 1995.

Delattre, Louis. *Le Pays Wallon*. [1905]. Brussels: Lebègue, 1929.

Delgado-P., Guillermo. "The Devil Mask." In *The Power of Symbols*, ed. N. Ross Crumrine and Marjorie Halpin, pp. 131–148. Vancouver: University of British Columbia Press, 1983.

Devoto, Daniel. "Folklore et politique au Château Ténébreux." In *Les Fêtes de la Renaissance*. 3 vols. Ed. Jean Jacquot, 2:311–328. Paris: Centre National de la Recherche Scientifique, 1960–75.

Dick, Kay. *Pierrot*. London: Hutchinson, 1960.

Dominguez Assiayn, Salvador. "Filosofía de los antiguos mexicanos." *Contemporáneos* 42–43 (1931): 209–225.

Dorsey, Joseph Carroll. "Puerto Rico and the Atlantic Slave Trade, 1815–1873." Ph.D. dissertation, University of California, Santa Barbara, 1988.

Doutrepont, Georges. *Les types populaires de la littérature française*. 2 vols. Brussels: Lambertin, 1926–1928.

Duchartre, Pierre Louis. *The Italian Comedy*. [1929]. Trans. Randolph T. Weaver. New York: Dover, 1966.

Duffy, Eamon. *The Stripping of the Altars*. New Haven, Conn.: Yale University Press, 1992.

[Echeverría, José de?]. "Diario del tumulto acaecido en la villa de Oruro en 10 de febrero de 1781 . . ." *Revista de Buenos Aires* 22 (1870): 270–312.

Epton, Nina. *Spanish Fiestas*. London: Cassell, 1968.

Esquivel y Navia, Diego de. *Noticias cronológicas de la gran ciudad del Cuzco*. [ca. 1749]. Ed. Félix Denegri Luna. 2 vols. Lima: Fundación Augusto N. Wiese, 1980.

Esses, Maurice. *Dance and Instrumental Diferencias in Spain during the Seventeenth and Early Eighteenth Centuries*. 3 vols. Stuyvesant, N.Y.: Pendragon Press, 1992.

Evrard, Jacques. *Binche: Le Carnaval*. Mons: Fédération du Tourisme de la Province du Hainaut, 1985.

Fahissa, Jaime. *Manuel de Falla*. Trans. Jean Wagstaff. London: Museum Press, 1954.

Farmer, David Hugh. *Oxford Dictionary of Saints*. 4th ed. Oxford: Oxford University Press, 1997.

Farràs, Jaume. *La Patum de Berga*. 2d ed. Barcelona: Editorial Labor, 1992.

Fernandez Calvo, A. "Las manifestaciones folklóricas del día de Corpus en Puertollano durante los siglos XVII y XVIII." *Cuadernos del Instituto de estudios manchegos* 15 (1984): 191–199.

Fiedler, Carol Ann. "Corpus Christi in Cuzco." Ph.D. dissertation, Tulane University, 1985.

Fita, Fidel. "La inquisición toledana." *Boletín de la Real Academia de la Historia* 11 (1887): 289–322.

Fletcher, Alan J. *Drama, Performance, and Polity in Pre-Cromwellian Ireland*. Toronto: University of Toronto Press, 2000.

Flores Barriento, Victor. "Breve noticia sobre la música de las comparsas del Carnaval de Oruro." In *Antología del Carnaval de Oruro*, 3 vols., ed. Alberto Guerra Gutiérrez, 1:131–136. Oruro: Quelco, 1970.

Flores Ochoa, Jorge A. "Historia, fiesta y encuentro en el Corpus Christi cuzqueño." In *La fiesta en el arte*, no ed., pp. 39–59. Lima: Banco de Crédito del Perú, 1994.

Flores Ochoa, Jorge A. and Eldi Flores Nájar. " 'Mamacha Nati. Mamita Nati.' Devoción intercultural a la Virgen Natividad." In *El Qosqo*, ed. Hiroyasu Tomeada and Jorge A. Flores Ochoa, pp. 277–308. Cusco: Centro de Estudios Andinos Cuzco, 1992.

Folklore in Wallonia. Brochure published by the Federation of Tourism of the Walloon Region, n.d.

Fortún, Julia Elena. *La danza de los diablos*. La Paz: Ministerio de Educación y Bellas Artes, 1961.

Forrest, John. *The History of Morris Dancing, 1485–1750*. Toronto: University of Toronto Press, 1999.

Fournel, Victor. *Les spectacles populaires et les artistes des rues*. Paris: Dentu, 1863.

Franceschini, Ezio. "Origine e stile della bolla 'Transiturus.'" *Aevum* 39 (1965): 218–243.

Frazer, James George. *The Golden Bough*. 3d ed. 12 vols. London: Macmillan, 1911–1915.

Fribourg, Jeanine. *Fêtes et littérature orale en Aragon*. Paris: L'Harmattan, 1996.

Fuentes, Manuel A. *Estadistica general de Lima*. Lima: M. N. Corpancho, 1858.

Furetière, Antoine. *Le dictionnaire universel . . .* [1690]. 3 vols. Paris: Robert, 1978.

García García, María Teresa. *Huexotla: Un sitio del Acolhuacan*. Mexico City: Instituto Nacional de Antropología e Historia, 1987.

García Rodero, Cristina and J. M. Caballero Bonald. *Festivals and Rituals of Spain*. Trans. Wayne Finke. New York: Harry N. Abrams, 1994.

Garcilaso de la Vega, El Inca. *Royal Commentaries of the Incas and General History of Peru*. 2 vols. Trans. Harold V. Livermore. Austin: University of Texas Press, 1966.

Garin, Adelson. *Binche et le Carnaval*. Charleroi: Imprimerie Provinciale du Hainaut, 1998.

Garmendia Larrañaga, Juan. *Carnaval en Navarra*. San Sebastian: Haranburu, 1984.

———. *Iñauteria/El Carnaval Vasco*. San Sebastian: Sociedad Guipuzcoana, 1973.

Gasol, Josep M. *Manresa*. Manresa: Gràfiques Montañà, 1971.

Gay, Derek. "A Brief History of the Steelpan." *Drama Review* 42, no. 3 (1998): 64–65.

Gibson, Walter S. *Hieronymus Bosch*. London: Thames and Hudson, 1973.

Giroux, Françoise, ed. *Carnavals et fêtes d'hiver*. Paris: Centre Georges Pompidou, 1984.

Gisbert, Teresa. *El paraíso de los pájaros parlantes: La imagen el otro en la cultura andina*. La Paz: Plural, 1999.

Glotz, Samuël. *Le Carnaval de Binche*. Gembloux: J. Duculot, 1975.

————. *Le Carnaval de Binche*. Mons: Fédération du Tourisme de la Province du Hainaut, 1983.

————. "Le Carnaval en Belgique francophone." In *Le Carnaval, la fête et la communication*, no ed., pp. 3–10. Nice: Editions Serre, 1985.

————. *De Marie de Hongrie aux Gilles de Binche*. Binche: Traditions et Parlers Populaires Wallonie-Bruxelles, 1995.

Goins, John F. "The Death of Atahuallpa." *Journal of American Folklore* 74 (1961): 252–257.

Golby, J. M. and A. W. Purdue. *The Making of the Modern Christmas*. Athens: University of Georgia Press, 1986.

González Anáhuac. "Los Concheros." In *Las danzas de conquista*. Vol. 1, *México contemporáneo*, ed. Jesús Jáuregui and Carlo Bonfiglioli, pp. 207–227. Mexico City: Consejo Nacional para la Cultura y las Artes, 1996.

González Casarrubios, Consolación. *Fiestas populares en Castilla–La Mancha*. Ciudad Real: Junta de Comunidades de Castilla–La Mancha, 1985.

Gonzalez Reboredo, Xosé M. and Xosé R. Mariño Ferro. *Entroido*. La Coruña: Editorial Diputación Provincial, 1987.

Gow, David D. "The Gods and Social Change in the High Andes." Ph.D. dissertation, University of Wisconsin–Madison, 1976.

Gras, Henk. "The *Ludus de Decem Virginibus* and the Reception of Represented Evil." In *Evil on the Medieval Stage*, ed. Meg Twycross, pp. 175–186. Lancaster: Medieval English Theatre, 1992.

Grinberg, Martine and Sam Kinser, "Les combats de Carnaval et de Carême." *Annales: Économies, Sociétés, Civilisations* 38 (1983): 65–98.

Guaman Pomo de Ayala, Felipe. *Nueva corónica y buen gobierno* [1615?]. Ed. Franklin Pease. 2 vols. Caracas: Biblioteca Ayacucho, 1980.

Gueullette, Thomas-Simon. *Théâtre des boulevards*. [1756]. Ed. Georges d'Heylli. 2 vols. Paris: Édouard Rouveyre, 1881.

Gutiérrez, Gustavo. *A Theology of Liberation*. Trans. Sister Caridad Inda and John Eagleson. Maryknoll, N.Y.: Orbis, 1973.

Hall, Tony. "Lennox Pierre." Interview. *Drama Review* 42, no. 3 (1998): 41.

Harrington, Patricia. "Mother of Death, Mother of Rebirth: The Mexican Virgin of Guadalupe." *Journal of the American Academy of Religion* 56 (1988): 25–50.

Harris, Max. "The Arrival of the Europeans: Folk Dramatizations of Conquest and Conversion in New Mexico." *Comparative Drama* 28 (1994): 141–165.

————. *Aztecs, Moors, and Christians: Festivals of Reconquest in Mexico and Spain*. Austin: University of Texas Press, 2000.

————. "Carnival in Galicia." *Drama Review* 44, no. 3 (2000): 154–170.

————. *The Dialogical Theatre*. London: Macmillan, 1993.

————. "The Impotence of Dragons: Playing Devil in the Trinidad Carnival." *Drama Review* 42, no. 3 (1998): 108–123.

————. "Moctezuma's Daughter: The Role of La Malinche in Mesoamerican Dance." *Journal of American Folklore* 109 (1996): 149–177.

————. "Muhammed and the Virgin: Folk Dramatizations of Battles between

Moors and Christians in Modern Spain." *Drama Review* 38, no. 1 (1994): 45–61.

Heartz, Daniel. "Un divertissement de palais pour Charles Quint à Binche." In *Les fêtes de la Renaissance.* 3 vols. Ed. Jean Jacquot, 2:329–342. Paris: Centre National de la Recherche Scientifique, 1960–1975.

Held, Robert. *Inquisition/Inquisición: A Bilingual Guide to the Exhibition of Torture Instruments from the Middle Ages to the Industrial Era . . .* Florence: Qua d'Arno, 1985.

Hemming, John. *The Conquest of the Incas.* New York: Harcourt Brace Jovanovich, 1970.

Hérelle, Georges. *Le théâtre comique.* Paris: Champion, 1925.

Herskovits, Melville J. "African Gods and Catholic Saints in New World Negro Belief." *American Anthropologist* n.s. 39 (1937): 635–643.

———. *The Myth of the Negro Past.* New York: Harper, 1941.

Hill, Errol. *The Trinidad Carnival.* Austin: University of Texas Press, 1972.

Honoré, Brian. "The Midnight Robber." *Drama Review* 42, no. 3 (1998): 124–131.

Huch i Guixer, Jaume, ed. *La Patum, què és?* [1950]. Berga: Casa Huch, 1981.

Hudson, William and John Cottingham Tingey, eds. *The Records of the City of Norwich.* 2 vols. Norwich: Jarrold, 1906–1910.

Huet, Michel and Claude Savary. *The Dances of Africa.* Trans. Dorothy Blair. New York: Harry N. Abrams, 1996.

Humphrey, Chris. *The Politics of Carnival.* Manchester: Manchester University Press, 2001.

Hutton, Ronald. *The Stations of the Sun.* Oxford: Oxford University Press, 1997.

Ingram, R. W., ed. *Coventry.* Records of Early English Drama. Toronto: University of Toronto Press, 1981.

Iribarren, José María. "Estampas del folklore navarro." *Principe de Viana* 5 (1944): 393–420.

Irigoien, Iñaki, Emilio X. Dueñas, and Josu Larrinaga. *Ihauteriak/Carnavales.* Bilbao: Euskal Arkeologia, Etnografia eta Kondaira Museoa, 1992.

Jacquot, Jean, ed. *Les fêtes de la Renaissance.* 3 vols. Paris: Centre National de la Recherche Scientifique, 1960–75.

Jáuregui, Jesús. "Santiago contra Pilatos." In *Las danzas de conquista.* Vol. 1, *México contemporáneo,* eds. Jesús Jáuregui and Carlo Bonfiglioli, pp. 165–204. Mexico City: Consejo Nacional para la Cultura y las Artes, 1996.

Jaye, Barbara H. and William P. Mitchell, "The Iconography of Audience in the Cuzco Corpus Christi Paintings." In *Iconography and Comparative Studies in Medieval Drama,* ed. Clifford Davidson and John H. Stroupe, pp. 94–103. Kalamazoo, Mich.: Medieval Institute Publications, 1991.

Jiménez de Gregorio, Fernando. "Panoramica geográfico-histórica de la villa manchega de Camuñas." *Beresit* 1 (1987): 143–162.

Johnson, Kim. "Introduction." In *Trinidad Carnival,* ed. Gerard A. Besson, pp. xi–xxii. Port of Spain: Paria, 1988.

Junyent i Maydeu, Francesc. *Manresa.* Manresa: Ajuntament de Manresa, 1993.

Kamen, Henry. *The Spanish Inquisition.* London: Weidenfeld and Nicolson, 1997.

Kelly, Joyce. *The Complete Visitor's Guide to Mesoamerican Ruins.* Norman: University of Oklahoma Press, 1982.

King, Pamela M. and Clifford Davidson, eds. *The Coventry Corpus Christi Plays.* Kalamazoo, Mich.: Medieval Institute Publications, 2000.

Kinser, Samuel. *Carnival, American Style.* Chicago: University of Chicago Press, 1990.

———. *Rabelais's Carnival.* Berkeley: University of California Press, 1990.

Klausner, David N., ed. *Herefordshire, Worcestershire.* Records of Early English Drama. Toronto: University of Toronto Press, 1990.

Knight, Alan E. "The Bishop of Fools and His Feasts in Lille." In *Festive Drama,* ed. Meg Twycross, pp. 157–166. Cambridge: D. S. Brewer, 1996.

Kolve, V. A. *The Play Called Corpus Christi.* Stanford: Stanford University Press, 1966.

Korotaj, W., J. Szwedkowska, and M. Szymanska, eds. *Programy teatru jezuickiego.* Vol. 2, pt. 1, of *Dramat staropolski od poczatków do powstania sceny narodowej. Bibliografia.* Wroclaw: Ossolineum, 1976.

Kuenzli, E. Gabrielle. "At the Interstices of Identity on Exhibit: The Politics of Ethnicity and Citizenship in the Festival Rituals of Bolivia." M.A. thesis, University of Wisconsin–Madison, 1998.

Ladurie, Emmanuel Le Roy. *Carnival in Romans.* Trans. Mary Feeney. New York: George Braziller, 1979.

La Fay, Howard. "Carnival in Trinidad." *National Geographic* 140 (1971): 690–701.

Lara, Jesús, ed. *Tragedia del fin de Atawallpa.* [1957]. Buenos Aires: Ediciones del Sol, 1989.

Larrea Palacín, Arcadio de. *El dance aragonés y las representaciones de moros y cristianos.* Tetuàn, Morocco: Editora Marroquí, 1952.

Laso de la Vega, Luis. *The Story of Guadalupe: Luis Laso de la Vega's Huei tlamahuicoltica of 1649.* Ed. and trans. Lisa Sousa, Stafford Poole, and James Lockhart. Stanford: Stanford University Press, 1998.

Latrobe, Charles. *The Rambler in Mexico.* New York: Harper, 1836.

Laza: Paisaje y Tradición. Typed handout distributed by the Ayuntamiento de Laza, n.d.

Lever, Maurice. *Le sceptre et la marotte.* Paris: Fayard, 1983.

Lleo Cañal, Vicente. *Fiesta grande.* Sevilla: Ayuntamiento de Sevilla, 1980.

Lockhart, James. *The Nahuas after the Conquest.* Stanford: Stanford University Press, 1992.

López Cantos, Angel. *Fiestas y juegos en Puerto Rico (siglo XVIII).* San Juan, PR: Centro de Estudios Avanzados de Puerto Rico y el Caribe, 1990.

López Estrada, Francisco. "Fiestas y literatura en los siglos de oro." *Bulletin hispanique* 84 (1982): 291–327.

López Gómez, Juan Estanislao. *La procesión del Corpus Christi de Toledo.* Toledo: Diputación Provincial de Toledo, 1993.

Lovelace, Earl. *The Dragon Can't Dance.* Harlow, Essex: Longman, 1979.

———. "The Emancipation-Jouvay Tradition and the Almost Loss of Pan." *Drama Review* 42, no. 3 (1998): 54–60.

———. *Salt.* London: Faber and Faber, 1996.

Lozano, Jesús, director. *Entroido en Laza.* Film. Madrid: Europ Documenta and New York University in Spain, 1989.

Lutterman-Aguilar, Ann. "The Virgin of Guadalupe: The Feminine Divine and Mexican Women's Liberation." Paper presented at the Annual Meeting of the American Academy of Religion, Nashville, November 2000.

Lynch, William F. *Christ and Apollo.* [1960]. Notre Dame: University of Notre Dame Press, 1975.

Malavé, Carlos H., director. *La tercera raíz.* Film. San Juan, PR: La Fundación Puertorriqueña de las Humanidades, 1994.

Mariátegui Oliva, Ricardo. *Pintura cuzqueña del siglo XVII.* Lima: Alma Mater, 1951.

———. *Pintura cuzqueña del siglo XVII en Chile.* Lima: Alma Mater, 1954.

Martin, Carol. "Trinidad Carnival Glossary." *Drama Review* 42, no. 3 (1998): 220–235.

Martin, Paul. *Military Costume.* Stuttgart: Franckh'sche Verlagshandlung, 1963.

Martínez Sosa, Luis, director. *Las Fiestas de Santiago Apóstol en Loíza.* Film. San Juan, PR: Producciones Vegigante and La Fundación Puertorriqueña de las Humanidades, 1982.

Mason, Peter. *Bacchanal! The Carnival Culture of Trinidad.* Philadelphia: Temple University Press, 1998.

Massip, Francesc. "El infierno en escena." *Euskera* 14 (1999): 239–265.

Mauleón Benítez, Carmen Cecilia. *El español de Loíza Aldea.* Madrid: Ediciones Partenon, 1974.

Mazoeur, Charles. "Théâtre et Carnaval en France jusqu'à la fin du XVIᵉ siècle." *Revue d'Histoire du Théâtre* 35 (1983): 147–161.

McFarren, Wendy. "El mascarero, Antonio Viscarra." In *Máscaras de los andes bolivianos,* ed. Peter McFarren, pp. 151–171. La Paz: Quipus, 1993.

Mendieta, Gerónimo de. *Historia eclesiástica indiana.* 2 vols. Mexico City: Cien de México, 1997.

Mendoza, Zoila S. *Shaping Society through Dance: Mestizo Ritual Performance in the Peruvian Andes.* Chicago: University of Chicago Press, 2000.

[Menéndez, Patricio Gabriel?]. "Relación trágica de los funestos y ruidosos acaecimientos de la Villa de Oruro." *Revista de Buenos Aires* 22 (1870): 312–325.

Mesa, José de and Teresa Gisbert. *Historia de la pintura cuzqueña.* 2 vols. Lima: Fundación Augusto N. Wiese, 1982.

Mesters, Carlos. *Defenseless Flower.* [1983]. Trans. Francis McDonagh. Maryknoll, N.Y.: Orbis, 1989.

Mic, Constant. *La Commedia dell'arte*. Paris: La Pléiade, 1927.

Milá y Fontanals, Manuel. "De algunas representaciones catalanas antiguas y vulgares." *Revista de Cataluña* 2 (1862): 19–31, 69–77, 119–128, 263–284.

———. *Obras completas*. 6 vols. Barcelona: Álvaro Verdaguer, 1889–1895.

Milne, Jean. *Fiesta Time in Latin America*. Los Angeles: Ward Ritchie Press, 1965.

Molinié, Antoinette. "La horca." In *Imagenes de una danza*, ed. Gabriel Romero Aranda, pp. 116–117. Toledo: Diputación Provincial de Toledo, 1994.

———. "Rite espagnol en clef de juif." *Terrain* 27 (1996): 131–146.

Montes Camacho, Niver. *Proceso intimo del carnaval de Oruro*. Oruro: Editorial Universitaria, 1986.

Montoya Castro, Jacobo. *Huexotla, un pueblo en transición*. Chapingo: Universidad Autónomo Chapingo, 1981.

Moreau, Celestin. *Bibliographie des Mazarinades*. 3 vols. Paris: Jules Renouard, 1850–1851.

Moreno Nieto, Luis. *Diccionario enciclopédico de Toledo y su provincia*. Toledo: n.p., 1974.

———. *La provincia de Toledo*. Toledo: Diputación Provincial, 1960.

Morera, Arturo. *La extro-historia de Salvador Sarinianus*. Sariñena: Asociación Cultural Quio, 1995.

Motolinía, Toribio de. *Historia de los indios de la Nueva España*. Ed. Edmundo O'Gorman. [1969]. 5th ed. Mexico City: Porrúa, 1990.

Muchembled, Robert. *Popular Culture and Elite Culture in France, 1400–1750*. [1978]. Trans. Lydia Cochrane. Baton Rouge: Louisiana State University Press, 1985.

Mullen, Robert J. *Architecture and Its Sculpture in Viceregal Mexico*. Austin: University of Texas Press, 1997.

Muller, Nazma. "Paramin Mountain Village." *Drama Review* 42, no. 3 (1998): 112–113.

Nash, June. *We Eat the Mines and the Mines Eat Us*. 2d ed. New York: Columbia University Press, 1993.

Neumann, Bernd. *Geistliches Schuaspiel im Zeugnis der Zeit*. 2 vols. Munich: Artemis, 1987.

Noch, Feliciti. "Mascareros de Oruro." In *Máscaras de los andes bolivianos*, ed. Peter McFarren, pp. 131–149. La Paz: Quipus, 1993.

Noguera i Canal, Josep. *Visió històrica de la Patum de Berga*. Barcelona: Rafael Dalmau, 1992.

Noyes, Dorothy Pettit. "The Mule and the Giants: Struggling for the Body Social in a Catalan Corpus Christi Festival." Ph.D. dissertation, University of Pennsylvania, 1992.

Oman, Charles. *A History of the Peninsular War*. 7 vols. Oxford: Clarendon Press, 1902–1930.

Orienti, Sandra and René de Solier. *Hieronymus Bosch*. [1976]. Trans. Roy Bloom. New York: Crescent Books, 1979.

Ortiz, Carmen. "The Uses of Folklore by the Franco Regime." *Journal of American Folklore* 112 (1999): 479–496.

Palma, Marigloria. *Muestras del folklore puertorriqueño.* San Juan, PR: Editorial Edil, 1981.

Panofsky, Dora. "Gilles or Pierrot? Iconographic Notes on Watteau." *Gazette des Beaux-Arts* 39 (1952): 319–340.

Parfaict, François. *Dictionnaire des théâtres de Paris.* 7 vols. Paris: Lambert, 1756.

Paz, Octavio. *The Labyrinth of Solitude.* Trans. Lysander Kemp. New York: Grove Press, 1961.

Pearse, Andrew. "Carnival in Nineteenth Century Trinidad." *Caribbean Quarterly* 4 (1956): 175–193. Reprinted in *Trinidad Carnival,* ed. Gerard A. Besson, pp. 4–41. Port of Spain: Paria, 1988.

Petit de Julleville, L. *Les comédiens en France au moyen âge.* [1885]. Geneva: Slatkine Reprints, 1968.

Pettit, Tom. "Protesting Inversions: Charivary as Folk Pageantry and Folk-Law." *Medieval English Theatre* 21 (1999): 21–51.

Pilco Loaiza, Amós David. *Danzas de la region del Cusco.* Cusco: n.p., 1998.

Poole, Deborah A. "Accommodation and Resistance in Andean Ritual Dance." *Drama Review* 34, no. 2 (1990): 98–126.

Poole, Stafford. *Our Lady of Guadalupe.* Tucson: University of Arizona Press, 1995.

Posner, Daniel. *Antoine Watteau.* Ithaca, N.Y.: Cornell University Press, 1984.

Pougin, Arthur. *Dictionnaire historique et pittoresque du théâtre et des arts qui s'y rattachent.* Paris: Firmin-Didot, 1885.

Procope, Bruce. "The Dragon Band or Devil Band." *Caribbean Quarterly* 4 (1956): 275–280. Reprinted in *Trinidad Carnival,* ed. Gerard A. Besson, pp. 186–196. Port of Spain: Paria, 1988.

Programa de la semana grande del Corpus (1997). Toledo: n.p., 1997.

Pujol, Francesc and Joan Amades. *Diccionari de la dansa, dels entremesos i dels instruments de música i sonadors.* Vol. 1: *Dansa.* Barcelona: Imprenta Elzeviriana, 1936.

Raboteau, Albert J. *Slave Religion.* Oxford: Oxford University Press, 1978.

Ramirez E., Juan Andrés. "La novena al Señor de Qoyllur Rit'i." *Allpanchis* 1 (1969): 61–88.

Ramírez, Maira and Itzel Valle. "Las coreografías de la conquista." In *Las danzas de conquista.* Vol. 1, *México contemporáneo,* ed. Jesús Jáuregui and Carlo Bonfiglioli, pp. 339–398. Mexico City: Consejo Nacional para la Cultura y las Artes, 1996.

Randall, Robert. "Qoyllur Rit'i, an Inca Fiesta of the Pleiades." *Bulletin de l'Institut Français d'Études Andines* 11, no. 1–2 (1982): 37–81.

Regalado, Mariana. "*Ounhas couces do nabizo*—A Few Kicks from the Donkey." M.A. thesis, New York University, 1992.

"Relación veridica en la que se da noticia de lo acaecido en la isla de Puerto Rico a fines del año de 45 y principios de el 47 con el motivo de llorar la muerte de N. Rey y Señor don Phelipe quinto y celebrar la exaltación a la corona de N. S. D. Fernando sexto . . ." *Boletín Histórico de Puerto Rico* 12 (1925): 148–193.

Revelard, Michel. "Le Carnaval de Binche (Belgique) et son Gilles." In *Le Carnaval, la fête et la communication,* no ed., pp. 239–245. Nice: Editions Serre, 1985.

Revelard, Michel and Petra Jarosova. "Le Musée International du Carnaval et du Masque." In *Carnavals du monde à travers les âges,* ed. Pierre Falicon and Annie Sidro, pp. 44–54. Nice: Espace Niçois d'Art et de Culture, 1984.

Ricard, Robert. *The Spiritual Conquest of Mexico.* Trans. Lesley Byrd Simpson. Berkeley: University of California Press, 1966.

Richards, Kenneth and Laura Richards. *The Commedia dell'Arte.* Oxford: Blackwell, 1990.

Riggio, Milla. "Geraldo Andrew Vieira." Interview. *Drama Review* 42, no. 3 (1998): 194–202.

———. "Resistance and Identity: Carnival in Trinidad and Tobago." *Drama Review* 42, no. 3 (1998): 7–23.

Risco, Vicente. "Etnografía: Cultura espiritual." In *Historia de Galicia,* ed. Ramón Otero Pedrayo, 1:255–777. 2 vols. Madrid: Akal, 1979.

———. "Notas sobre las fiestas de Carnaval en Galicia." *Revista de Dialectologia y Tradiciones Populares* 4 (1948): 163–196, 339–368.

Robins, Nicholas A. *El mesianismo y la rebelión indigena.* Trans. Luz Mariela Escobar R. La Paz: Hisbol, 1997.

Roca Huallparimachi, Demetrio. "San Jerónimo y su participación en el Corpus Christi del Cuzco." *Folklore: Revista de Cultura Tradicional* 1 (1966): 3–39.

Rodríguez, Áurea E. *African Diaspora in Puerto Rico.* New York: Caribbean Cultural Center, 1991.

Rohlehr, Gordon. " 'We Getting the Kaiso That We Deserve': Calypso and the World Music Market." *Drama Review* 42, no. 3 (1998): 82–95.

Roma Riu, Josefina. *Aragón y el Carnaval.* Zaragoza: Guara Editorial, 1984.

Romero Aranda, Gabriel, ed. *Imagenes de una danza: Camuñas-Pecados y Danzantes.* Toledo: Diputación Provincial de Toledo, 1994.

Romero de Terreros, Manuel. "Huexotla." *Anales del Instituto de Investigaciones Esteticas* 7, no. 26 (1957): 51–54.

Rostas, Susanna. "The Production of Gendered Imagery: The Concheros of Mexico." In *Machos, Mistresses, Madonnas,* ed. Marit Melhuus and Kristi Anne Stølen, pp. 207–229. London: Verso, 1996.

Rubin, Miri. *Corpus Christi.* Cambridge: Cambridge University Press, 1991.

Rudlin, John. *Commedia dell'Arte.* London: Routledge, 1994.

Rumbo i Soler, Albert. *Història dels gegants de Berga.* Berga: Patronat Centre d'Estudis del Berguedâ, 1995.

Sahagún, Bernardino de. *Florentine Codex: General History of the Things of New Spain.* Ed. and trans. Arthur J. O. Anderson and Charles E. Dibble. 12 books in 13 vols. Salt Lake City: University of Utah Press, 1950–1982.

———. *Historia general de las cosas de Nueva España.* 5 vols. Mexico City: Pedro Robredo, 1938.

Sallnow, Michael J. *Pilgrims of the Andes*. Washington, D.C.: Smithsonian Institution Press, 1987.

Santisteban Ochoa, Julian, ed. "Documentos para la historia del Cuzco existentes en el Archivo General de Indias de Sevilla." *Revista del Archivo Histórico del Cuzco* 11 (1963): 1–118.

Sardans i Farràs, Jordi. "De la República als nostres dies." In *Història de les comarques de Catalunya: Bages*, ed. Llorenç Ferrer i Alòs, vol. 1, pp. 421–458. [1986]. 2d ed. Manresa: Parcir, 1987.

Sarret i Arbós, Joaquim. *Historia de Manresa*. Manresa: Sant Josep, 1921.

———. *Historia religiosa de Manresa*. Manresa: Sant Josep, 1924.

Scarano, Francisco. "The *Jíbaro* Masquerade and the Subaltern Politics of Creole Identity Formation in Puerto Rico, 1745–1823." *American Historical Review* 101 (1996): 1398–1431.

Schneider, Karin, ed. *Das Eisenacher Zehnjungfrauenspiel*. Texte des späten Mittelalters und der frühen Neuzeit 17. Berlin: Erich Schmidt, 1964.

Schwartz, Regina M. *The Curse of Cain*. Chicago: University of Chicago Press, 1997.

Sciorra, Joseph. "'We're not here just to plant. We have culture.' An Ethnography of the South Bronx Casita Rincón Criollo." *New York Folklore* 20, nos. 3–4 (1994): 19–41.

Scott, James C. *Domination and the Arts of Resistance*. New Haven: Yale University Press. 1990.

Scott, Kenneth, ed. "Charles Walker's Letters from Puerto Rico, 1835–1837." *Caribbean Studies* 5, no. 1 (1965): 37–50.

Seeger, Peter. "The Steel Drum." *Journal of American Folklore* 71 (1958): 52–57.

Seward, Desmond. *The Monks of War*. [1972]. Rev. ed. London: Penguin, 1995.

Shergold, N. D. *A History of the Spanish Stage from Medieval Times to the End of the Seventeenth Century*. Oxford: Clarendon Press, 1967.

Siles Guevara, Juan. "Los sucesos del 10 de febrero de 1781 en Oruro, según un diario anónimo poco conocido." In *Perfiles de Oruro*, ed. Elias Delgado Morales, pp. 35–51. Oruro: Alea, 1987.

Silverman-Proust, Gail. "Representación gráfica del mito Inkarrí en los tejidos Q'ero." *Boletín de Lima*, no. 48 (November 1986): 59–71.

Sire, H. J. A. *The Knights of Malta*. New Haven: Yale University Press, 1994.

Somaize, Antoine Baudeau de. *Les véritables précieuses*. [1660]. In *Comédies et pamphlets sur Molière*, ed. Goerges Mongrédien, pp. 9–66. Paris: A.-G. Nizet, 1986.

Somerset, J. Alan B., ed. *Shropshire*. 2 vols. Records of Early English Drama. Toronto: University of Toronto Press, 1994.

Sonesson, Birgit. *Catalanes en las Antillas*. Colombre, Asturias: Archivo de Indianos, 1995.

Southworth, John. *Fools and Jesters at the English Court*. Stroud: Sutton, 1998.

Stegassy, Ruth. "John Cupid." Interview. *Drama Review* 42, no. 3 (1998): 96–107.

Steinberg, Leo. *The Sexuality of Christ in Renaissance Art and Modern Oblivion.* [1983]. Rev. and expanded ed. Chicago: University of Chicago Press, 1996.

Stone, Martha. *At the Sign of Midnight: The Concheros Dance Cult of Mexico.* Tucson: University of Arizona Press, 1975.

Storey, Robert F. *Pierrot.* Princeton: Princeton University Press, 1978.

Sued Badillo, Jalil and Angel López Cantos. *Puerto Rico Negro.* Río Piedras, PR: Editorial Cultural, 1986.

Taboada Chivite, Xesús. *Etnografía galega.* Vigo: Editorial Galaxia, 1972.

———. *Ritos y creencias gallegas.* A Coruña: Salvora, 1980.

Taylor, William B. *Magistrates of the Sacred: Priests and Parishioners in Eighteenth-Century Mexico.* Stanford: Stanford University Press, 1996.

Tenorio, Nicolás. *La aldea gallega.* [1914]. Vigo: Xerais, 1982.

Thomas, Hugh. *Conquest.* London: Hutchinson, 1993.

———. *The Slave Trade.* New York: Touchstone, 1997.

———. *The Spanish Civil War.* [1961]. Rev. and expanded ed. New York: Harper and Row, 1977.

Thomson, Guy P. C. "The Ceremonial and Political Roles of Village Bands, 1846–1974." In *Rituals of Rule, Rituals of Resistance,* ed. William H. Beezley, Cheryl English Martin, and William E. French, pp. 307–342. Wilmington, Del.: SR Books, 1994.

Tilliot, Jean-Bénigne Lucotte du. *Memoires pour servir à histoire de la fête des foux.* Geneva: Bousquet, 1741.

Toledo, Francisco de. *Fundación española del Cusco y ordenanzas para su gobierno.* Ed. Horacio H. Urteaga and Carlos A. Romero. Lima: Talleres Gráficos Sanmartí, 1926.

Torras i Serra, Marc. "Festes i costums manresans." In *Història de les comarques de Catalunya: Bages,* ed. Llorenç Ferrer i Alòs, vol. 1, pp. 477–486. [1986]. 2d ed. Manresa: Parcir, 1987.

———. *Manresa: Festes i tradicions.* Manresa: Ajuntament de Manresa, 1990.

Turner, Alice K. *The History of Hell.* San Diego, Calif.: Harcourt Brace, 1993.

Ungerleider Kepler, David. *Las fiestas de Santiago Apóstol en Loíza.* San Juan, PR: Isla Negra, 2000.

Unzueta, Mario. *Valle.* Cochabamba: La Epoca, 1945.

Urquiza Vázquez del Mercado, Gabriela. *Convento Huexotla: Reflejo de la mística franciscana.* Mexico City: Plaza y Valdés, 1993.

Vargas, Manuel. "El Carnaval de Oruro." In *Máscaras de los andes bolivianos,* ed. Peter McFarren, pp. 81–113. La Paz: Quipus, 1993.

Vargas Luza, Jorge Enrique. *La diablada de Oruro.* La Paz: Plural, 1998.

Verger, Pierre. *Fiestas y danzas en el Cuzco y en los Andes.* 2d ed. Buenos Aires: Editorial Sudamericana, 1951.

———. *Indians of Peru.* Introd. by Luis E. Valcárcel. Lake Forest, Ill.: Pocahontas Press, 1950.

Very, Francis George. *The Spanish Corpus Christi Procession.* Valencia: Editorial Castalia, 1962.

Vetancurt, Agustin de. *Teatro Mexicano.* 4 vols. Madrid: Jose Porrua Turanzas, 1960–1961.

Vidal, Mary. *Watteau's Painted Conversations.* New Haven: Yale University Press, 1992.

Vilhena, Maria da Conceição. "Sobre a origem dos foliões." *Boletim do Instituto Histórico da Ilha Terceira* 43 (1985): 227–241.

Villarroel, Emeterio. "Novena de la Virgen del Socavón." [1908]. In *Antología del Carnaval de Oruro,* 3 vols., ed. Alberto Guerra Gutiérrez, 2:23–28. Oruro: Quelco, 1970.

Villasante Ortiz, Segundo. *Paucartambo.* Vol. 2, *Provincia Folklórica Mamacha Carmen.* Cusco: Editorial León, 1980.

Vissepo, Mario, director. *La herencia de un tambor.* Film. San Juan, P.R.: Cinetel, 1980.

Wachtel, Nathan. *The Vision of the Vanquished.* Trans. Ben and Siân Reynolds. New York: Barnes and Noble, 1977.

Walsh, Martin. "Jouvay Mornin' with the Merry Darceuils." *Drama Review* 42, no. 3 (1998): 132–146.

Wangermée, Robert. *Flemish Music and Society in the Fifteenth and Sixteenth Centuries.* Trans. Robert Erich Wolf. New York: Frederick A. Praeger, 1968.

Wasson, John M., ed. *Devon.* Records of Early English Drama. Toronto: University of Toronto Press, 1986.

Webster, Susan Verdi. *Art and Ritual in Golden-Age Spain.* Princeton: Princeton University Press, 1998.

Ysursa, John M. *Basque Dance.* Boise, Id.: Tamarack Books, 1995.

Yugo Santacruz, Pedro. *Danzantes y pecados de Camuñas: El triunfo de la gracia sobre el pecado.* Toledo: Diputación Provincial, 1985.

Zaconeta, José Victor. "La Virgen del Socavón y la corte infernal." [1925]. In *Antología del Carnaval de Oruro,* 3 vols., ed. Alberto Guerra Gutiérrez, 2:69–88. Oruro: Quelco, 1970.

Zaragoza, Edward C. *St. James in the Streets: The Religious Processions of Loíza Aldea, Puerto Rico.* Lanham, Md.: Scarecrow Press, 1995.

Zika, Charles. "Hosts, Processions and Pilgrimages: Controlling the Sacred in Fifteenth-Century Germany." *Past and Present* 118 (1988): 25–64.

Index